Islamic Democracy

Islamic Democracy

Dr P Quereshi

MD Publications Pvt Ltd
New Delhi
www.mdppl.com

Published by :

MD Publications Pvt Ltd
"MD House", 11, Darya Ganj,
New Delhi-110 002
Phone : +91-11-41563325 (Customer Service)
+91-11-41562846 (Editorial)
E-mail (orders) : order@mdppl.com
Website : www.mdppl.com

ISBN : 978-81-7533-215-7

Published and Printed by Mr. Pranav Gupta on behalf of MD Publications Pvt Ltd at Printext, New Delhi.

Preface

Most Islamic democracies fall under the first definition, leading many analysts to dismiss the compatibility of Islam with democracy. Critics of the concept of Islamic democracy argue that Islam and secularism are opposite forces, that theocracy is incompatible with democracy, and that Muslim culture lacks the liberal social atitudes of democratic societies. Others agrue that the concepts of liberalism and democratic participation were already present in the medieval Islamic world.

Muslim democrats argue that the Qu'ran insists on *shura,* that is "mutual consultation", in deciding communal affairs (Aal 'Imran 3:159, Ash-Shura 42:38), which may include electing leaders to represent and govern on the community's behalf. This viewpoint, however, requires radical modification of Islam's fundamental tenets, although it is accepted by some Liberal movements within Islam. Government by the people is not therefore necessarily incompatible wth the rule of Islam, whilst it has also been argued that rule by a religious authority is not the same as rule by a representative of Allah.

Islamic democratic regimes have the same human rights issues as any other democracies, but some matters which may cause friction include appeasing anti-democratic Islamic radicals, non-Muslim religious minorities, the role of Islam in state education (especially with regard to Sunni and Shia traditions), women's rights, and similar matters. Nonetheless, Islamic feminism does exist.

In addition, while some Islamic democracies ban alcohol outright, as it is against the religion, other governments allow the individual to choose whether to trangress Islam themselves. In these instances, while the act will be considered wrong by strict Muslims, the penalty is seen to be a spiritual not worldly one.

I am very grateful to Mr. Pranav Gupta, Director of MD Publications Pvt Ltd, New Delhi for his cooperation and support for this book.

Dr P Qureshi

CONTENTS

1

Islamic Democracy
An Introduction

Democracy is a commonly known word all over the world. Most of the political movements in the world have made it their goal to establish this system in their respective countries. Democracy is the most popular and accepted political system in the modern world. Yet, there exists some difference of opinion among the Islamic groups on democracy. Democracy and human rights have occupied very important position in the political agenda of many of the Islamic parties. However, some of the parties and people do not accept it, since democracy speaks of sovereignty of the people.

In this context, we need careful and deep analysis on this issue. We need to understand the issue avoiding the minor technicalities. As we see, Islamic parties and Islamic scholars of the modern world think of a political system wherein government will run the country through Parliament. They also want freedom of expression, voting right of the people, rule of law, independent & free judiciary, free press, fundamental human rights etc. These are also the prerequisites of the democratic system. It is therefore, apparent on a deeper analysis that the concept of state and govt. of Islamic Parties are in conformity with the principles of democracy.

Theoretically speaking, Islam speaks of sovereignty of Allah, while western democracy advocates that sovereignty belongs to people. However, all political thinkers do not share the same view of sovereignty. Some political scientists even argue that there is no need of concept sovereignty at all. Even the concept of sovereignty is not highlighted in the books which discuss democracy though sovereignty is discussed in great detail as a political concept in the books of political science. In this context, we feel it necessary to quote from the writings of Allama Yousuf Al Qardawi, an eminent Islamic scholar of the present time. He wrote:

The fear of some people here that democracy makes the people a source of power and even legislation (although legislation is Allah's alone) should not be heeded here, because we are supposed to be speaking of a people that in its majority and has accepted Allah as its Lord, Mohammad as its Prophet and Islam as its Religion. Such a people would not be expected to pass a legislation that contradicts Islam and its incontestable principles and conclusive rules.

Anyway, these fears can be overcome by one article stipulating that any legislation contradicting the incon-testable provisions of Islam shall be null and void because Islam is the religion of the State and the source of legitimacy of all its institutions and therefore may no be contradicted, as a branch may not run against the main stream.?

It should be known that the acceptance of the principle that legislation or rule belong to Allah does not rob the Nation of its right to seek for itself the codes necessary to regulate its ever-changing life and earthly affairs.

What we seek is that legislations and codes be within the limits of the flawless texts and the over all objectives of Sharia and the Islamic Message. The binding texts are very few, while the area of permissibility or legislative free space is quite wide and the texts themselves are as flexible and capacious as to accommodate more than one under-standing and accept more than one interpretation, which leads to the existence of several schools and philosophies within the expansive framework of Islam.

We find many Islamic scholars accepted the idea of democracy in Islam though under certain conditions. Dr. Abu Said Nuruddin has written in his book *Mohakobi Iqbal,* (Iqbal the Great Poet) that Allama Iqbal was not happy with the democratic system because of its secularist stance but he suggested in his writings that there was no alternative to democracy. In his 6th speech on Reconstruction of religious thought in Islam, Allama Iqbal stated that Islamic state is established on the principles of freedom, equality, and the absolute principles of stability. Therefore the principles of democratic rule are not only similar with the fundamental aspects of Islam rather the executing powers are enhanced in the Muslim world.

Iqbal observed, should the foundation of democracy rests upon spiritual and moral values, it would be the best political system. He wrote in the "The New Era" on its 28th July, 1917 issue: that democracy was born in Europe from economic renaissance that took place in most of its societies. But Islamic democracy is not developed from the idea of economic advancement rather it is a spiritual principle that comes from the principle that everybody is a source of power whose possibilities can be developed through virtue and character. That means according to Iqbal Islam prescribes democracy under the law of Allah.

We see Moulana Maududi, fifty years ago from now, in his book Political theory of Islam used the term Theo-democracy for Islamic state. He didn't deny the term democracy. Rather he accepted democracy while this system will work under the sovereignty of Allah. We also see that in the first Islamic constitution of the present world, the term democracy was accepted with the consent of Islamic scholars (ulema). In the preamble, the term democracy was accepted in the following manner:

Wherein the principles of democracy, freedom, equality, tolerance and social justice as enunciated by Islam should be fully observed.

In the 1973 constitution the same position was maintained.

Wherein the principles of democracy, freedom, equality, tolerance and social justice as enunciated by Islam shall be fully observed.

This means that democracy has been accepted within the limits of Islam so that in the name of democracy Islamic principles cannot be violated. Islamic Scholars and Islamic Politicians have come to accept the word democracy and what it means within these limits.

Allama Yousuf Al Qardawi in his book *Priorities of the Islamic Movement in the Coming Phase* has titled one of its chapters as The Movement and Political Freedom and Democracy. In this book he has shown that Islam does not allow any kind of autocracy or monarchy. He also showed that Islam spreads through political freedom. He stated that Islam unlike democracy is a complete code of life, which encompasses many more vital issues of human needs. Above all, he thinks democracy is consistent with Islam and the fundamental rights of mankind prescribed in Islam can be ensured through democracy. He has advocated in favor of democratic system and political freedom. But he suggested introducing a clause in the constitution to the effect that no law will be passed contrary to the injunctions of the Quran and Sunnah. This clause will act as guarantee against the fear of some people that anti Islamic law may be passed under the cover of democracy. Dr. Qardawi writes: It is the duty of the (Islamic) Movement in the coming phase to stand firm against totalitarian and dictatorial rule, political despotism and usurpation of people's rights. The movement should always stand by political freedom, as represented by true, not false, democracy. It should flatly declare its refusal of tyrants and steer clear of all dictators, even if some tyrant appears to have good intentions towards it for some gain and for a time that is usually short, as has been shown by experience.

The Prophet (SAWS) said, when you see my Nation fall victim to fear and does not say to wrong-doer, you are wrong, and then you may lose hope in them. So how about a regime that forces people to say to a conceited wrongdoer, how just, how great you are. O our hero, our savior and our liberator!?

The Quran denounces tyrants such as Nimrudh, Pharoah, Haman and others, but it also dispraises those who follow tyrants and obey their orders. This is why Allah dispraises the people of Noah by saying, but they follow (men) whose wealth and children give them no increase but only loss.

Allah also says of Ad, people of Hud, And followed the command of every powerful, obstinate transgressor.

See also what the Quran says about the people of Pharoah, but they followed the command of Pharaoh, and the command of Pharoah was not rightly guided. Thus he made fools of his people, and they obeyed him: truly they were a people rebellious (against Allah).

A closer look at the history of the Muslim Nation and the Islamic Movement in modern times should show clearly that the Islamic idea, the Islamic Movement and the Islamic Awakening have never flourished or borne fruit unless in an atmosphere of democracy and freedom, and have withered and become barren only at the times of oppression and tyranny that trod over the will of the people by force which clung to Islam. Such oppressive regimes imposed their Secularism, Socialism, or Communism on their people by force and coercion, using covert torture and public executions, and employing those devilish tools that tore flesh, shed blood, crushed bone and destroyed the soul.

On the other hand, we saw the Islamic Movement and the Islamic Awakening bear fruit and flourish at the times of freedom and democracy, and in the wake of the collapse of imperial regimes that ruled peoples with fear and oppression.

However, the tools and guarantees created by democracy are as close as can ever be to the realization of the political principles brought to this earth by Islam to put a leash on the ambitions and whims of rulers. These principles are: shura (consultation), good advice enjoining what is proper and forbidding what is evil, disobeying illegal orders, resisting unbelief and changing wrong by force whenever possible. It is only in democracy and political freedom that the power of

Parliament is evident and that people's deputies can withdraw confidence from any government that breaches the Constitution, and it is only in such an environment that the strength of free press, free Parliament, opposition and the masses is most felt.

It is evident from the above discussion that Islamic thinkers and Muslim people want their right to vote, rule of law, and a government that is to be elected by the people. The term democracy means all these things. Taking everything into consideration, we can say that there is no problem to accept the term democracy under certain conditions. We see different constitutions and Islamic scholars conditionally accepted the term 'democracy'. Muslim community can accept this term. This will help to remove misunderstandings about Islam that it is for violence and dictatorships.

The relationship between Islam and democracy in the contemporary world is complex. The Muslim world is not ideologically monolithic. It presents a broad spectrum of perspectives ranging from the extremes of those who deny a connection between Islam and democracy to those who argue that Islam requires a democratic system. In between the extremes, in a number of countries where Muslims are a majority, many Muslims believe that Islam is a support for democracy even though their particular political system is not explicitly defined as Islamic.

Throughout the Muslim world in the twentieth century, many groups that identify themselves explicitly as Islamic attempted to participate directly in the demo-cratic processes as regimes were overthrown in Eastern Europe, Africa, and elsewhere. In Iran such groups controlled and defined the system as a whole; in other areas, the explicitly Islamic groups were participating in systems that were more secular in structure. The participation of self-identified islamically oriented groups in elections and in democratic processes in general, aroused considerable controversy. People who believe that secular approaches and a separation of religion and politics are an essential part of democracy argue that Islamist groups only advocate democracy as a tactic to gain political power. They say Islamist groups support "one man, one vote, one time." In Algeria and Turkey, following electoral successes by parties thought to be religiously threatening to the existing political regimes, the Islamic political parties were restricted legally or suppressed.

The relationship between Islam and democracy is strongly debated among the people who identify with the Islamic resurgence in the late twentieth century and the beginning of the twenty-first. Some of these Islamists believe that "democracy" is a foreign concept that has been imposed by Westernizers and secular reformers upon Muslim societies. They often argue that the concept of popular sovereignty denies the fundamental Islamic affirmation of the sovereignty of God and is, therefore, a form of idolatry. People holding these views are less likely to be the ones participating in elections. Many limit themselves to participating in intellectual debates in the media, and others hold themselves aloof from the political dynamics of their societies, hoping that their own isolated community will in some way be an inspiration to the broader Muslim community. Many prominent Islamic intellectuals and groups, however, argue that Islam and democracy are compatible. Some extend the argument to affirm that under the conditions of the contemporary world, democracy can be considered a requirement of Islam. In these discussions, Muslim scholars bring historically important concepts from within the Islamic tradition together with the basic concepts of democracy as understood in the modern world.

The process in the Muslim world is similar to that which has taken place within other major religious traditions. All of the great world faith traditions represent major bodies of ideas, visions, and concepts fundamental to understanding human life and destiny.

Many of these significant concepts have been used in different ways in different periods of history. The Christian tradition, for example, in pre-modern times provided a conceptual foundation for divine right monarchy; in contemporary times, it fosters the concept that Christianity and democracy are truly compatible.

In all traditions, there are intellectual and ideological resources that can provide the justification for absolute monarchy or for democracy. The controversies arise regarding how basic concepts are to be understood and implemented.

A relatively neutral starting point for Muslims is presented in a 1992 interview in the London Observer with the Tunisian Islamist leader and political exile, Rashid Ghanoushi: "If by democracy is meant the liberal model of government prevailing in the West, a system under which the people freely choose their representatives and leaders, in which there is an alternation of power, as well as all freedoms and human rights for the public, then Muslims will find nothing in their religion to oppose democracy, and it is not in their interests to do so." Many Muslims, including Ghanoushi himself, go beyond this and view democracy as an appropriate way to fulfill certain obligations of the faith in the contemporary world.

The Islamic tradition contains a number of key concepts that are presented by Muslims as the key to "Islamic democracy." Most would agree that it is important for Muslims not simply to copy what non-Muslims have done in creating democratic systems, emphasizing that there are different forms that legitimate democracy can take. Iran's President Mohammad Khatami, in a television interview in June before that country's presidential elections, noted that "the existing democracies do not necessarily follow one formula or aspect. It is possible that a democracy may lead to a liberal system. It is possible that democracy may lead to a socialist system. Or it may be a democracy with the inclusion of religious norms in the government. We have accepted the third option." Khatami presents a view common among the advocates of Islamic democracy that "today world democracies are suffering from a major vacuum, which is the vacuum of spirituality," and that Islam can provide the framework for combining democracy with spirituality and religious government.

The synthesis of spirituality and government builds on a fundamental affirmation at the heart of Islam: the proclamation that "There is no divinity but The God" and the affirmation of the "oneness" of God. This concept, called tawhid, provides the foundation for the idea that one cannot separate different aspects of life into separate compartments. Ali Shariati, who made important contributions to the ideological development of the Islamic revolution in Iran, wrote in On the Sociology of Islam, that tawhid "in the sense of oneness of God is of course accepted by all monotheists. But tauhid as a world view... means regarding the whole universe as a unity, instead of dividing it into this world and the here-after... spirit and body." In this worldview, the separation of religion from politics creates a spiritual vacuum in the public arena and opens the way for political systems that have no sense of moral values. From such a perspective, a secular state opens the way for the abuse of power. The experiences of Muslim societies with military regimes that are secularist in ideological origin, such as the Baath Arab Socialist regime of Saddam Hussein in Iraq, reinforce this mistrust of separating religious values from politics.

Advocates of Islamic democracy argue that the Oneness of God requires some form of democratic system; conservatives contend that the idea of the sovereignty of the people contradicts the sovereignty of God; often the alternative then becomes some form of a monarchical system. The response to this is an affirmation of tawhid, as expressed by a Sudanese intellectual, Abdelwahab El-Affendi, in the October 2000 edition of Islam 21: "No Muslim questions the sovereignty of God or the rule of Shari'ah [the Islamic legal path]. However, most Muslims do (and did) have misgivings about any claims by one person that he is sovereign. The sovereignty of one man contradicts the sovereignty of God, for all men are equal in front of God.... Blind obedience to one-man rule is contrary to Islam." In this way, it is argued that the doctrine of tawhid virtually requires a democratic system because humans are all created equal and any system that denies that equality is not Islamic.

There are a number of specific concepts that Muslims cite when they explain the relationship between Islam and democracy. In the Qur'an, the righteous are described as those people who, among other things, manage their affairs through "mutual consultation" or shura. This is expanded through traditions of the Prophet and the sayings and actions of the early leaders of the Muslim community to mean that it is obligatory for Muslims in managing their political affairs to engage in mutual consultation. Contemporary Muslim thinkers ranging from relatively conservative Islamists to more liberal modernists to Shi'ite activists emphasize the importance of consultation. There would be little disagreement with the view of Ayatollah Baqir al-Sadr, the Iraqi Shi'ite leader who was executed by Saddam Hussein in 1980, who said in Islamic Political System, that the people "have a general right to dispose of their affairs on the basis of the principle of consultation." What this meant for the constitutional system of the Islamic Republic of Iran, which was influenced by al-Sadr's thought, was affirmed by President Khatami in last June's interview: the "people play a fundamental role in bringing a government to power, in supervising the government and possibly the replacement of the government without any tension and problems."

Another basic concept in the development of Islamic democracy is "caliph." In contemporary discussions, traditional political usage of the term caliph has been redefined. Historically the term caliph was used as the title of the monarchs who ruled the medieval Muslim empire. When medieval Muslim political philosophers spoke of the institutions of caliph rule, the caliphate, they were analyzing the political institution of the successors to the Prophet Muhammad as the leader of the Muslim community. However, this concept of the caliphate was something that developed after the death of the Prophet.

In the Qur'an, the Arabic words for caliph (khalifah) and caliphate (khilafah) have a different meaning. These terms in the Qur'an have the more general meaning of steward and stewardship or trustee and trusteeship. In this way, Adam, as the first human, is identified as God's caliph or steward on earth. Muhammad is instructed to remind humans that God made them the caliphs (stewards or trustees) of the earth. In this way, in the Qur'an, the term caliphate refers to the broad responsibilities of humans to be the stewards of God's creation.

By the late twentieth century, long after the last vestiges of the political caliphate had been abolished by the reforms of Ataturk in Turkey in 1924, Muslim intellectuals began to see the importance of the concept of all humans as "caliphs" or God's stewards. As the intellectual dimensions of the late twentieth-century Islamic resurgence became more clearly defined, Ismail al-Faruqi, a scholar of Palestinian origins, outlined an ambitious project in a small book, Islamization of Knowledge. The concept of the caliphate involved responsibilities for all humans, in all dimensions of life, but especially the political: "Rightly, Muslims understand khilafah as directly political.... Islam requires that every Muslim be politicized (i.e., awakened, organized, and mobilized)."

The implications of this reassertion of a more explicitly Qur'anic meaning of human stewardship for Islamic democracy were spelled out by the South Asian Islamist leader, Abu al-Ala Mawdudi in The Islamic Way of Life: "The authority of the caliphate is bestowed on the entire group of people, the community as a whole.... Such a society carries the responsibility of the caliphate as a whole and each one of its individual[s] shares the Divine Caliphate. This is the point where democracy begins in Islam. Every person in an Islamic society enjoys the rights and powers of the caliphate of God and in this respect all individuals are equal."

In theory and concept, Islamic democracy is, at the beginning of the twenty-first century, quite well developed and persuasive. In actual practice the results have been less encouraging. Authoritarian rulers such as Ja'far Numayri in Sudan and Zia al-Haqq in Pakistan initiated formal programs of Islamization of the law and political system in the 1980s with results that were not encouraging for democracy. A military coup brought a combination of military and civilian Islamists to rule in Sudan in 1989 and despite the proclaimed goal of creating an Islamic democracy, the regime's human rights record in terms of treatment of non-Muslim minorities and Muslim opposition groups is deplorable.

International human rights groups have also been critical of the treatment of non-Muslim minorities in Iran, where the Shah was overthrown in 1979. During its first decade, the Islamic Republic set narrow limitations on political participation. However, the end of the nineties saw the unprecedented presidential election victory of Mohammad Khatami, who had not been favored by the conservative religious establishment. He was reelected by an over-whelming majority again in 2001.

Although there are continuing grounds for criticizing Iran in terms of its repression of opposition and minorities, increasing numbers of women and youth are voting in elections. Instead of "one man, one vote, one time," the "one man" is being joined by "one woman" as a voting force.

Beyond the formally proclaimed Islamic political systems, there has also been an increasing role for democracy with an Islamic tone. In many Muslim countries, who are not activist Islamists had participated in electoral processes and brought a growing sense of need for morality and Islamic awareness in the political arena.

In an era when politics in many countries is becoming "desecularized," leaders of Islamic organizations play important roles in electoral political systems that are not explicitly identified as Islamic. When the military regime of Suharto in Indonesia was brought to an end, the person who became president in 1999 as a result of the first open elections was Abd al-Rahman Wahid, the leader of Nahdat ul-Ulama, perhaps the largest Islamic organization in the world. He did not campaign on a platform of Islamizing the political system, even though he participated in the democratic system as a clearly identifiable Islamic leader. When he was removed as president this year, it was by a process of orderly replacement, and neither his followers nor his opponents engaged in religious warfare.

Similarly, islamically oriented political parties have operated successfully in the secular electoral politics of Turkey, with the leader of one such party, Necmettin Erbakan, serving as prime minister briefly in 1996-1997. Although in succession, the islamically oriented Turkish parties have been suppressed and many of their leaders jailed, the response of the people in the parties has simply been to form new parties and try again within the political system rather than withdrawing into a violent underground opposition.

The Turkish experience reflects the fact that many Muslims, whether living in formally secular or formally Islamic states, see democracy as their main hope and vehicle of effective political participation. One important dimen-sion of this participation is that despite conservative Muslim opposition to the idea of rule by a woman, the three largest Muslim states in the world - Indonesia, Bangladesh, and Pakistan - have had or now have elected women as their heads of government. None of these women was explicitly Islamist and one was directly opposed by an Islamist party.

In this complex context, it is clear that Islam is not inherently incompatible with democracy. "Political Islam" is sometimes a program for religious democracy and not primarily an agenda for holy war or terrorism.

The solutions to the many problems of the world are in our classrooms, and global peace can be best achieved by promoting the spirit of democracy in our schools. In the history of American education, schools have always been used as tools of reform, and the most important lessons of the 21st century (in addition to teaching the advancement of technology and science) would be to teach the skills of living in peace and harmony in the world. At the heart of democracy lies the ideals of equality, justice, and fairness for all; democracy is not a form of government or theory but rather a way of life. In no other time in the history of our nation have our democratic principles been put to the test than it is today; hence, it is more important to teach about democracy today!

As educators begin to focus on teaching the different forms of government to our young citizens, the future leaders, it is vital that they give a fair picture of democracy. The Muslim world and Islam today have been distorted greatly, and one of the forms of distortion is the misinfor-mation or lack of information about Islamic history. It may surprise many to hear that democracy has been at the cornerstone of Islam; unfortunately today this information is covered by the debris of terrorism and fundamentalism, the wars and destructions around the Muslim world and the Middle East. Organizations such as Council of American Islamic Relations (CAIR), Florida Law Related Education (FLREA), and State Bar of Texas can help educate to clear such misunderstandings.

Although only 15% of the total Muslim population of the world consists of Arabs, Islam and Arab have become synonymous after the recent attacks of September 11, 2001. More focus has been laid on the area of Middle East than any other part of the Muslim world. Asad AbuKhalil in his article "The Islamic World Needs Secularism", states that Islam has been used by governments for centuries for political purposes, and it has consequently affected various aspects of Muslim life. But the questions of Islam and democracy as well as of Islam and secularism are often discussed in ways that imply a peculiar anti-democratic streak in Islam. Hence it becomes even more important for the west, and especially the United States a leading nation to gain more knowledge about the two from an unbiased perspective.

The last decade has brought political changes in several Arab countries that "are now leading to democratization of one form or another.

Democratization of the political system occurred in Jordan, Algeria, Yemen and Lebanon, in spite of the many limitations and challenges of these countries. Abu Khalil emphasizes that "Democracy, as an aspiration and not as a political actuality, is now sweeping the entire region. Since the early 1980s, Arab men and women have clearly voiced their deep desire for democratic changes in their respective countries." "The subject of democracy and openness has been the focus of Arab intellectual debates since before the demise of communist rule. Recent events in the Arab world have also forced them to believe that nationalism or "unity without democracy will be short-lived." The ideological debate in the Arab world today, particularly in the scholarly writings, focuses on the way in which Islam, Arab nationalism and democracy can be linked together harmoniously.

Unfortunately, Islam has been seen as a hindrance to democracy and a threat to the west. The division of east and west has for long been seen on opposite ends and against each other, is it cultures or ideologies; educating one's self and others about the uniqueness and different perspectives would help ease tensions between the western and eastern countries. The next few years will be as important for democracy's evolution as for Islam's.

For two millennia democracy has taken root only in Western cultures. One of the next major global challenges will be determining whether democracy is adaptable to Eastern countries, including Islamic and Confucian societies, and vice versa. This is a moment to encourage, rather than obstruct, Islam's expression in pluralist forms." "The Islamic resurgence clearly presents a challenge to the West. But it also provides enormous opportunity." A time for opportunity to also educate the students, both Americans and Muslim-Americans about the truth about Islam and Democracy, and that democracy in the United States should mean the same to all Americans, regardless of their religion, ethnicity and cultural background.

Democracy is not new to Islam. The foundation of the first government in the history of Islam was laid on democracy. "That Muslims attach great significance to their organization as a political community can be seen in the fact that their calendar is dated neither from the birth nor the death of the Prophet, but from the establishment of the first Muslim policy in the city-state of Madina in 622.

Before Madina was founded, the Arabs had no state to "establish justice, insure domestic tranquility, provide for the common defense, promote the general welfare, and secure the blessings of liberty."

President Bush had rightly stated in his speech during the 20th anniversary of the National Endowment for Democracy in Washington D.C. on November 6, 2003:

It should be clear to all that Islam-the faith of one-fifth of humanity – is consistent with democratic rule. Democ-ratic progress is found in many predominantly Muslim countries – in Turkey and Indonesia, and Senegal and Albania, Niger and Sierra Leone. Muslim men and women are good citizens of India and South Africa, of the nations of Western Europe, and of the United States of America.

More than half of all the Muslims in the world live in freedom under democratically constituted governments. They succeed in democratic societies, not in spite of their faith, but because of it. A religion that demands individual moral accountability, and encourages the encounter of the individual with God, is fully compatible with the rights and responsibilities of self-government.

President Bush further stated that the challenges that the Middle East is going through during the present times, whether it be poverty or the lack of rights for women, should not be misunderstood that this is due to Islam but it was the result of colonialism leading to the establishment of dictatorships. He emphasizes that "These are not the failures of a culture or a religion. These are the failures of political and economic doctrines." He further states that any "working democracies always need time to develop – as did our own. We've taken a 200-year journey toward inclusion and justice – and this makes us patient and understanding as other nations are at different stages of this journey".

There are certain important points to remember as one searches democracy in the history of Islam. The concept of democracy is present in the Qur'an as the Qur'an covers everyday life, including the political structure. Since Islam is a way of life, democracy fits in well with it – freedom of speech, religion, equality, are the rights of the people as long as they are well balanced.

Prophet Muhammad applied democratic principles in the establishment of the Muslim community 1500 years ago. The two major principles of democracy practiced during this time were: The concept of Bay'ah (voting) where the Qur'an says that the "ruler cannot rule without the consent of the people." For example, Abu Bakr was the first elected Khalifa. He was democratically elected in the same way the earlier U.S. president George Washington was elected. A large number of Sahaba (companions of the prophet) would gather in the Saqifa where different parties would put forward different nominations open for debate and then would pick out a single nominee like the caucuses in the different parties in a constitutional democracy. At the time of Abu Bakr there were not two parties but three, and each party came up with their own nomination (Al Muhajeroon with candidate Abu Baker; Alansar with Saad bin Ubada; and Ali Bin Abi Talib and Abdullah Ibn Alzubir in a mixture of Muhajeroon and Ansar as the third party). After the individual caucuses the three major groups met in the Saqifa of Banu Saeda and agreed on Abu Bakr after much heated debates. Abu Bakr finally emerged as the nominee and he was presented to the masses as the candidate for them to make a final vote. In other words Abu Bakr did not become the Khalifa until the masses gave him the Biya, similar to the Democratic and Republican parties. Thus, "Abu Bakr's election as the first caliph demonstrates the acceptability of the Electoral College as a method of electing the head of state."

Also, lack of a single model of elections described in the Quran shows that the model is not intended to be one stagnant for all times but it should always have an element of shura or democracy.

The concept of the Shura (consultation) is very similar to the democratic principle of debate and agreement. It is the community as a whole, not an individual that owns or exercises power. In a chapter on Al-Shura the Qur'an describes Muslim societies as one in which individuals manage their affairs through consultation. Shura is similar to direct democracy and is considered as a personal duty, which no one can perform on behalf of another. Shura is obligatory on Muslims as the five daily prayers are; like prayers Muslims are urged to practice shura in their daily work, family lives, and community affairs. John Voll and John Esposito, 1995 in their article Islam Has Strong Democratic Traditions, emphasize on the Operational Concepts for Islamic Democracy. "Several Islamic concepts have a key role in the development of Islamic democracy: consultation (shura), consensus (ijma), and independent interpretive judgment (ijtihad)." These interpretations, like the "interpreted concepts such as citizens and parliament in the Western tradition, they have become crucial concepts for the articulation of Islamic democracy." Thus, "Consultation, consensus, and independent judgment provide the basic concepts for understanding the relationship between Islam and democracy in the contemporary world, and an effective foundation to build an Islamic basis for democracy."

The first constitution during the prophet's life was the Charter of Medina which was drawn by Prophet Muhammad 500-600 years before the Magna Carta. It laid out a federal role over the tribes. It was a pact signed by the Prophet and the main non-Muslim tribes – some pagans and Christians, but mostly Jews. This charter became a way of life for the citizens of Medina. A comparison is drawn below between the Charter of Medina and the US Constitution by using a few examples from the time of the Prophet Muhammad's life:

a. Right to equality before law- It established equality, where it said all citizens of Medina were equal.

b. Due process of law- One may not punish someone by guilt association.

c. Minority Rights- The charter forbids giving any advantage to someone influential in executing punishments.

d. Freedom of speech- People were free to provide consultation and criticism to the extent that free discussion was encouraged through ijtihad (interpretation of the Quran).

e. Bill of Rights- Hilf ul Fudool or a covenant was signed by Prophet Muhammad to protect those who are weak and to make sure that business dealings were conducted in all fairness.

f. Right to vote- Women as a minority had the right to vote and women of Medina voted for the Prophet.

g. Socio-economic structure was developed to maintain equality through zakat (charity) system where 2.5% of the total savings had to pay to help the needy and improve the standard of living for all.

h. Right to religious freedom- Where the Jewish tribes were allowed to live according to their own rules and were not required to follow the rules of Islam. "Christian minorities in Muslim society have always had access to wine (which they need for their sacrament), despite the fact that Islamic law prohibits." Thus, there was respect for diversity in religions and cultures as the Quran mentions, "We have made you into nations and tribes so that ye may understand each other and not despise each other. Verily the most honored among you is one that is most righteous." Prophet Muhammad posed no religious test in the Medina Covenant. The Jews and Christians have held high positions in Muslim governments. While the "American restriction is one of geography, the Islamic restriction is one of declared commitment to the source of the law." True, anyone "can alter his or her religion but no one can alter his or her place of birth."

Causes for the decline of democracy after the prophet

1. Differences arose among successors of the Prophet. (The Prophet did not assign a successor during his lifetime but left it to the people to decide their leader, thus setting an example – Sunnah).

2. People who were not pious took power and rulers went against the Islamic doctrine and "politics began to suppress religions, rather than religion suppressing politics".
3. Long history of colonialism was prevalent around the Muslim world where colonial powers chose weak leader who acted more as puppets than true leaders. "European colonial rule and post-independence govern-ments headed by military officers, ex-military men, and monarchs have contributed to a legacy in which political participation and the building of democratic institutions are of little concern."
4. Colonialism also led to the reform in the education system where Arabic and Quran were eradicated from the schools. Thus people lacked the knowledge of the Quran and were denied to engage in ijtihad (process of interpreting the Quran).
5. Lack of knowledge from the Quran and Sunnah led to misleading information that was more cultural than religious. (Women began to be oppressed, rulers became dictators, and inequality and corruption soon became the rule of the land).
6. The misconception that Islam is against democracy has its roots in the history of Muslim dictators who did not want to awaken the people to the truth about Islam. (Mughuls in India, Abbasid in Baghdad, and the Turks were all dynastic rulers not real rulers based on the principles described in the Quran & Sunnah.
7. Lack of successful democracies today has made it even harder for the Muslim countries to return to the true democratic and Islamic governments of the past.

Although the concept of democracy is not introduced to the Muslims by the west, the west will be given credit for bringing its 'renaissance' be it in the Middle East or any other parts of the Muslim world. John Esposito, a practicing Christian professor reminds his fellow citizens to learn lessons from "a past in which fear of a monolithic Soviet threat often blinded the United States to the Soviet bloc's diversity, led to uncritical support for (anti-Communist) dictatorships, and enabled the "free world" to tolerate the suppression of legitimate dissent and massive human rights violations by governments that labeled the opposition "communist" or "socialist". The risk today is that exaggerated fears will lead to a double standard in the promotion of democracy and human rights in the Muslim world as can be witnessed by the Western concern about and action to support democracy..."Support for democracy and human rights is more effective if it is consistent around the world. Treating Islamic experiences as exceptional is an invitation to long-term conflict."

Voll and Esposito have rightly stated that the global dynamics of democratization reflect the dramatic changes of the present. True, throughout the world—including the Western democracies-the effort to create more effective democratic structures continues apace and the Muslim countries are not an exception.

"Movements like an-Nahda in Tunisia, the Muslim Brethren of Jordan and Egypt, and the Jamaat-i-Islami in Pakistan affirm that democratization consists of more than simply importing a set model from the West." "Muslims have important contributions to make in the process of reconceptualizing democracy, especially in the area of consensual participation and non-adversarial democratic structures." Educational seminars and workshops such as this would be a first step towards strengthening the culture and movement of democracy and helping towards the gradual evolution of democracy in today's world.

2

Islam and Civil Society

A Historical Analysis

In the political science and thought literature, civil society and state are defined as distinct spheres, which nonetheless complement each other. Under conditions in which civil society has developed sufficiently in a given society, the state is likely to have limited activities, act in a non-partisan manner and abide by law. This is indeed an instrumental state. Conversely, in societies where civil society is weak and deficient, all sorts of political, economic and ideological power remains in the hand of the state, which exerts absolute monopoly over all walks of social life. In such a milieu, the state is not only seen to be acting as a political organisation but is seen as a metaphysical and abstract entity which is beyond the grasp of ordinary individuals. The development of civil society is closely linked to the size and activities of the state.

A ripening civil society replaces the state in the performance of certain functions and compels the state to turn into an impartial institution in relation to different segments of society. Wherever civil society is advanced far enough, the state, rather than commanding the society to adopt a particular ideology or way of life, is transformed into an instrumental organisation, which seeks to serve the individuals and protect their basic rights.

There are three prerequisites for the development of civil society: differentiation, forming organisations, creation of an autonomous sphere. All sorts of social differentiation should be encouraged if civil society is to strengthen. Accordingly, the society ought to be differentiated along sociological categories such as ethnic, cultural, religious, ideological, occupational and other linkages. The second necessary requirement for the strengthening of civil society is the accordance of freedom for all those representing different formations, which are willing to engage in politics. Social organisations in this sense act as an intermediary for the enjoyment of individual rights.

Finally, the strengthening of civil society requires that the social groups, identities and categories enjoy an 'autonomous' status vis-à-vis the state. In other words, social groups and categories should have the right to determine their 'self' and translate this into practice without the intervention of the state. In short, today, the term 'civil society' implies the existence of a democratic society and state characterised by the rule of law in which the primary goals are securing maximum freedoms enjoyed by individuals, widespread participation in social and political life, and individual self-determination.

In the sense defined above, civil society obtained the chance of development only after the industrial revolution in the West. The notion of 'world state' set up by the Catholic Church had resulted in the restriction of individual rights and freedoms and had opened all the realms of social life into the hegemony of the state. The process of social differentiation, which occurred as a by-product of industrial revolution inevitably, resulted in the process of political differentiation; together they set the course on the path of democracy. Therefore, the concepts of democracy and civil society have simultaneously evolved in the West. The lack of democracy always meant the absence of civil society. The rigid, centralising, totalitarian and tyrannical states, built on socialist principles in Eastern Europe in this century, were also characterised by the conspicuous absence of civil societies.

Universal Islamic Declaration of Democracy

Human Rights

Islam gave to mankind [what many Muslims believe to be] an ideal code of human rights fourteen centuries ago. These rights aim at conferring honour and dignity on mankind and eliminating exploitation, oppression and injustice.

Human rights in Islam are firmly rooted in the belief that God, and God alone, is the Law Giver and the Source of all human rights [so mankind can have no say in the promulgation of new laws not in conformity with God's law]. Due to their Divine origin, no ruler, government, assembly or authority can curtail or violate in any way the human rights conferred by God, nor can they be surren-dered [nor extended or enlarged upon in the light of human experience].

Human rights in Islam are an integral part of the overall Islamic order and it is obligatory on all Muslim governments and organs of society to implement them in letter and in spirit within the framework of that order.

It is unfortunate that human rights are being trampled upon with impunity in many countries of the world, including some Muslim countries. Such violations are a matter of serious concern and are arousing the conscience of more and more people throughout the world.

This Declaration of Human Rights is the second fundamental document proclaimed by the Islamic Council to mark the beginning of the 15th Century of the Islamic era, the first being the Universal Islamic Declaration announced at the International Conference on The Prophet Muhammad (peace and blessings be upon him) and his Message, held in London from 12 to 15 April 1980. The Universal Islamic Declaration of Human Rights is based on the Qur'an and the Sunnah and has been compiled by eminent Muslim scholars, jurists and representatives of Islamic movements and thought. May God reward them all for their efforts and guide us along the right path.

- Paris 21 Dhul Qaidah 1401 Salem Azzam
- 19th September 1981 Secretary General

O men! Behold, we have created you all out of a male and a female, and have made you into nations and tribes, so that you might come to know one another. Verily, the noblest of you in the sight of God is the one who is most deeply conscious of Him. Behold, God is all-knowing, all aware.

Whereas the age-old human aspiration for a just world orders wherein people could live, develop and prosper in an environment free from fear, oppression, exploitation and deprivation, remains largely unfulfilled;

Whereas the Divine Mercy unto mankind reflected in its having been endowed with super-abundant economic sustenance is being wasted, or unfairly or unjustly withheld from the inhabitants of the earth;

Whereas Allah (God) has given mankind through His revelations in the Holy Qur'an and the Sunnah of His Blessed Prophet Muhammad an abiding legal and moral framework within which to establish and regulate human institutions and relationships;

Whereas the human rights decreed by the Divine Law aim at conferring dignity and honour on mankind and are designed to eliminate oppression and injustice;

Whereas by virtue of their Divine source and sanction these rights can neither be curtailed, abrogated or disregarded by authorities, assemblies or other institutions, nor can they be surrendered or alienated;

Therefore we, as Muslims, who believe:

a. In God, the Beneficent and Merciful, the Creator, the Sustainer, the Sovereign, the sole Guide of mankind and the Source of all Law [and reject all man-made laws not in conformity therewith];
b. In the Viceregency (Khilafah) of man who has been created to fulfill the Will of God on earth;
c. In the wisdom of Divine guidance brought by the Prophets, whose mission found its culmination in the final

Divine message that was conveyed by the Prophet Muhammad (Peace be upon him) to all mankind;

d. That rationality by itself without the light of revelation from God can neither be a sure guide in the affairs of mankind nor provide spiritual nourishment to the human soul, and, knowing that the teachings of Islam represent the quintessence of Divine guidance in its final and perfect form, [therefore reject the idea that useful knowledge can be obtained independently from any other source, and] feel duty-bound to remind man of the high status and dignity bestowed on him by God;

e. In inviting all mankind to the message of Islam;

f. That by the terms of our primeval covenant with God our duties and obligations have priority over our rights, and that each one of us is under a bounden duty to spread the teachings of Islam by word, deed, and indeed in all gentle ways, and to make them effective not only in our individual lives but also in the society around us [and therefore have a corresponding duty to prevent the teaching of any other religion or philosophy of life];

g. In our obligation to establish an Islamic order:

- Wherein all human beings shall be equal and none shall enjoy a privilege or suffer a disadvantage or discrimination by reason of race, colour, sex, origin or language [although discrimination on the grounds of belief shall be permissible];
- Wherein all human beings are born free [but are not free to change their religion if they are born a Muslim];
- Wherein slavery and forced labour are abhorred [but not banned outright];
- Wherein conditions shall be established such that the institution of family shall be preserved, protected and honoured as the basis of all social life [and all alternative life-styles strongly discouraged];
- Wherein the rulers and the ruled alike are subject to, and equal before, the Law;

- Wherein obedience shall be rendered only to those commands that are in consonance with the Law; [i.e. the Sharia only]
- Wherein all worldly power shall be considered as a sacred trust, to be exercised within the limits prescribed by the Law and in a manner approved by it, and with due regard for the priorities fixed by it;
- Wherein all economic resources shall be treated as Divine blessings bestowed upon mankind, to be enjoyed by all in accordance with the rules and the values set out in the Qur'an and the Sunnah [but not in conformity with any man-made law, treaty or other contractual obligation];
- Wherein all public affairs shall be determined and conducted, and the authority to administer them shall be exercised after mutual consultation (Shura) [but only] with the believers qualified to contribute to a decision which would accord well with the Law and the public good;
- Wherein everyone shall undertake obligations proportionate to his capacity and shall be held responsible pro rata for his deeds;
- Wherein everyone shall, in case of an infringement of his rights, be assured of appropriate remedial measures in accordance with the Law;
- Wherein no one shall be deprived of the rights assured to him by the Law except by its authority and to the extent permitted by it;
- Wherein every individual shall have the right to bring legal action against anyone who commits a crime against society as a whole or against any of its members;
- Wherein every effort shall be made to
  a. Secure unto mankind deliverance from every type of exploitation, injustice and oppression,

b. Ensure to everyone security, dignity and liberty in terms set out and by methods approved and within the limits set by the Law;

Do hereby, as servants of Allah and as members of the Universal Brotherhood of Islam, at the beginning of the Fifteenth Century of the Islamic Era, affirm our commit-ment to uphold the following inviolable and inalienable human rights that we consider are enjoined by Islam.

Right to Life

Human life is sacred and inviolable and every effort shall be made to protect it. In particular no one shall be exposed to injury or death, except under the authority of the Law [which may not actually be codified but open to interpretation by jurists and may invoke penalties incompatible with internationally agreed standards of justice].

Just as in life, so also after death, the sanctity of a person's body shall be inviolable. It is the obligation of believers to see that a deceased person's body is handled with due solemnity.

Right to Freedom

Man is born free. No inroads shall be made on his right to liberty except under the authority and in due process of the Law.

Every individual and every people has the inalienable right to freedom in all its forms- physical, cultural, economic and political- [but not religious] and shall be entitled to struggle by all available means against any infringement or abrogation of this right; and every oppressed individual or people has a legitimate claim to the support of other individuals and/or peoples in such a struggle.

Right to Equality and Prohibition against Impermissible Discrimination

All persons are equal before the Law and are entitled to equal opportunities and protection of the Law [except for women,

Christians, Jews, Hindus and nonbelievers for whom neither opportunities nor protection are equal].

All persons shall be entitled to equal wage for equal work. No person shall be denied the opportunity to work or be discriminated against in any manner or exposed to greater physical risk by reason of religious belief, colour, race, origin, sex or language.

Right to Justice

Every person has the right to be treated in accordance with the Law and only in accordance with the Law [and shall therefore have the right not to be treated in accordance with any law which does not conform to the Sharia].

Every person has not only the right but also the obligation to protest against injustice; to recourse to remedies provided by the Law in respect of any unwarranted personal injury or loss; to self-defence against any charges that are preferred against him and to obtain fair adjudication before an independent judicial tribunal in any dispute with public authorities or any other person.

It is the right and duty of every person to defend the rights of any other person and the community in general (Hisbah).

No person shall be discriminated against while seeking to defend private and public rights [but only those rights which conform to the Sharia]

It is the right and duty of every Muslim to refuse to obey any command which is contrary to the Law, no matter by whom it may be issued. [So Muslims have the right and duty to disobey any man-made law which does not conform to the Sharia]

Right to Fair Trial

No person shall be adjudged guilty of an offence and made liable to punishment except after proof of his guilt before an independent judicial tribunal. [However the word of a Muslim shall count as the word of two non-Muslims and the word of a Muslim man shall count as the word of two Muslim women].

No person shall be adjudged guilty except after a fair trial and after reasonable opportunity for defence has been provided to him. Punishment shall be awarded in accordance with the Law, in proportion to the seriousness of the offence and with due consideration of the circumstances under which it was committed.

No act shall be considered a crime unless it is stipulated as such in the clear wording of the Law.

Every individual is responsible for his actions. Responsibility for a crime cannot be vicariously extended to other members of his family or group, who are not otherwise directly or indirectly involved in the commission of the crime in question.

Right to Protection against Abuse of Power

Every person has the right to protection against harassment by official agencies. He is not liable to account for himself except for making a defence to the charges made against him or where he is found in a situation wherein a question regarding suspicion of his involvement in a crime could be reasonably raised

Right to Protection against Torture

No person shall be subjected to torture in mind or body, or degraded, or threatened with injury either to himself or to anyone related to or held dear by him, or forcibly made to confess to the commission of a crime, or forced to consent to an act which is injurious to his interests.

Right to Protection of Honour and Reputation

Every person has the right to protect his honour and reputation against calumnies, groundless charges or deliberate attempts at defamation and blackmail.

Right to Asylum

Every persecuted or oppressed person has the right to seek refuge and asylum. This right is guaranteed to every human being irrespective of race, religion, colour and sex.

Al Masjid Al Haram (the sacred house of Allah) in Mecca is a sanctuary for all Muslims.

Rights of Minorities

The Qur'anic principle "There is no compulsion in religion" shall govern the religious rights of non-Muslim minorities.

In a Muslim country religious minorities [but not nonbelievers] shall have the choice to be governed in respect of their civil and personal matters by Islamic Law, or by their own laws.

Right and Obligation to Participate in the Conduct and Management of Public Affairs

Subject to the Law, every individual in the community (Ummah) is entitled to assume public office [provided they are a Muslim]

Process of free consultation (Shura) is the basis of the administrative relationship between the government and the people. People also have the right to choose and remove their rulers in accordance with this principle.

Right to Freedom of Belief, Thought and Speech

Every person has the right to express his thoughts and beliefs so long as he remains within the limits prescribed by the Law [i.e. does not criticize Islam or the prophet]. No one, however, is entitled to disseminate falsehood [i.e. anything which does not conform to Islamic belief] or to circulate reports which may outrage public decency, or to indulge in slander, innuendo or to cast defamatory aspersions on other persons.

Pursuit of knowledge and search after truth is not only a right but a duty of every Muslim [provided that it does not conflict with a) above].

It is the right and duty of every Muslim to protest and strive (within the limits set out by the Law) against oppression even if it involves challenging the highest authority in the state.

There shall be no bar on the dissemination of information provided it does not endanger the security of the society or the state and is confined within the limits imposed by the Law [i.e. does not criticism or conflict with the teachings of Islam, the Prophet or with the decisions of any cleric].

No one shall hold in contempt or ridicule the religious beliefs of others or incite public hostility against them. [To criticism verbally or in writing any aspect of the Law shall be deemed to be inciting public hostility to the religious beliefs of others.] Respect for the religious feelings of others is obligatory on all Muslims.

Right to Freedom of Religion

Every person has the right to freedom of conscience and worship in accordance with his religious beliefs.

Right to Free Association

Every person is entitled to participate individually and collectively in the religious, social, cultural and political life of his community and to establish institutions and agencies meant to enjoin what is right (ma'roof) and to prevent what is wrong (munkar). [This extends to a right to control personal, private conduct].

Every person is entitled to strive for the establishment of institutions whereunder an enjoyment of these rights would be made possible. Collectively, the community is obliged to establish conditions so as to allow its members full development of their personalities.

The Economic Order and the Rights Evolving Therefrom

In their economic pursuits, all persons are entitled to the full benefits of nature and all its resources. These are blessings bestowed by God for the benefit of mankind as a whole.

All human beings are entitled to earn their living according to the Law.

Every person is entitled to own property individually or in association with others. State ownership of certain economic resources in the public interest is legitimate.

The poor have the right to a prescribed share in the wealth of the rich, as fixed by Zakah, levied and collected in accordance with the Law. [This tax is limited to 5% of income].

All means of production shall be utilised in the interest of the community (Ummah) as a whole, and may not be neglected or misused.

In order to promote the development of a balanced economy and to protect society from exploitation, Islamic Law forbids monopolies, unreasonable restrictive trade practices, usury, the use of coercion in the making of contracts and the publication of misleading advertisements.

All economic activities are permitted provided they are not detrimental to the interests of the community (Ummah) and do not violate Islamic laws and values.

Right to Protection of Property

No property may be expropriated except in the public interest and on payment of fair and adequate compensation.

Status and Dignity of Workers

Islam honours work and the worker and enjoins Muslims not only to treat the worker justly but also generously. He is not only to be paid his earned wages promptly, but is also entitled to adequate rest and leisure.

Right to Social Security

Every person has the right to food, shelter, clothing, education and medical care consistent with the resources of the community. This obligation of the community extends in particular to all individuals who cannot take care of themselves due to some temporary or permanent disability.

Right to Found a Family and Related Matters

Every person is entitled to marry, to found a family and to bring up children in conformity with his religion, traditions and culture. Every spouse is entitled to such rights and privileges and carries such obligations as are stipulated by the Law.

Each of the partners in a marriage is entitled to respect and consideration from the other.

Every husband is obligated to maintain his wife and children according to his means.

Every child has the right to be maintained and properly brought up by its parents, it being forbidden that children are made to work at an early age or that any burden is put on them which would arrest or harm their natural development. If parents are for some reason unable to discharge their obligations towards a child it becomes the responsibility of the community to fulfill these obligations at public expense. Every person is entitled to material support, as well as care and protection, from his family during his childhood, old age or incapacity. Parents are entitled to material support as well as care and protection from their children.

Motherhood is entitled to special respect, care and assistance on the part of the family and the public organs of the community (Ummah).

Within the family, men and women are to share in their obligations and responsibilities according to their sex, their natural endowments, talents and inclinations, bearing in mind their common responsibilities toward their progeny and their relatives. No person may be married against his or her will, or lose or suffer diminutions of legal personality on account of marriage.

Rights of Married Women

Every married woman is entitled to:

a. Live in the house in which her husband lives [but not to live apart from her husband];
b. Receive the means necessary for maintaining a standard of living which is not inferior to that of her spouse, and, in the event of divorce, receive during the statutory

period of waiting (iddah) [but no longer than that,] means of maintenance commensurate with her husband's resources, for herself as well as for the children she nurses or keeps, irrespective of her own financial status, earnings, or property that she may hold in her own rights;

c. Seek and obtain dissolution of marriage (Khul'a) in accordance with the terms of the Law [i.e. a lesser right to divorce than her husband]. This right is in addition to her right to seek divorce through the courts.

d. Inherit from her husband, her parents, her children and other relatives according to the Law. [In the case of her husband - and if they have children - a maximum of one eighth part of his estate to be shared jointly with any other wives.]

e. Strict confidentiality from her spouse, or ex-spouse if divorced, with regard to any information that he may have obtained about her, the disclosure of which could prove detrimental to her interests.

   A similar responsibility rests upon her in respect of her spouse or ex-spouse [thereby inhibiting her ability to give evidence against him in support of her divorce].

Right to Education

Every person is entitled to receive education in accordance with his natural capabilities.

Every person is entitled to a free choice of profession and career and to the opportunity for the full development of his natural endowments.

Right of Privacy

Every person is entitled to the protection of his privacy.

Right to Freedom of Movement and Residence

In view of the fact that the World of Islam is veritably Ummah Islamia, every Muslim shall have the right to freely move in and out of any Muslim country [but the right of a non-Muslim to settle in or become a full citizen of any Islamic country may be denied].

No one shall be forced to leave the country of his residence, or be arbitrarily deported therefrom without recourse to due process of Law.

Right of citizens in an islamic state

We have discussed the human rights in general. Now we would like to take up the question of rights of the citizens in an Islamic State. As these rights are more extensive than the general human rights which have been described earlier, they need separate treatment.

The Security of Life and Property

In the address which the Prophet delivered on the occasion of the Farewell Hajj, he said: "Your lives and properties are forbidden to one another till you meet your Lord on the Day of Resurrection." God Almighty has laid down in the Holy Quran: "Anyone who kills a believer deliberately will receive as his reward (a sentence) to live in Hell for ever. God will be angry with him and curse him, and prepare dreadful torment for him" (4:93). The Prophet has also said about the dhimmis (the non-Muslim citizens of the Muslim State): "One who kills a man under covenant (i.e. a dhimmi) will not even smell the fragrance of Paradise" (al-Bukhari and Abu Dawud).

Islam prohibits homicide but allows only one exception, which the killing is done in the due process of law which the Quran refers to as bi al-haqq (with the truth). Therefore a man can be killed only when the law demands it, and it is obvious that only a court of law can decide whether the execution is being carried out with justice or without justification. In case of war or insurrection a just and righteous government alone, which follows the ari'ah or the Islamic Law, can decide whether a war is just or unjust, whether taking of a life is justified or not; and whether a person is a rebel or not and who can be sentenced to death as a punishment.

These weighty decisions cannot be left in the hands of a court which has become heedless to God and is under the influence of the administration.

A judiciary like this may miscarry justice. Nor can the crimes of state be justified on the authority of the Holy Quran or Traditions (hadith) when the state murders its citizens openly and secretly without any hesitation or on the slightest pretext, because they are opposed to its unjust policies and actions or criticize it for its misdeed, and also provides protection to its hired assassins who have been guilty of the heinous crime of murder of an innocent person resulting in the fact, that neither the police take any action against such criminals nor can any proof or witnesses against these criminals be produced in the courts of law. The very existence of such a government is a crime and none of the killings carried out by them can be called "execution for the sake of justice" in the phraseology of the Holy Quran.

Along with security of life, Islam has with equal clarity and definiteness conferred the right of security of ownership of property, as mentioned earlier with reference to the address of the Farewell Hajj.

On the other hand, the Holy Quran goes so far as to declare that the taking of people's possessions or property is completely prohibited unless they are acquired by lawful means as permitted in the Laws of God. The Law of God categorically declares "Do not devour one another's wealth by false and illegal means" (2:188).

The Protection of Honour

The second important right is the right of the citizens to the protection of their honour. In the address delivered on the occasion of the Farewell Hajj, to which I have referred earlier, the Prophet did not only prohibit the life and property of the Muslims to one another, but also any encroachment upon their honour, respect and chastity were forbidden to one another. The Holy Quran clearly lays down:

a. "You who believe, do not let one (set of) people make

fun of another set.

b. Do not defame one another.

c. Do not insult by using nicknames.

d. And do not backbite or speak ill of one another".

This is the law of Islam for the protection of honour which is indeed much superior to and better than the Western Law of Defamation. According to the Islamic Law if it is proved that someone has attacked the honour of another person, then irrespective of the fact whether or not the victim is able to prove himself a respectable and honourable person the culprit will in any case get his due punishment. But the interesting fact about the Western Law of Defamation is that the person who files suit for defamation has first to prove that he is a man of honour and public esteem and during the interrogation he is subjected to the scurrilous attacks, accusations and innuendoes of the defence council to such an extent that he earns more disgrace than the attack on his reputation against which he had knocked the door of the court of law.

On top of it he has also to produce such witnesses as would testify in the court that due to the defamatory accusations of the culprit, the accused stands disgraced in their eyes. Good Gracious! What a subtle point of law, and what an adherence to the spirit of Law! How can this unfair and unjust law be compared to the Divine law? Islam declared blasphemy as a crime irrespective of the fact whether the accused is a man of honour or not, and whether the words used for blasphemy have actually disgraced the victim and harmed his reputation in the eyes of the public or not. According to the Islamic Law the mere proof of the fact that the accused said things which according to common sense could have damaged the reputation and honour of the plaintiff, is enough for the accused to be declared guilty of defamation.

The Sanctity and Security of Private Life

Islam recognizes the right of every citizen of its state that there should be no undue interference or encroachment on the privacy of his life. The Holy Quran has laid down the injunction: "Do not spy on one another" (49:12). "Do not enter any houses except your own homes unless you are sure of their occupants' consent" (24:27). The Prophet has gone to the extent of instructing his followers that a man should not enter even his own house suddenly or surreptitiously.

He should somehow or other informs or indicates to the dwellers of the house that he is entering the house, so that he may not see his mother, sister or daughter in a condition in which they would not like to be seen, nor would he himself like to see them in that condition. Peering into the houses of other people has also been strictly prohibited, so another person secretly peering into his house, and he blinds his eye or eyes as a punishment then he cannot be called to question nor will he be liable to prosecution.

The Prophet has even prohibited people from reading the letters of others, so much so that if a man is reading his letter and another man casts sidelong glances at it and tries to read it, his conduct becomes reprehensible. This is the sanctity of privacy that Islam grants to individuals. On the other hand in the modern civilized world we find that not only the letters of other people are read and their correspondence censored, but even their photostat copies are retained for future use or blackmail. Even bugging devices are secretly fixed in the houses of the people so that one can hear and tape from a distance the conversation taking place behind closed doors. In other words it means that there is no such thing as privacy and to all practical purposes the private life of an individual does not exist.

This espionage on the life of the individual cannot be justified on oral grounds by the government saying that it is necessary to know the secrets of the dangerous persons. Though, to all intents and purposes, the basis of this policy is the fear and suspicion with which modern governments look at their citizens who are intelligent and dissatisfied with the official policies of the government. This is exactly what Islam has called as the root cause of mischief in politics. The injunction of the Prophet is: "When the ruler begins to search for the causes of dissatisfaction amongst his people, he spoils them" (Abu Dawud).

The Amir Mu'awiyah has said that he himself heard the Prophet saying: "If you try to find out the secrets of the people, then you will definitely spoil them or at least you will bring them to the verge of ruin." The meaning of the phrase 'spoil them' is that when spies (C.I.D. or F.B.I. agents) are spread all around the country to find out the affairs of men, then the people begin to look at one another with suspicion, so much so that people are afraid of talking freely in their houses lest some word should escape from the lips of their wives and children which may put them in embarrassing situations. In this manner it becomes difficult for a common citizen to speak freely, even in his own house and society begins to suffer from a state of general distrust and suspicion.

The Security of Personal Freedom

Islam has also laid down the principle that no citizen can be imprisoned unless his guilt has been proved in an open court. To arrest a man only on the basis of suspicion and to throw him into a prison without proper court proceedings and without providing him a reasonable opportunity to produce his defence is not permissible in Islam. It is related in the hadith that once the Prophet was delivering a lecture in the mosque, when a man rose during the lecture and said: "O Prophet of God, for what crime have my neighbours been arrested?" The Prophet heard the question and continued his speech. The man rose once again and repeated the same question. The Prophet again did not answer and continued his speech. The man rose for a third time and repeated the same question. Then the Prophet ordered that the man's neighbours be released. The reason why the Prophet had kept quiet when the question was repeated twice earlier was that the police officer was present in the mosque and if there were proper reasons for the arrest of the neighbours of this man, he would have got up to explain his position. Since the police officer gave no reasons for these arrests the Prophet ordered that the arrested persons should be released. The police officer was aware of the Islamic law and therefore he did not get up to say: "the administration is aware of the charges against the arrested men, but they cannot be disclosed in public. If the Prophet would inquire about their guilt in camera I would enlighten him." If the police officer had made such a statement, he would have been dismissed then and there.

The fact that the police officer did not give any reasons for the arrests in the open court was sufficient reason for the Prophet to give immediate orders for the release of the arrested men. The injunction of the Holy Quran is very clear on this point. "Whenever you judge between people, you should judge with (a sense of) justice" (4:58). And the Prophet has also been asked by God: "I have been ordered to dispense justice between you." This was the reason why the Caliph 'Umar said: "In Islam no one can be imprisoned except in pursuance of justice." The words used here clearly indicate that justice means due process of law. What has been prohibited and condemned is that a man be arrested and imprisoned without proof of his guilt in an open court and without providing him an opportunity to defend himself against those charges. If the Government suspects that a particular individual has committed a crime or he is likely to commit an offence in the near future then they should give reasons for should be allowed to produce his defence in an open court, so that the court may decide whether the suspicion against him is based on sound grounds or not and if there is good reason for suspicion, then he should be informed of how long he will be in preventive detention. This decision should be taken under all circumstances in an open court, so that the public may hear the charges brought by the government, as well as the defence made by the accused and see that the due process of law is being applied to him and he is not being victimized.

The correct method of dealing with such cases in Islam is exemplified in the famous decision of the Prophet which took place before the conquest of Makkah. The Prophet was making preparations for the attack on Makkah, when one of his

Companions, Hatib ibn Abi Balta'ah sent a letter through a woman to the authorities in Makkah informing them about the impending attack. The Prophet came to know of this through a Divine inspiration. He ordered 'Ali and Zubayr:

"Go quickly on the route to Makkah, at such and such place, you will find a woman carrying a letter. Recover the letter from her and bring it to me." So they went and found the woman exactly where the Prophet had said. They recovered the letter from her and brought it to the Prophet. This was indeed a clear case of treachery. To inform the enemy about a secret of an army and that too at the time of a war is a very serious offence tantamount to treachery. In fact one cannot think of a more serious crime during war than giving out a military secret to one's enemy. What could have been a more suitable case for a secret hearing; a military secret had been betrayed and common sense demanded that he should be tried in camera. But the Prophet summoned Hatib to the open court of the Mosque of the Prophet and in the presence of hundreds of people asked him to explain his position with regard to his letter addressed to the leaders of Quraysh which had been intercepted on its way.

The accused said: "O God's Messenger (may God's blessings be on you) I have not revolted against Islam, nor have I done this with the intention of betraying a military secret. The truth of the matter is that my wife and children are living in Makkah and I do not have my tribe to protect them there. I had written this letter so that the leaders of Quraysh may be indebted to me and may protect my wife and children out of gratitude." 'Umar rose and respectfully submitted: "O Prophet, please permit me to put this traitor to the sword." The Prophet replied: "He is one of those people who had participated in the Battle of Badr, and the explanation he has advanced in his defence would seem to be correct."

Let us look at this decision of the Prophet in perspective. It was a clear case of treachery and betrayal of military secrets. But the Prophet acquitted Hatib on two counts. Firstly, that his past records were very clean and showed that he could not have betrayed the cause of Islam, since on the occasion of the Battle of Badr when there were heavy odds against the Muslims, he had risked his life for them.

Secondly, his family was in fact in danger at Makkah. Therefore, if he had shown some human weakness for his children and written this letter, then this punishment was quite sufficient for him that his secret offence was divulged in public and he had been disgraced and humiliated in the eyes of the believers. God has referred to this offence of Hatib in the Holy Quran but did not propose any punishment for him except rebuke and admonition.

The attitude and activities of the Kharijis in the days of the Caliph 'Ali are well-known to the students of Muslim history. They used to abuse the Caliph openly, and threaten him with murder. But whenever they were arrested for these offences, 'Ali would set them free and tell his officers "As long as they do not actually perpetrate offences against the State, the mere use of abusive language or the threat of use of force are not such offences for which they can be imprisoned." The imam Abu Hanifah has recorded the following saying of the Caliph 'Ali (A): "As long as they do not set out on armed rebellion, the Caliph of the Faithful will not interfere with them." On another occasion 'Ali was delivering a lecture in the mosque when the Kharijis raised their special slogan there. 'Ali said: "We will not deny you the right to come to the mosques to worship God, nor will we stop to give your share from the wealth of the State, as long as you are with us (and support us in our wars with the unbelievers) and we shall never take military action against you as long as you do not fight with us."

One can visualize the opposition which 'Ali was facing; more violent and vituperative opposition cannot even be imagined in a present-day democratic State; but the freedom that he had allowed to the opposition was such that no government has ever been able to give to its opposition. He did not arrest even those who threatened him with murder nor did he imprison them.

The Right to Protest against Tyranny

Amongst the rights that Islam has conferred on human beings is the right to protest against government's tyranny. Referring to it the Quran says: "God does not love evil talk in public unless it is by someone who has been injured thereby" (4:148). This means that God strongly disapproves of abusive language or strong words of condemnation, but the person who has been the victim of injustice or tyranny, God gives him the right to openly protest against the injury that has been done to him. This right is not limited only to individuals. The words of the verse are general.

Therefore if an individual or a group of people or a party usurps power, and after assuming the reins of authority begins to tyrannize individuals or groups of men or the entire population of the country, then to raise the voice of protest against it openly is the God-given right of man and no one has the authority to usurp or deny this right. If anyone tries to usurp this right of citizens then he rebels against God. The talisman of Section 1444 may protect such a tyrant in this world, but it cannot save him from the hell-fire in the Hereafter.

Freedom of Expression

Islam gives the right of freedom of thought and expression to all citizens of the Islamic State on the condition that it should be used for the propagation of virtue and truth and not for spreading evil and wickedness. This Islamic concept of freedom of expression is much superior to the concept prevalent in the West. Under no circumstances would Islam allow evil and wickedness to be propagated. It also does not give anybody the right to use abusive or offensive language in the name of criticism. The right to freedom of expression for the sake of propagating virtue and righteousness is not only a right in Islam but an obligation.

One who tries to deny this right to his people is openly at war with God, the All-Powerful. And the same thing applies to the attempt to stop people from evil. Whether this evil is perpetrated by an individual or by a group of people or the government of one's own country or the government of some other country; it is the right of a Muslim and it is also his obligation that he should warn and reprimand the evil-doer and try to stop him from doing it. Over and above, he should openly and publicly condemn it and show the course of righteousness which that individual, nation or government should adopt.

The Holy Quran has described this quality of the Faithful in the following words: "They enjoin what is proper and forbid what is improper".

In contrast, describing the qualities of a hypocrite, the Quran mentions: "They bid what is improper and forbid what is proper". The main purpose of an Islamic Government has been defined by God in the Quran as follows: "If we give authority to these men on earth they will keep up prayers, and offer poor-due, bid what is proper and forbid what is improper". The Prophet has said:

"If any one of you comes across an evil, he should try to stop it with his hand (using force), if he is not in a position to stop it with his hand then he should try to stop it by means of his tongue (meaning he should speak against it). If he is not even able to use his tongue then he should at least condemn it in his heart. This is the weakest degree of faith" (Muslim).

This obligation of inviting people to righteousness and forbidding them to adopt the paths of evil is incumbent on all true Muslims. If any government deprives its citizens of this right, and prevents them from performing this duty, then it is in direct conflict with the injunction of God. The government is not in conflict with its people, but is in conflict with God. In this way it is at war with God and is trying to usurp that right of its people which God has conferred not only as a right but as an obligation.

As far as the government which itself propagates evil, wickedness and obscenity and interferes with those who are inviting people to virtue and righteousness is concerned, according to the Holy Quran it is the government of the hypocrites.

Freedom of Association

Islam has also given people the right to freedom of association and formation of parties or organizations. This right is also subject to certain general rules. It should be exercised for propagating virtue and righteousness and should never be used for spreading evil and mischief.

We have not only been given this right for spreading righteousness and virtue, but have been ordered to exercise this right. Addressing the Muslims, the Holy Quran declares: You are the best community which has been brought forth for mankind. You command what is proper and forbid what is improper and you believe in God...

This means that it is the obligation and duty of the entire Muslim community that it should invite and enjoin people to righteousness and virtue and forbid them from doing evil. If the entire Muslim community is not able to perform this duty then "let there be a community among you who will invite (people) to (do) good, command what is proper and forbid what is improper, those will be prosperous" This clearly indicates that if the entire Muslim nation collectively begins to neglect its obligation to invite people to goodness and forbid them from doing evil then it is absolutely essential that it should contain at least a group of people which may perform this obligation.

As has been said before this is not only a right but an obligation and on the fulfillment of which depends success and prosperity here as well as in the Hereafter. It is an irony with the religion of God that in a Muslim country the assembly and association that is formed for the purposes of spreading evil and mischief should have the right to rule over the country and the association and party which has been formed for propagating righteousness and virtue should live in perpetual fear of harassment and of being declared illegal. Conditions here are just the reverse of what has been prescribed by God. The claim is that we are Muslims and this is an Islamic State but the work that is being done is directed to spreading evil, to corrupt and morally degrade and debase the people while there is an active and effective check on the work being carried out for reforming society and inviting people to righteousness. Moreover the life of those who are engaged in spreading righteousness and checking the spread of evil and wickedness is made intolerable and hard to bear.

Freedom of Conscience and Conviction

Islam also gives the right to freedom of conscience and conviction to its citizens in an Islamic State. The Holy Quran has laid down the injunction: "There should be no coercion in the matter of faith". Though there is no truth and virtue greater than the religion of Truth-Islam, and Muslims are enjoined to invite people to embrace Islam and advance arguments in favour of it, they are not asked to enforce this faith on them. No force will be applied in order to compel them to accept Islam. Whoever accepts it he does so by his own choice. Muslims will welcome such a convert to Islam with open arms and admit him to their community with equal rights and privileges. But if somebody does not accept Islam, Muslims will have to recognize and respect his decision, and no moral, social or political pressure will be put on him to change his mind.

Protection of Religious Sentiments

Along with the freedom of conviction and freedom of conscience, Islam has given the right to the individual that his religious sentiments will be given due respect and nothing will be said or done which may encroach upon this right. It has been ordained by God in the Holy Quran: "Do not abuse those they appeal to instead of God" (6:108). These instructions are not only limited to idols and deities, but they also apply to the leaders or national heroes of the people. If a group of People holds a conviction which according to you is wrong, and holds certain persons in high esteem which according to you is not deserved by them, then it will not be justified in Islam that you use abusive language for them and thus injure their feelings. Islam does not prohibit people from holding debate and discussion on religious matters, but it wants that these discussions should be conducted in decency. "Do not argue with the people of the Book unless it is in the politest manner" says the Quran. This order is not merely limited to the people of the Scriptures, but applies with equal force to those following other faiths.

Protection from Arbitary Imprisonment

Islam also recognizes the right of the individual that he will not be arrested or imprisoned for the offences of others. The Holy Quran has laid down this principle clearly: "No bearer of burdens shall be made to bear the burden of another". Islam believes in personal responsibility. We ourselves are responsible for our acts, and the consequence of our actions cannot be transferred to someone else. In other words this means that every man is responsible for his actions. If another man has not shared this action then he cannot be held responsible for it, nor can he be arrested. It is a matter of great regret and shame that we are seeing this just and equitable principle which has not been framed by any human being, but by the Creator and Nourisher of the entire universe, being flouted and violated before our eyes. So much so that a man is guilty of a crime or he is a suspect, but his wife being arrested for his crime. Things have gone so far that innocent people are being punished for the crimes of others. To give a recent example, in Karachi (Pakistan), a man was suspected of being involved in a bomb throwing incident. In the course of police investigation he was subjected to horrible torture in order to extract a confession from him. When he insisted on his innocence, then the police arrested his mother, his wife, daughter and sister and brought them to the police station. They were all stripped naked in his presence and he was stripped naked of all his clothes before their eyes so that a confession of the crime could be extracted from him. It appears as if for the sake of investigation of crime it has become proper and legal in our country to strip the innocent women folk of the household in order to bring pressure on the suspect. This is indeed very outrageous and shameful.

The Right to Basic Necessities of Life

Islam has recognized the right of the needy people that help and assistance will be provided for them. "And in their wealth there is acknowledged right for the needy and the destitute" (51:19). In this verse, the Quran has not only conferred a right on every man who asks for assistance in the wealth of the Muslims, but has also laid down that if a Muslim comes to know that a certain man is without the basic necessities of life, then irrespective of the fact whether he asks for assistance or not, it is his duty to reach him and give all the help that he can extend. For this purpose Islam has not depended only on the help and charity that is given voluntarily, but has made compulsory charity, zakat as the third pillar of Islam, next only to profession of faith and worship of God through holding regular prayers. The Prophet has clearly instructed in this respect that: "It will be taken from their rich and given to those in the community in need" (al-Bukhari and Muslim).

In addition to this, it has also been declared that the Islamic State should support those who have nobody to support them. The Prophet has said: "The Head of state is the guardian of him, who has nobody to support him" (Abu Dawud, al-Tirmidhi). The word wali which has been used by the Prophet is a very comprehensive word and has a wide range of meanings. If there is an orphan or an aged man, if there is a crippled or unemployed person, if one is invalid or poor and has no one else to support him or help him, then it is the duty and the responsibility of the state to support and assist him. If a dead man has no guardian or heir, then it is the duty of the state to arrange for his proper burial. In short the state has been entrusted with the duty and responsibility of looking after all those who need help and assistance. A truly Islamic State is therefore a truly welfare state which will be the guardian and protector of all those in need.

Equality before Law

Islam gives its citizens the right to absolute and complete equality in the eyes of the law. As far as the Muslims are concerned, there are clear instructions in the Holy Quran and hadith that in their rights and obligations they are all equal: "The believers are brothers (to each other)" (49:10). "If they (disbelievers) repent and keep up prayer and pay the poor-due, they are your brothers in faith" (9:11). The Prophet has said that: "The life and blood of Muslims are equally precious". In another hadith he has said:

"The protection given by all Muslims are equal and even an ordinary man can grant protection to any man". In another more detailed Tradition of the Prophet, it has been said that those who accept the Oneness of God, believe in the Prophet hood of His Messenger, give up primitive prejudices and join the Muslim community and brotherhood, "then they have the same rights and obligations as other Muslims have" (al-Bukhari; al-Nisa'i). Thus there is absolute equality between the new converts to Islam and the old followers of the Faith.

This religious brotherhood and the uniformity of their rights and obligations is the foundation of equality in Islamic society, in which the rights and obligations of any person are neither greater nor lesser in any way than the rights and obligations of other people. As far as the non- Muslim citizens of the Islamic State are concerned, the rule of Islamic Shari'ah (law) about them has been very well expressed by the Caliph 'Ali in these words: "They have accepted our protection only because their lives may be like our lives and their properties like our properties". In other words, their (of the dhimmis) lives and properties are as sacred as the lives and properties of the Muslims. Discrimination of people into different classes was one of the greatest crimes that, according to the Quran, Pharaoh used to indulge in: "He had divided his people into different classes,"... "And he suppressed one group of them (at the cost of others)".

Rulers not above the Law

Islam clearly insists and demands that all officials of the Islamic State, whether he is the head or an ordinary employee, are equal in the eyes of the law. None of them is above the law or can claim immunity. Even an ordinary citizen in Islam has the right to put forward a claim or file a legal complaint against the highest executive of the country. The Caliph 'Umar said, "I have myself seen the Prophet, may God's blessings be on him, taking revenge against himself (penalizing himself for some shortcoming or failing)." On the occasion of the Battle of Badr, when the Prophet was straightening the rows of the Muslim army he hit the belly of a soldier in an attempt to push him back in line. The soldier complained "O Prophet, you have hurt me with your stick." The Prophet immediately bared his belly and said: "I am very sorry, you can revenge by doing the same to me." The soldier came forward and kissed the abdomen of the Prophet and said that this was all that he wanted.

A woman belonging to a high and noble family was arrested in connection with a theft. The case was brought to the Prophet, and it was recommended that she may be spared the punishment of theft. The Prophet replied: "The nations that lived before you were destroyed by God because they punished the common men for their offences and let their dignitaries go unpunished for their crimes; I swear by Him (God) who holds my life in His hand that even if Fatimah, the daughter of Muhammad, has committed this crime then I would have amputated her hand." During the caliphate of 'Umar, Muhammad the son of 'Amr ibn al-'As the Governor of Egypt, whipped an Egyptian. The Egyptian went to Medina and lodged his complaint with the Righteous Caliph, who immediately summoned the Governor and his son to Medina. When they appeared before him in Medina, the Caliph handed a whip to the Egyptian complainant and asked him to whip the son of the Governor in his presence. After taking his revenge when the Egyptian was about to hand over the whip to 'Umar, he said to the Egyptian:

"Give one stroke of the whip to the Honourable Governor as well. His son would certainly have not beaten you were it not for the false pride that he had in his father's high office." The plaintiff submitted: "The person, who had beaten me, I have already avenged myself on him."

'Umar said: "By God, if you had beaten him (the Governor) I would not have checked you from doing so. You have spared him of your own free will." Then he ('Umar) angrily turned to 'Amr ibn al-'As and said: "O 'Amr, when did you start to enslave the people, though they were born free of their mothers?" When the Islamic State was flourishing in its pristine glory and splendour, the common people could equally lodge complaints against the caliph of the time in the court and the caliph had to appear before the qadi to answer the charges. And if the caliph had any complaint against any citizen, he could not use his administrative powers and authority to set the matter right, but had to refer the case to the court of law for proper adjudication.

The Right to Avoid Sin

Islam also confers this right on every citizen that he will not be ordered to commit a sin, a crime or an offence; and if any government, or the administrator, or the head of department orders an individual to do a wrong, then he has the right to refuse to comply with the order. His refusal to carry out such crime or unjust instructions would not be regarded as an offence in the eyes of the Islamic law.

On the contrary giving orders to one's subordinates to commit a sin or do a wrong is itself an offence and such a serious offence that the officer who gives this sinful order whatever his rank and position may be, is liable to be summarily dismissed. These clear instructions of the Prophet are summarized in the following hadith: "It is not permissible to disobey God in obedience to the orders of any human being".

In other words, no one has the right to order his subordinates to do anything against the laws of God. If such an order is given, the subordinate has the right to ignore it or openly refuse to carry out such instructions. According to this rule no offender will be able to prove his innocence or escape punishment by saying that this offence was committed on the orders of the government or superior officers. If such a situation arises then the person who commits the offence and the person who orders that such an offence be committed, will both be liable to face criminal proceedings against them. And if an officer takes any improper and unjust measures against a subordinate who refuses to carry out illegal orders, then the subordinate has the right to go to the court of law for the protection of his rights, and he can demand that the officer be punished for his wrong or unjust orders.

The Right to Participate in the Affairs of State

According to Islam, governments in this world are actually representatives (khulafa') of the Creator of the universe, and this responsibility is not entrusted to any individual or family or a particular class or group of people but to the entire Muslim nation. The Holy Quran says: "God has promised to appoint those of you who believe and do good deeds as (His) representatives on earth". This clearly indicates that khilafah is a collective gift of God in which the right of every individual Muslim is neither more nor less than the right of any other person. The correct method recommended by the Holy Quran for running the affairs of the state is as follows: "And their business is (conducted) through consultation among themselves".

According to this principle it is the right of every Muslim that either he should have a direct say in the affairs of the state or a representative chosen by him and other Muslims should participate in the consultation of the state. Islam, under no circumstance, permits or tolerates that an individual or a group or party of individuals may deprive the common Muslims of their rights, and usurps powers of the state. Similarly, Islam does not regard it right and proper that an individual may put up a false show of setting up a legislative assembly and by means of underhand tactics such as fraud, persecution, bribery, etc., gets himself and men of his choice elected in the assembly.

This is not only a treachery against the people whose rights are usurped by illegal and unfair means, but against the Creator Who has entrusted the Muslims to rule on this earth on His behalf, and has prescribed the pro-legislative assembly has no other meaning except that:

1. The executive head of the government and the members of the assembly should be elected by free and independent choice of the people.
2. The people and their representatives should have the right to criticize and freely express their opinions.
3. The real conditions of the country should be brought before the people without suppressing any fact so that they may be able to form their opinion about whether the government is working properly or not.
4. There should be adequate guarantee that only those people who have the support of the masses should rule over the country and those who fail to win this support should be removed from their position of authority.

Right of Enemies at War

After dealing with the rights of the citizens of an Islamic State, let's have a brief discussion on the rights which Islam has conferred on its enemies. In the days when Islam came into focus the world was completely unaware of the concept of humane and decent rules of war. The West became conscious of this concept for the first time through the works of the seventeenth century thinker, Grotius. But the actual codification of the 'international law' in war began in the middle of the war was found in the West. All forms of barbarity and savagery were perpetrated in war, and the rights of those at war were not even recognized, let alone respected. The laws which were framed in this field during the nineteenth century or over the following period up to the present day cannot be called 'laws' in the real sense of the word. They are only in the nature of conventions and agreements and calling them 'international law' is actually a kind of misnomer, because no nation regards them binding when they are at war, unless, of course, when the adversaries also agree to abide by them. In other words, these civilized laws imply that if our enemies respect them then we shall also abide by them, and if they ignore these human conventions and take recourse to barbaric and cruel ways of waging war, then we shall also adopt the same or similar techniques. It is obvious that such a course which depends on mutual acceptance and agreement cannot be called 'law'. And this is the reason why the provisions of this so-called 'international law' have been flouted and ignored in every way, and every time they have been revised, additions or deletions have been made in them.

Law of War and Peace in Islam

The rules which have been framed by Islam to make war civilized and humane, are in the nature of law, because they are the injunctions of God and His Prophet which are followed by Muslims in all circumstances, irrespective of the behaviour of the enemy. It is now for the scholars to find out how far the West has availed of the laws of war given by Islam thirteen hundred years ago; and even after the adaptation of some of the laws of Islam how far the West attained those heights of civilized and humane methods of warfare which Muslims reached through the blessings of Islam. Western writers have often asserted that the Prophet had borrowed everything in his teachings from the Jews and the Christians. Instead of saying anything in its refutation I will only recommend the reader to refer to the Bible so that he can see which methods of war are recommended by the sacred Book of these Western clai-mants to civilization and culture. We have examined in some detail the basic human rights that Islam has conferred on man. Let us now find out what rights and obligations Islam recognizes for an enemy.

The Rright of the Non-Combatants

Islam has first drawn a clear line of distinction between the combatants and the non-combatants of the enemy country. As far as the non-combatant population is concerned such as women, children, the old and the infirm, etc., the instructions of the Prophet are as follows: "Do not kill any old person, any child or any woman". "Do not kill the monks in monasteries" or "Do not kill the people who are sitting in places of worship".

During a war, the Prophet saw the corpse of a woman lying on the ground and observed: "She was not fighting. How then she came to be killed?" From this statement of the Prophet the exegetists and jurists have drawn the principle that those who are non-combatants should not be killed during or after the war.

The Right of the Combatants

1. *Torture with Fire:* In the hadith there is a saying of the Prophet that: "Punishment by fire does not behove anyone except the Master of the Fire". The injunction deduced from this saying is that the adversary should not be burnt alive.
2. *Protection of the Wounded:* "Do not attack a wounded person"-thus said the Prophet. This means that the wounded soldiers not fit to fight, nor actually fighting, should not be attacked.
3. *The Prisoner of War should not be Slain:* "No prisoner should be put to the sword"-a very clear and unequivocal instruction given by the Prophet (S).
4. *No one should be Tied to be Killed:* "The Prophet has prohibited the killing of anyone who is tied or is in captivity."
5. *No Looting and Destruction in the Enemy's Country:* Muslims have also been instructed by the Prophet that if they should enter the enemy's territory, they should not indulge in pillage or plunder nor destroy the residential areas, nor touch the property of anyone except those who are fighting with them. It has been narrated in the hadith: "The Prophet has prohibited the believers from loot and plunder". His injunction is: "The loot is no more lawful than the carrion". Abu Bakr al-Siddiq used to instruct the soldiers while sending them to war, "Do not destroy the villages and towns, do not spoil the cultivated fields and gardens,

and do not slaughter the cattle." The booty of war which is acquired from the battleground is altogether different from this. It consists of the wealth, provisions and equipment captured only from the camps and military headquarters of the combatant armies.

6. *Sanctity of Property:* The Muslims have also been prohibited from taking anything from the general public of a conquered country without paying for it. If in a war the Muslim army occupies an area of the enemy country, and is encamped there, it does not have the right to use the things belonging to the people without their consent. If they need anything, they should purchase it from the local population or should obtain permission from the owners. Abu Bakr al-Siddiq, while instructing the Muslim armies being despatched to the battlefront would go to the extent of saying that Muslim soldiers should not even use the milk of the milch cattle without the permission of their owners.
7. *Sanctity of a Dead Body:* Islam has categorically prohibited its followers from disgracing or mutilating the corpses of their enemies as was practised in Arabia before the advent of Islam. It has been said in the hadith: "The Prophet has prohibited us from mutilating the corpses of the enemies". The occasion on which this order was given is highly instructive. In the Battle of Uhud the disbelievers mutilated the bodies of the Muslims, who had fallen on the battlefield and sacrificed their lives for the sake of Islam, by cutting off their ears and noses, and threading them together to put round their necks as trophies of war. The abdomen of Hamzah, the uncle of the Prophet, was ripped open by Quraysh, his liver was taken out and chewed by Hind, the wife of Abu Sufyan, the leader of the Meccan army. The Muslims were naturally enraged by this horrible sight. But the Prophet asked his followers not great example of forbearance and restraint is sufficient to convince any reasonable man who is not blinded by prejudice or bias that Islam is really the religion sent down by the Creator

of the universe, and that if human emotions had any admission in Islam, then this horrible sight on the battlefield of Uhud would have provoked the Prophet to order his followers to mutilate the bodies of their enemy in the same manner.

8. *Return of Corpses of the Enemy:* In the Battle of Ahzab a very renowned and redoubtable warrior of the enemy was killed and his body fell down in the trench which the Muslims had dug for the defence of Medina. The unbelievers presented ten thousand Dinars to the Prophet and requested that the dead body of their fallen warrior may be handed over to them. The Prophet replied "I do not sell dead bodies. You can take away the corpse of your fallen comrade."
9. *Prohibition of Breach of Treaties:* Islam has strictly prohibited treachery. One of the instructions that the Prophet used to give to the Muslim warriors while sending them to the battlefront was: "Do not be guilty of breach of faith."

   This order has been repeated in the Holy Quran and the hadith again and again, that if the enemy acts treacherously let him do so, you should never go back on your promise. There is a famous incident in the peace treaty of Hudaybiyyah, when after the settlement of the terms of the treaty, Abu Jandal, the son of the emissary of the unbelievers who had negotiated this treaty with the Muslims, came, fettered and blood-stained, rushing to the Muslim camp and crying for help. The Prophet told him "Since the terms of the treaty have been settled, we are not in a position to help you out. You should go back with your father. God will provide you with some other opportunity to escape this persecution." The entire Muslim army was deeply touched and grieved at the sad plight of Abu Jandal and many of them were moved to tears. But when the Prophet declared that "We cannot break the agreement", not even a single person came forward to help the unfortunate prisoner, so the unbelievers forcibly dragged him back to Makkah. This is an unparalleled example of the observance of the terms of agreement by the Muslims, and Islamic history can show many examples of a similar nature.

10. *Rules About Declaration of War:* It has been laid down in the Holy Quran: "If you apprehend breach of treaty from a people, then openly throw the treaty at their faces". In this verse, Muslims have been prohibited from opening hostilities against their enemies without properly declaring war against them, unless of course, the adversary has already started aggression against them. Otherwise the Quran has clearly given the injunction to Muslims that they should intimate to their enemies that no treaty exists between them, and they are at war with them. The present day 'interna-tional law' has also laid down that hostilities should not be started without declaration of war, but since it is a man-made rule, they are free to violate it whenever it is convenient. On the other hand, the laws for Muslims have been framed by God, hence they cannot be violated.

This is a brief sketch of those rights which fourteen hundred years ago Islam gave to man, to those who were at war with each other and to the citizens of its state, which every believer regards as sacred as law. On the one hand, it refreshes and strengthens our faith in Islam when we realize that even in this modern age which makes such loud claims of progress and enlightenment, the world has not been able to produce juster and more equitable laws than those given 1400 years ago. On the other hand it hurts one's feelings that Muslims are in possession of such a splendid and comprehensive system of law and yet they look forward for guidance to those leaders of the West who could not have dreamed of attaining those heights of truth and justice which was achieved a long time ago. Even more painful than this is the realization that throughout the world the rulers who claim to be Muslims have made disobedience to their God and the Prophet as the basis and foundation of their government. May God have mercy on them and give them the true guidance.

Compatibility with Democracy and Modernity

It is frequently argued that because many Islamic countries are monarchies or dictatorships - or because of certain events that have taken place within their borders - Islam is not compatible with either democracy or modernity. Some would maintain that Islamic culture is itself a stumbling block to a democratic polity and modernistic society and can accommodate neither. To maintain such a position is to misunderstand not only religion, but society, history and the operation of social forces.

If the same logic were applied elsewhere then Christianity too would still be under a cloud. The Christian Church also opposed democracy, secularism and modernity until the 18th century. A great struggle ensued between the church and princely rulers on the one hand, and between Christian and secular elements in society on the other. It was finally only during 19th century that democracy and modernity became acceptable within western, Christian society.

However, even some well-known scholars and orientalists have accepted such a superficial view of Islam and Islamic society. The western media, partly for political reasons and partly from ignorance of the social and material forces at work, have been instrumental in propagating such views about Islam and Islamic societies. But in order to understand the reality requires deeper insight into the social processes at work and it is necessary to view the issue from a number of perspectives: sociological, political and historical.

Recently a debate took place on the web regarding these issues. Ten questions were posed and responded to by the participants:

1. Is Islam incompatible with democracy?
2. Can Shari'ah laws with their harsh punishments and democracy go together?
3. Is it possible in Islamic countries to separate religion and state?
4. Can Islam support individual rights i.e. human rights?

5. Has the United States contributed to hampering democracy in countries like Saudi Arabia, Egypt, etc?
6. Is Islam opposed to modernity and does it refuse to come to terms with it?
7. Can religious texts be used as blueprints for the structure of a modern society?
8. Do women hold an inferior position in Muslim society, and can equality for women only be ensured through secular laws?
9. Is Islam tolerant and progressive, given that Islamic countries ban music and T.V., cinema posters etc?

In order to understand these questions it is not enough simply to look at what is happening in Muslim countries today and ascribe it to religion and religious teachings. Religion may appear to be a dominant cause but often it is not. Much happens under the cover of religion but there are all sorts of interests, particularly political and economic, that is more determinative and cannot be ignored. One also has to remember that there is no single interpretation of any religion. And one's interpretation is deeply influenced by one's sociopolitical inclination and turn of mind. Contemporary forces also play an important role in the interpretation of religion. Contemporary Islam is being interpreted in multiple ways. And the roles of history, of historical forces, of culture and of cultural heritage are all factors in the interpretation of religion.

Islam and Democracy

The first question is whether Islam is incompatible with democracy. It certainly is not but the Qur'an lays emphasis on what it calls shura' (consultation). Even the messenger of Allah is required to consult his people in worldly matters and Muslims are required to consult each other in their secular affairs. Now it is true that such consultation and modern day representative democracy may not be exactly similar. However, the idea of modern democracy and the Qur'anic injunction to consult people is the same in spirit. New institutions are continually developing and human societies, depending on their worldly experiences, continually change and refine these institutions. The Qur'anic text not only gives us the concept of shura' (democratic consultation) but cannot be said to support even remotely the ideas of dictatorship and authoritarianism.

Some commentators try to use the Qur'anic verse 4:59 to justify obedience to any kind of authority including a monarch, a caliph or a military dictator. This is certainly not the spirit of the verse. One has to see it in its historical context. The verse is addressed to Bedouins who were nomads and were not used to submitting to any authority. The Prophet sent his representatives to these Bedouin tribes and they refused to follow his instructions. The verse exhorted them to obey these authorities. It cannot be used to justify submission to illegitimately constituted authority. And, read in conjunction with the verses 3:159 and 42:38, it implies strongly that one has to submit to properly and democratically constituted authority. Authority has to be legitimate and properly constituted.

In the contemporary world the concept of shura' should mean democratic process and the constitution of proper democratic institutions - for which elections are a necessary requirement. In Islam no authority forcibly constituted, or acquired by power of swords or arms, can have any legitimacy whatsoever. The institution of monarchy or military dictatorship did not exist during the time of the Prophet. They are subsequent developments and were legitimized by the 'Ulama in order to prevent anarchy. Thus the 'Ulama conferred some legitimacy on monarchy not in the light of Islamic teachings but only to prevent anarchy. Some of them also became part of the power structure but their pronouncements had no Islamic legitimacy. One sees this today in most of the Islamic countries. The 'Ulama in Saudi Arabia are very much part of the monarchical power structure and legitimize everything the Saudi rulers do.

Thus the absence of democracy in Muslim countries is by means on account of Islamic teachings or the incompatibility of democracy with Islam but due to a host of factors: political, historical and cultural. The imperialist powers, first of Europe and then of the United States, have also played their role. The early Islamic democracy breathed its last within thirty years of the Holy Prophet's death. The institution of monarchy crept in under Roman influence. It is important to note that the capital of Islam had shifted from Medina to Kufa in Iraq and then to Damascus in Syria, once part of the Roman Empire. Mu'awiyah who seized power without the consent of the Muslims operated from Damascus and adopted Roman monarchical ways. Thus deeper historical and cultural influences must be taken into account in order to understand the political institutions in many Muslim countries today. American and British interests also play their role in shaping the power structures in these countries. In many Islamic countries including the Saudi Arabia and Egypt there is a deep longing among the people for democracy and popular government but it is frustrated by the heavy hand of authoritarian rule. It is not Islam that stands in the way of establishing democracy in these countries. It is powerful vested interests - both internal and external – that are preventing democracy from being established.

Divine Mercy and the Shari'ah

The next question is of implementation of Shari'ah law in Muslim countries. Many theologians and their followers believe sincerely that the problems confronting their countries and societies can be solved by enforcing Shari'ah laws and the punishments prescribed therein. Also, they believe these laws must be enforced as they were developed by the early jurists (fuqaha') without any rethinking. This is certainly not the spirit of the Qur'anic injunctions. Many Qur'anic verses were revealed in and relate to particular situations and this has to be kept in mind when applying these laws. The fundamental principle is to prevent crime and crime can be prevented in number of ways. At times harsh punishments may be necessary while at other times reformative efforts may be more relevant. When the Qur'anic injunctions about crimes like murder, theft, robbery, rebellion, rape and adultery are considered carefully this becomes quite obvious.

For example, the verse on cutting off of hands, 5:38 is immediately followed by verse 5:39 which says, "But whoever repents after his wrongdoing and reforms, Allah will turn to him (mercifully). Surely Allah is Forgiving, Merciful." Thus emphasis is on reform and repentance, not on harsh punishment. It may be awarded only in extreme cases. Also, if verse 5:39 is read in conjunction with the verse 5:33 where punishment for "those who wage war against Allah and His Messenger and strive to make mischief in the land is that they should be murdered, or crucified, or their hands and their feet should be cut off on opposite sides, or they should be imprisoned", it should become obvious that one must distinguish between ordinary and ultimate crime. When the punishment for mischief in the land or waging war against Allah and His Messenger could be imprisonment, how can the cutting off of hands be justified for mere theft?

Cutting off of hands can also be interpreted metaphorically, to mean taking measures that will prevent the miscreant from committing theft in future. Cutting off the tongue could mean silencing some one, not literally cutting off the tongue. Also, one has to keep in mind the historical context. This was the traditional, pre-Islamic punishment meted out at that time and when some tribes indulged in crimes for their survival. The Qur'an invokes the then prevalent punishment but also adds the concept of reform and repentance and speaks of Allah's Forgiveness and Mercy. A criminal, if he repents and reforms should be forgiven and shown mercy. Thus the Qur'an accepts the then prevalent punishment but improves upon it. The real purpose of Qur'anic justice is to reform the criminal but not to spare him if he persists despite being given the opportunity for a better life.

Separation of Religion and State

Another question relates to the separation of state and religion. Muslims generally believe that it is not possible to separate Islam and the state. This belief has acquired almost doctrinal status among Muslims. However, it has no such doctrinal position in the Qur'an. In fact it has been pointed out that the Qur'an does not even mention the concept of the state, only the concept of a just society. There was no state in Arabia at the time that Islam appeared and the Prophet laid down a bare framework of administration for the newly emerging society. There was no paid police, army or bureaucracy during his time.

It was during the time of 2nd Caliph Umar that a register (Diwan) of paid army soldiers was started. It is mere historical coincidence that a state structure came into existence along with the religious movement. The Shari'ah law provided a cohesive and logical legal structure where before there had been a legal vacuum and thus was a great advance. Hence Shari'ah law acquired a very high status in Islam.

Integration of state and religion is therefore a historical coincidence rather than a result of religious doctrine. Over time Shari'ah law, which had been the result of a dynamic process, became stagnant. Some modern scholars tried to infuse the principle of dynamism by invoking the concept of ijtihad but did not succeed because of the stagnation inherent in most Islamic states.

The authoritarian rulers in Muslim countries find legitimization only through the support of the 'Ulama and the 'Ulama insist on retaining the Sahri'ah law as inherited from the past. If Shari'ah law were to be rethought or reinterpreted in the light of modern conditions, the orthodox 'Ulama would risk losing their grip over the power structures. The collaboration between authoritarian rulers and the orthodox 'Ulama has thus resulted in total social, political and legal stagnation in many Muslim countries.

In some Muslim countries it may not be possible to attempt a total separation between state and religion, where for example, non-separation has become an integral part of the historical legacy, and one should begin by taking gradual steps in that direction.

There cannot be any universal recipe since much will depend on the specific conditions in each country. An overall

Islamic moral framework can be retained - as had happened in many western countries, including the USA, where an overall Christian moral framework has influenced law making. There are few countries in the West that have discarded such influence totally. Among Muslim countries Turkey has achieved separation of state from religion. But it must also be borne in mind that forcible imposition of modernization and separation of state and religion failed in countries like Afghanistan during the thirties and in Iran during the time of the Shah. Such attempts resulted in Islamic revolution and the imposition of Shari'ah law from above.

Islam and Human Rights

Individual rights are fundamental to the functioning of any liberal democracy. In fact the concept of individual rights or human rights has evolved along with the evolution of democratic power structures. Since there is no fully fledged democracy in any Muslim country there is little respect for the concept of individual rights. Indeed, many authoritarian rulers in Muslim countries reject the very concept of human rights denouncing them as western and secular in origin.

Thus one has to struggle for democratic power in order to usher in the concept of individual rights in Muslim countries. Human rights activists in some Muslim countries such as Saudi Arabia and Egypt are dubbed as western agents, persecuted and thrown into jail. Anyone who holds a different political opinion faces persecution and someone who advocates changes in the Shari'ah laws in the light of changed conditions, or attempt to reconceptualise Islamic philosophical doctrine to face severe persecution. There is little respect for individual rights and individual dignity. Full respect for individual rights and dignity are only possible under a fully democratic system. For that there is a basic need for a democratic polity.

Freedom of conscience and freedom of speech have never been denied by the Qur'an or the Prophet. The Prophet never suppressed individual freedom or discouraged differences of opinion. He even said that difference of opinion in the Islamic ummah was a matter of grace and mercy. However, with the evolution of feudal and monarchical culture differences of opinion were not permitted and were ruthlessly suppressed. During the early Abbasid period a controversy raged whether the Qur'an was created or is coeternal with God.

The Abbasid who supported the Mu'tazilah viewpoint that the Qur'an was created forcibly suppressed the other point of view that the Qur'an is coeternal with God and flogged a person of the stature of Imam Abu Hanifa for holding a contrary view. This authoritarian culture remains unchanged in many Muslim countries today. Many Islamic scholars have had to leave Egypt, Pakistan and other Muslim countries for western universities.

The suppression of free speech and freedom of conscience go hand-in-hand with the suppression of freedom of inquiry. It is for this reason that no Muslim country today has a strong tradition in the social or physical sciences. For the sciences to flourish one needs a liberal democratic culture. Muslim countries will remain far behind in these fields if their authoritarian power structures are not demolished and replaced with democratic ones. Unfortunately there is no such movement in sight. The United States has always propped up corrupt and authoritarian rulers in the Middle East who suppress freedom of expression and many of these countries remain totally dependent on the west. They cannot develop even to the extent that India has developed. No Muslim country can boast of any modern scientific discovery.

Religious Texts and Modern Society

It is true that some religious texts pose serious problems for modern society. But it need not be so with the Qur'anic texts if they are properly understood and are interpreted in the correct spirit. At the same time one should not obstruct worthwhile democratic, social and political change simply because some text is problematic. The religious texts were revealed or evolved in a very different social environment and one must take today's relevance into account. One need not reject religious texts per se but examine their suitability or otherwise for modern societies.

Status of Women

Many Muslim societies treat women as inferior to men and try to justify this treatment by quoting from religious texts including the Qur'an. But they quote very selectively to prove women's subordination to men. The Qur'an, if approached holistically, promotes the equal status of women. The verse often quoted by theologians to show women's inferior status is 4:34, but they ignore verses like 2:228, 33:35 and several others or try to explain them away as promoting merely spiritual equality. This is incorrect. The Qur'an taken as a whole is far more supportive of equality of the sexes.

Modern Islamic scholars now totally reject the orthodox interpretation of verse 4:34 made in a social environment in which male superiority was considered as quite natural, socially and biologically.

But one has to wage a serious struggle to promote sexual equality in contemporary Muslim societies where Muslim women suffer many severe disabilities. Again, it should be a part of the democratic struggle. One can break the stranglehold of the conservative 'Ulama only in a tolerant, pluralistic modern democracy. It is not Islamic teaching that stands in the way, it is the orthodox 'Ulama on the one hand, and authoritarian power structures on the other. The Qur'an, can in fact, can become a great asset in promoting sexual equality.

What we need is not only modern interpretation of the Qur'anic text but also female theologians fully conscious of their rights.

Freedom of Religion and Belief

Freedom of religion and belief does not mean merely the freedom to have a faith but also the freedom to change one's religion or belief. But under the Sharia, apostasy (either advocating the rejection of Islamic belief or announcing such rejection by word or deed) is not permitted and for a man may be punishable by death. The punishment for a woman may be more lenient, although opinions differ. She might be spared, but only to stay in prison until she reverts, however long it takes. Even when the death penalty is not applied, those accused of apostasy can be subject to the most violent treatment. This discrimination is clearly contrary to freedom of religion and belief and to the principle that religion should be a private matter for the individual. In a feeble attempt to disguise the Islamic attitude to apostasy, apologists often quote the Koranic verse: "There shall be no compulsion in religion". For a Muslim wishing to leave Islam this is simply not true.

The Islamic position on apostasy has been described as: "total disbelief that any sane person could possibly have a genuine reason for leaving 'the most perfect religion'. He or she must therefore, by definition, be acting in bad faith".

Belief in any religion should be voluntary and a private matter, but more often than not it is a collective statement and part of our identity. Typically, we inherit our religious belief from our parents, and share the beliefs of the community of which we are part. For most of us, our religion is more a matter of tradition, loyalty and custom than of deeply held belief. But for Muslims there is the added incentive of the severest penalties for any who wish to leave. One may ask the question of how strong a religion is if it has to force its adherents to stay under penalty of death.

Freedom of Expression

Under the Sharia and where Political Islam holds sway, writers, thinkers, philosophers, activists, and artists are frequently denied freedom of expression. Islamic regimes are notorious for the violent suppression of free thought. Often, as a government aligns itself closely with Islam, any critics of the government will be accused of heresy, blasphemy or insulting Islam. Under the Sharia people are deprived of many pleasures such as drinking alcohol, playing music, even of reading literature or philosophy, and are denied the opportunity of fully expressing their sexuality or of enjoying the arts.

Non-Muslims and the Sharia

In addition to its imposition of Islamic morality on non-Muslims, Sharia law dictates that there shall be no equality between Muslims and non-Muslims. Under strict Sharia law only Muslims can be full citizens of an Islamic state. Many states shamelessly discriminate against non-Muslims. In Saudi Arabia and Kuwait being Muslim is a precondition of naturalization.

Christians and Jews have limited rights but they may not participate in public life or hold positions of authority over Muslims. Anyone other than a Muslim, Christian or Jew is deemed to be an unbeliever and is not permitted to reside permanently in an Islamic state. The Koran only recognizes the People of the Book as religious communities. Others are pagans and must be excluded. In criminal prosecutions non-Muslims are given harsher punishments than Muslims. Crimes against Muslims are often punished more severely than crimes against others. In court under the Sharia the testimony of a non-Muslim carries less weight than that of a Muslim. In the multicultural world of which we are now part there can be no justification for discrimination on religious grounds.

Imagine the howls of protest if Muslims living in the west were to be treated as second-class citizens under the law. One of the great lessons we can learn from the west is the idea of secular that is neutral, laws that discriminate against no-one.

3

The Political Framework of Islam

The political system of Islam is based on the three principles of towhid (Oneness of Allah), risala (Prophet-hood) and Khilifa (Caliphate). Towhid means that one Allah alone is the Creator, Sustainer and Master of the universe and of all that exists in it - organic or inorganic. He alone has the right to command or forbid. Worship and obedience are due to Him alone. No aspect of life in all its multifarious forms ¾ our own organs and faculties, the apparent control which we have over physical objects or the objects themselves ¾ has been created or acquired by us in our own right. They are the bountiful provisions of Allah and have been bestowed on us by Him alone.

Hence, it is not for us to decide the aim and purpose of our existence or to set the limits of our worldly authority; nor does anyone else have the right to make these decisions for us. This right rests only with Allah. This principle of the Oneness of Allah makes meaningless the concept of the legal and political sovereignty of human beings. No individual, family, class or race can set themselves above Allah. Allah alone is the Ruler and His commandments constitute the law of Islam.

Risala is the medium through which we receive the law of Allah. We have received two things from this source: the Qur'an, the book in which Allah has expounded His law, and the authoritative interpretation and exemplification of that Book by the Prophet Muhammad (blessings of Allah and peace be upon him), through word and deed, in his capacity as the representative of Allah. The Qur'an laid down the broad principles on which human life should be based and the Prophet of Allah, in accordance with these principles, established a model system of Islamic life. The combination of these two elements is called the shari'a (law).

Khilifa means "representation". Man, according to Islam, is the representative of Allah on earth, His vice-gerent; that is to say, by virtue of the powers delegated to him by Allah, and within the limits prescribed, he is required to exercise Divine authority.

To illustrate what this means, let us take the case of an estate of yours which someone else has been appointed to administer on your behalf. Four conditions invariably obtain: First, the real ownership of the estate remains vested in you and not in the administrator; secondly, he administers your property directly in accordance with your instructions; thirdly, he exercises his authority within the limits prescribed by you; and fourthly, in the administration of the trust he executes your will and fulfils your intentions and not his own. Any representative who does not fulfill these four conditions will be abusing his authority and breaking the covenant which was implied in the concept of "representation".

This is exactly what Islam means when it affirms that man is the representative (khalifa) of Allah on earth. Hence, these four conditions are also involved in the concept of Khalifa. The state that is established in accordance with this political theory will in fact be a caliphate under the sovereignty of Allah. The above explanation of the term Khilafa also makes it clear that no individual or dynasty or class can be Khalifa: the authority of Khilafa is bestowed on the whole of any community which is ready to fulfill the conditions of representation after subscribing to the principles of towhid and Risala. Such a society carries the responsibility of the Khilafa as a whole and each one of its individuals shares in it.

This is the point where democracy begins in Islam. Every individual in an Islamic society enjoys the rights and powers of the caliphate of Allah and in this respect all individuals are equal. No-one may deprive anyone else of his rights and powers. The agency for running the affairs of the state will be formed by agreement with these individuals, and the authority of the state will only be an extension of the powers of the individuals delegated to it. Their opinion will be decisive in the formation of the government, which will be run with their advice and in accordance with their wishes.

Whoever gains their confidence will undertake the duties and obligations of the caliphate on their behalf; and when he loses this confidence he will have to step down. In this respect the political system of Islam is as perfect a dorm of democracy as there can be.

What distinguishes Islamic democracy from Western democracy, therefore, is that the latter is based on the concept of popular sovereignty, while the former rests on the principle of popular Khilafa. In Western democracy, the people are sovereign; in Islam sovereignty is vested in Allah and the people are His caliphs or representatives. In the former the people make their own; in the latter they have to follow and obey the laws (shari'a) given by Allah through His Prophet. In one the government undertakes to fulfill the will of the people; in the other the government and the people have to fulfill the will of Allah.

The Purpose of the Islamic State

The Holy Qur'an clearly states that the aim and purpose of this state is the establishment, maintenance and development of those virtues which the Creator wishes human life to be enriched by and the prevention and eradication of those evils in human life which He finds abhorrent. The Islamic state is intended neither solely as an instrument of political administration nor for the fulfillment of the collective will of any particular set of people; rather, Islam places a high ideal before the state for the achievement of which it must use all the means at its disposal.

This ideal is that the qualities of purity, beauty, goodness, virtue, success and prosperity which Allah wants to flourish in the life of His people should be engendered and developed and that all kinds of exploitation, injustice and disorder which, in the sight of Allah, are ruinous for the world and detrimental to the life of His creatures, should be suppressed and prevented. Islam gives us a clear outline of its moral system by stating positively the desired virtues and the undesired evils. Keeping this outline in view, the Islamic state can plan its welfare programme in every age and in any environment.

The constant demand made by Islam is that the principles of morality must be observed at all costs and in all walks of life. Hence, it lays down as an unalterable policy that the state should base its policies on justice, truth and honesty. It is not prepared, under any circumstances, to tolerate fraud, falsehood and injustice for the sake of political, administrative or national expediency. Whether it be relations between the rulers and the ruled within the state, or the relations of the state with other states, precedence must always be given to truth, honesty and justice.

Islam imposes similar obligations on the state and the individual: to fulfill all contracts and obligations; to have uniform standards in dealings; to remember obligations along with rights and not to forget the rights of others when expecting them to fulfill their obligations; to use power and authority for the establishment of justice and not for the perpetration of injustice; to look upon duty as a sacred obligation and to fulfill it scrupulously; and to regard power as a trust from Allah to be used in the belief that one has to render an account of one's actions to Him in the life Hereafter.

Fundamental Rights

Although an Islamic state may be set up anywhere on earth, Islam does not seek to restrict human rights or privileges to the boundaries of such a state. Islam has laid down universal fundamental rights for humanity which are to be observed and respected in all circumstances. For example, human blood is sacred and may not be spilled without strong justification;

it is not permissible to oppress women, children, old people, the sick or the wounded; women's honour and chastity must be respected; the hungry must be fed, the naked clothed and the wounded or diseased treated medically irrespective of whether they belong to the Islamic community or are from amongst its enemies. These and other provisions have been laid down by Islam as fundamental rights for every man by virtue of his status as a human being.

Nor, in Islam, are the rights of citizenship confined to people born in a particular state. A Muslim ipso facto becomes the citizen of an Islamic state as soon as he sets foot on its territory with the intention of living there and thus enjoys equal rights along with those who acquire its citizenship by birth. And every Muslim is to be regarded as eligible for positions of the highest responsibility in an Islamic state without distinction of race, colour or class.

Islam has also laid down certain rights for non-Muslims who may be living within the boundaries of an Islamic state and these rights necessarily form part of the Islamic constitution. In Islamic terminology, such non-Muslims are called dhimmis (the covenanted), implying that the Islamic state has entered into a covenant with them and guaranteed their protection. The life, property and honour of a dhimmis are to be respected and protected in exactly the same way as that of a Muslim citizen. Nor is there difference between a Muslim and a non-Muslim citizen in respect of civil or criminal law.

The Islamic state may not interfere with the personal rights of non-Muslims, who have full freedom of conscience and belief and are at liberty to perform their religious rites and ceremonies in their own way. Not only may they propagate their religion, they are even entitled to criticize Islam within the limits laid down by law and decency.

These rights are irrevocable. Non-Muslims cannot be deprived of them unless they renounce the covenant which grants them citizenship. However much a non-Muslim state may oppress its Muslim citizens it is not permissible for an Islamic state to retaliate against its non-Muslim subjects; even if all the Muslims outside the boundaries of an Islamic state are massacred, that state may not unjustly shed the blood of a single non-Muslim citizen living within its boundaries.

Executive and Legislature

The responsibility for the administration of the government in an Islamic state is entrusted to an amir (leader) who may be compared to the president or the prime minister in a Western democratic state. All adult men and women who subscribe to the fundamentals of the constitution are entitled to vote for the election of the amir.

The basic qualifications for an amir are that he should command the confidence of the majority in respect of his knowledge and grasp of the spirit of Islam, that he should possess the Islamic quality of fear of Allah and that he should be endowed with qualities of statesmanship. In short, he should have both virtue and ability.

A shoora (advisory council) is also elected by the people to assist and guide the amir. It is incumbent on the amir to administer his country with the advice of this shoora; the amir may retain office only so long as he enjoys the confidence of the people and must relinquish it when he loses that confidence. Every citizen has the right to criticize the amir and his government and all reasonable means for the ventilation of public opinion must be available.

Legislation in an Islamic state is to be carried out within the limits prescribed by the law of the shari'a. The injunctions of Allah and His Prophet are to be accepted and obeyed and no legislative body may alter or modify them or make any law contrary to them. Those commandments which are liable to two or more interpretations are referred to a sub-committee of the advisory council comprising men learned in Islamic law. Great scope remains for legislation on questions not covered by specific injunctions of the shari'a and the advisory council or legislature is free to legislate in regard to these matters.

In Islam the judiciary is not places under the control of the executive. It derives its authority directly from the shari'a and is answerable to Allah. The judges are appointed by the government but once a judge occupies the bench he has to administer justice impartially according to the law of Allah; the organs and functionaries of the government are not outside his legal jurisdiction, so that even the highest executive authority of the government is liable to be called upon to appear in a court of law as a plaintiff or defendant. Rulers and ruled are subject to the same law and there can be no discrimination on the basis of position, power or privilege, Islam stands for equality and scrupulously adheres to this principle in social, economic and political realms alike.

Human Rights - The West and Islam

The Western Apporach

People in the West have the habit of attributing every beneficial development in the world to themselves. For example, it is vociferously claimed that the world first derived the concept of basic human rights from the Magna Carta of Britain - which was drawn up six hundred years after the advent of Islam. But the truth is that until the seventeenth century of no-one dreamt of arguing that the Magna Carta contained the principles of trial by jury, Habeas Corpus and control by Parliament of the right of taxation. If the people who drafted the Magna Carta were living today they would be greatly surprised to be told that their document enshrined these ideals and principles.

To the best of my knowledge, the West had no concept of human and civic rights before the seventeenth century; and it was not until the end of the eighteenth century that the concept took on practical meaning in the constitutions of America and France.

After this, although there appeared references to basic human rights in the constitutions of many countries, more often than not these rights existed only on paper. In the middle of the present century, the United Nations, which may now be more aptly described as the Divided Nations, made a Declaration of Universal Human Rights, and passed a resolution condemning genocide; regulations were framed to prevent it. But there is not a single resolution or regulation of the United Nations which can be enforced if the country concerned wants to prevent it. They are just expressions of pious hopes. They have no sanctions behind them, no force, physical or moral, to enforce them. Despite all the high-sounding resolutions of the United Nations, human rights continue to be violated and trampled upon.

The Islamic Approach

When we speak of human rights in Islam we mean those rights granted by Allah. Rights granted by kings or legislative assemblies can be withdrawn as easily as they are conferred; but no individual and no institution has the authority to withdraw the rights conferred by Allah.

The charter and the proclamations and the resolutions of the United Nations cannot be compared with the rights sanctioned by Allah; the former are not obligatory on anybody, while the latter are an integral part of the Islamic faith. All Muslims and all administrators who claim to be Muslim have to accept, recognize and enforce them. If they failed to enforce them or violate them while paying lip-service to them, the verdict of the Holy Qur'an is unequivocal:

"Those who do not judge by what Allah has sent down are the disbelievers (Kafirun)."

The following verse also proclaims:

- "They are the wrong-doers (zalimoon)".

A third verse in the same chapter says:

- "They are the perverse and law-breakers (fasiqoon)."

In other words, if temporal authorities regard their own words and decisions as right and those given by Allah as wrong, they are disbelievers. If, on the other hand, they regard Allah's commands as right but deliberately reject them in favour of their owns decisions, then they are wrong-doers. Law-breakers are those who disregard the bond of allegiance.

4

Democracy in Islamic Political Thought

Democracy has preoccupied Arab political thinkers since the dawn of the modern Arab renaissance about two centuries ago. Since then, the concept of democracy has changed and developed under the influence of a variety of social and political developments. The discussion of democracy in Arab Islamic literature can be traced back to Rifa'a Tahtawi, the father of Egyptian democracy according to Lewis Awad, who shortly after his return to Cairo from Paris published his first book, Takhlis Al-Ibriz Ila Talkhis Bariz, in 1834. The book summarized his observations of the manners and customs of the modern French, and praised the concept of democracy as he saw it in France and as he witnessed its defence and reassertion through the 1830 Revolution against King Charles X. Tahtawi tried to show that the democratic concept he was explaining to his readers was compatible with the law of Islam. He compared political pluralism to forms of ideological and jurisprudential pluralism that existed in the Islamic experience.

Religious freedom is the freedom of belief, of opinion and of sect, provided it does not contradict the fundamentals of religion. The same would apply to the freedom of political practice and opinion by leading administrators, who endeavour to interpret and apply rules and provisions in accordance with the laws of their own countries. Kings and ministers are licensed in the realm of politics to pursue various routes that in the end serve one purpose: good administration and justice.

One important landmark in this regard was the contribution of Khairuddin At-Tunisi (1810-99), leader of the 19th-century reform movement in Tunisia, who, in 1867, formulated a general plan for reform in a book entitled Aqwam Al-Masalik Fi Taqwim Al- Mamalik (The Straight Path to Reforming Governments). The main preoccupation of the book was in tackling the question of political reform in the Arab world. While appealing to politicians and scholars of his time to seek all possible means in order to improve the status of the community and develop its civility, he warned the general Muslim public against shunning the experiences of other nations on the basis of the misconception that all the writings, inventions, experiences or attitudes of non-Muslims should be rejected or disregarded. Khairuddin further called for an end to absolutist rule, which he blamed for the oppression of nations and the destruction of civilizations.

Ghannouchi believes that neither Khairuddin nor any of the Islamic scholars of his time had intended to cast doubt on Islam or introduce changes to it. They only sought to understand Islam better and explore new means and methods to implement it, relying on the explanations of both ancient and contemporary scholars. They sought to legitimize borrowing from the West on the basis that '... wisdom (or knowledge) is a believer's long-cherished objective', that '... religion has been revealed for the benefit of the creation', and that '... [the] Shari'a and the vital interests of the community are fully compatible'. To implement his reform plan, Khairuddin established the As-Sadiqiyah School for teaching modern arts and sciences within an Islamic framework. The purpose of the School, according to the founding declaration, was: 'To teach the Qur'an, writing and useful knowledge, i.e. juridical sciences, foreign languages, and the rational sciences that might be of use to Muslims being at the same time not contrary to the faith. The professors must inculcate in the students love of the faith by showing them its beauties and excellence, in telling them the deeds of the Prophet, the miracles accomplished by him, the virtues of the holy men...' Khairuddin At-Tunisi believed that '...

kindling the Umma's potential liberty through the adoption of sound administrative procedures and enabling it to have a say in political affairs, would put it on a faster track toward civilization, would limit the rule of despotism, and would stop the influx of European civilization that is sweeping everything along its path.'

In his search for the causes of decline in the Muslim world, Jamal ad-Deen Al-Afghani (1838-97) diagnosed that it was due to the absence of 'adl (justice) and shura (council) and non-adherence by the government to the constitution.

One of his main demands was that the people should be allowed to assume their political and social ryle by participating in governing through shura and elections. In an article entitled 'The Despotic Government', published in Misr on 14 February 1879, Al-Afghani attributed the decline to despotism which is the reason why thinkers in the Eastern (Muslim) countries could not enlighten the public about the essence and virtues of the 'republican government'? 'For those governed by it', he stresses, 'it is a source of happiness and pride'. He goes further, to insist that '... those governed by a republican form of government, alone deserve to be called human; for a true human being is only subdued by a true law that is based on the foundations of justice and that is designed to govern man's moves, actions, transactions and relations with others in a manner that elevates him to the pinnacle of true happiness.' To Al-Afghani, a republican government is a 'restricted government' that is accountable to the public, and that is thus the antithesis of the absolutist one. It is a government that consults the governed, relieves them of the burdens laid upon them by despotic governments and lifts them from the state of decay to the first level of perfection.

Muhammad Abduh (1849-1905) believed that Islam's relationship with the modern age was the most crucial issue that Islamic communities needed to deal with. In an attempt to reconcile Islamic ideas with Western ones, he suggested that maslaha (interest) in Islamic thought corresponded to manfa'a (utility) in Western thought. Similarly, he equated shura with democracy and ijma' with consensus. Addressing the question of authority, Abduh denied the existence of a theocracy in Islam and insisted that the authority of the hakim (governor) or that of the qadi (judge) or that of the mufti was civil. He strongly believed that ijtihad should be revived because '... emerging priorities and problems, which are new to the Islamic thought, need to be addressed'. He was a proponent of the parliamentary system and defended pluralism, refuting claims that it would undermine the unity of the umma. He argued that European nations were not divided by it. 'The reason', he concludes, 'is that their objective is the same. What varies is the method they pursue toward accomplishing it'.

Abdurrahman Al-Kawakibi (1849-1903) wrote two books on the subject, Taba'i' Al- Istibdad (The Characteristics of Tyranny) and Umm Al-Qura (The Mother of Villages). The first is dedicated to defining despotism and explaining the various forms it may take, with much of the discussion focusing on political despotism. The relationship between religion and despotism and what he calls the 'inseparable tie' between politics and religion are discussed. While stressing that Islam as a religion is not responsible for the forms of despotic government that have emerged and reigned in its name, Al-Kawakibi concludes that 'Allah, the omniwise, has intended nations to be responsible for the actions of those whom they choose to be governed by. When a nation fails in its duty, God causes it to be subdued by another nation that will govern it, just as happens in a court of law when a minor or an incompetent is put under the care of a curator. When, on the other hand, a nation matures and appreciates the value of liberty, it will restore its might; and this is only fair.' The entire book is an attempt to explain the reasons why the Muslim umma declined and became easy prey for 19th-century colonial powers.

Like Al-Afghani and Abduh, Al-Kawakibi attributed the success of Western nations to '... the adoption of logical and well-practised rules that have become social duties in these advanced nations which are not harmed by what appears to be a division into parties and groups, because such a division is only over the methods of applying the rules and not over them.' In his other book, Al-Kawakibi constructs a series of dialogues involving fictional characters whom he describes as thinkers each belonging to a known town in the Muslim world, all summoned to a conference organized in Makka (Umm al-Qura) during the pilgrimage (hajj) season to discuss the causes of decline of the Muslim umma. One character, Al-Baligh Al-Qudsi, says: 'It seems to me that the cause of tepidity is the change in the nature of Islamic politics. It was parliamentary and socialist, that is perfectly democratic. But due to the escalation of internal feuds, after the Guided ones (the first four Caliphs) it was transformed into a monarchy restrained by the basic rules of Shari'a, and then it became almost completely absolute.' Ar-Rumi says: 'The calamity has been our loss of liberty.' In conclusion, Al-Kawakibi stresses that progress is linked to accountability while regress is linked to despotism.

Muhammad Rashid Rida (1865-1935) saw that the reason for the backwardness of the umma was that '... the Muslims have lost the truth of their religion, and this has been encouraged by bad political rulers, for the true Islam involves two things, acceptance of the unity of God and consultation in matters of State, and despotic rulers have tried to make Muslims forget the second by encouraging them to abandon the first.' He stressed that the greatest lesson the people of the Orient can learn from Europeans is to know what government should be like. In his book Al-Khilafa (The Caliphate) he stresses that Islam is guidance, mercy and social-civic policy.

About the latter, which he seems to use as a synonym for politics, he says: 'As for the social-civic policy, Islam has laid its foundations and set forth its rules, and has sanctioned the exertion of opinion and the pursuit of ijtihad in matters related to it because it changes with time and place and develops as architecture and all other aspects of knowledge develop. Its foundations include that authority belongs to the umma, that decision-making is through shura, that the government is a form of a republic, that the ruler is not favoured in a court of law to the layman - for he is only employed to implement Shari'a and public opinion, and that the purpose of this policy is to preserve religion and serve the interests of the public...'

Nineteenth-century Islamic political thinkers, who were clearly influenced by European democratic thought and practice, tried to establish a resemblance between democracy and the Islamic concept of shura. Faced with a crisis of government augmented by the autocracy and corrupt conduct of Muslim rulers, they sought to legitimize the borrowing of aspects of the Western model they believed were compatible with Islam and capable of resolving the crisis. However, the trend changed in the aftermath of the First World War and following the demise of the khilafa (Caliphate), whose abrogation, in 1924, shocked the Muslims in spite of the fact that many of them had suffered greatly at the hands of some Ottoman rulers. The khilafa was an administrative legacy that for many centuries represented a moral shield and a political entity. The challenge was no longer despotism. The Muslims had already lost their symbol of unity, which they had been trying to reform. The European democracies, which provided inspiration and were greatly admired by reformists in the East, had colonized much of the Arab world, dividing its territories among them as booties. The Western colonizers' endeavours to Westernize the Muslims was viewed as a serious threat to the Arab-Islamic identity, and, thus, liberating Muslim lands from colonialism became a priority. Hence, the call for reform was replaced by one for revival.

During this period, Rashid Rida, Abduh's disciple, published the Al-Manar Journal which attracted a readership of Islamic intellectuals who shared Rida's specific additions to the thoughts of his masters Al-Afghani and Abduh, namely the condemnation of innovations in doctrine and worship and the acceptance of the rights of reason and public welfare in matters of social morality. A young man who frequented Rida's circle and regularly read his Journal, then attempted to carry it on after Rida's death. His name was Hasan Al-Banna (1904-49). Trained by his father Ahmad Al-Banna, a graduate of Al-Azhar University and author of an encyclopaedia of Hadith and Islamic Jurisprudence, young Hasan grew up to become the founder of the largest and first international Islamic movement in modern times, the al-Ikhwan al-Muslimun (Muslim Brotherhood).

Established as a study circle, known as Madrasat at-Tahdhib (The School of Refinement), in 1928 in the Egyptian port city of Al-Isma'iliyya - the headquarters of the Suez Canal Company and the British forces in Egypt - the group grew rapidly and spread to other parts of the country within a short period of time. Its growth accelerated by the 1936 Anglo-Egyptian Treaty and the Arab Revolt in Palestine against the British Mandate and Zionist colonisation; the movement quickly transformed itself into a political entity. By 1939 a series of rasa'il (messages or articles), mostly authored by Al-Banna, were circulated explaining the Ikhwan's mission, clarifying its ideas and underlining its method. In the first of these articles, entitled Bayn al-Ams wa'l-Yawm (Between Yesterday and Today), Hasan Al-Banna diagnosed the situation in the Muslim world as follows:

European power expanded, thanks to discoveries, expeditions, and travels to far and distant lands as far as many of the remote Islamic countries like India, as well as some of the neighbouring Islamic provinces. Europe began to work earnestly at dismembering the powerful and far-flung Islamic state proposing numerous plans toward this end, referring to them at times as 'the Eastern question' and at others as 'dividing up the inheritance of the Sick Man of Europe'. Every state began to seize any opportunity as it arose, adopting the flimsiest of excuses to attack the peaceful yet careless Islamic state, and to reduce its periphery or demolish parts of its integral fabric.

This onslaught continued over a long period of time, during which the Ottoman Empire was stripped of much of its Islamic territory which then fell under European domination, e.g., Morocco and North Africa. Many non-Islamic areas previously under Ottoman rule became independent during this time, e.g., Greece and the Balkan States. The final round of this struggle was the First World War, from 1914 to 1918, which ended in the defeat of Turkey and her allies, providing a perfect opportunity for the strongest nations of Europe, (England and France, and under their patronage, Italy). They laid their hands on the huge legacy left behind by the Islamic nations, imposing their rule over them under the various titles of occupation, colonialism, trusteeship or mandate dividing them up in the following manner: North Africa (Morocco, Algeria, and Tunis) became French colonies lying in between a zone of international influence in Tangier and a Spanish colony in the Rif; Tripoli and Barca became Italian colonies in which Italy did not wish a single trace of Islam to remain. She forced Italian citizenship upon the people giving it the name of 'South Italy' and filling it with thousands of hungry families and wild beasts in human form (Italian outcasts); Egypt and the Sudan fell under English authority, neither one possessing a shred of independent authority; Palestine became an English colony, which England took the liberty of selling to the Jews so that they might establish therein a national Zionist homeland; Syria became a French colony; Iraq became an English colony; the Hijaz (the Western Province of Arabia) possessed a weak, unstable government dependent on charity and clinging to false treaties and worthless covenants; Yemen possessed an outmoded government and a poverty stricken populace exposed to attack anywhere and at any time; the remaining nations of the Arabian peninsula consisted of small emirates whose rulers lived under the wing of the British consuls and who fought one another for the crumbs falling from their tables, their breasts burning with mutual resentment and hatred.

This was the case despite the reassuring promises and binding treaties drawn up by the Allies with the mightiest monarch of the Peninsula, King Hussein, stating that they would help him achieve the Arab independence and support the authority of the Arab Caliphate; Iran and Afghanistan possessed shaky governments beset by power hungry people on every side, they would be under the wing of one nation at one time and under that of another at other times; India was an English colony; Turkistan and the adjoining regions were Russian colonies, subjected to the bitter harshness of the Bolshevik authorities.

Apart from these, there were also the Islamic minorities scattered across many countries, knowing no state to whose protection they might have recourse, nor any well armed government to defend their nationality, as, e.g., the Muslims in Ethiopia, China, the Balkans, and the lands of Central, South, East and West Africa. Under such conditions, Europe won in the political struggle, and finally accomplished her goal in dismembering the Islamic empire, annihilating the Islamic state and erasing it politically, from the list of powerful, living nations.'

Al-Banna notes that as each of these nations struggled to regain its freedom and the right to exist as an independent entity, concepts of localized nationalism arose, and many states working towards this revival purposely ignored the idea of unity. From that moment the Muslim Brotherhood launched the struggle for the return of the Islamic empire as a unified state embracing the Muslims that had been scattered around the world, raising the banner of Islam and carrying its message. At this stage, the Europeans ceased to be a model. On the contrary, they were blamed for the ills of the Muslim umma. 'The Europeans', Hasan Al-Banna wrote: worked assiduously in trying to immerse (the world) in materialism, with its corrupting traits and murderous germs, to overwhelm those Muslim lands that their hands stretched out to... they were able to alter the basic principles of government, justice, and education, and infuse in the most powerful Islamic countries, their own peculiar political, judicial, and cultural systems. They imported their semi-naked women into these regions, together with their liquors, their theatres, their dance halls, their amusement arcades, their stories, their newspapers, their novels, their whims, their silly games, and their vices. Here they allowed for crimes intolerable in their own countries and beautified this tumultuous world to the deluded, naive eyes of wealthy Muslims and those of rank and authority. This was not enough for them, so they built schools and scientific cultural institutes, casting doubt and heresy within the hearts of people. They taught them how to demean themselves, to vilify their religion and their homeland, to detach themselves from their beliefs, and to regard anything Western as sacred, in the belief that only that which is European can be emulated. These schools were restricted to the upper class, the ruling body, the powerful and the future leaders. Those who were unsuccessful in such places were sent abroad to complete their studies. This drastic, well organised social campaign was tremendously successful since it appealed to the mind. It will continue to exert its strong intellectual influence over a long period of time. Thus, it was far more dangerous than any political or military campaign. Some Islamic countries went overboard in their admiration for the European civilisation and their dissatisfaction with the Islamic one, to the point that Turkey declared itself a non-Islamic state, imitating the Europeans in everything that they did. Aman Allah Khan, King of Afghanistan, tried this, but the attempt cost him his throne. In Egypt the manifestations of this mimicry increased and became so serious that one of her intellectual leaders could openly say that the only path to progress was to adopt this civilisation: good or evil, bitter or sweet, praiseworthy or reprehensible. From Egypt it spread with strength and speed into the neighbouring countries, to the extent that it reached Morocco and encircled the holy sanctuaries within the midst of Hijaz.

Explaining that his movement's mission is one of reawakening and deliverance, Al-Banna declared that the goals of his organization were: ' (1) Freeing the Islamic homeland from all foreign authority, for this is a natural right belonging to every human being which only the unjust oppressor will deny. (2) The establishment of an Islamic state within this homeland, which acts according to the precepts of Islam, applies its social regulations, advocates its sound principles, and broadcasts its mission to all of mankind.' Al-Banna warned the Muslims, in general, and the members of his group, in particular: 'As long as this state does not emerge, every Muslim is sinning and Muslims are responsible before

Allah the Almighty for their failure and slackness to establish it. In these bewildering circumstances, it is against the interests of humanity that a state advocating injustice and oppression should arise, while there should be no one at all working for the advent of a state founded on truth, justice, and peace. We want to accomplish these two goals in the Nile Valley and the Arab Kingdom, and in every land which Allah has blessed with the Islamic creed: uniting all the Muslims.'

The leaders of the Muslim Brotherhood took a special interest in stressing that their movement was set up in response to the downfall of the khilafa. 'When the khilafa was brought down', Mustafa Mashhoor, deputy leader of the Brotherhood explained: 'Imam Hasan Al-Banna rose up and proclaimed the restoration of the khilafa to be a religious duty incumbent upon every single Muslim man and woman.' In a message sent to the heads of Muslim states in June 1947, Hasan Al-Banna demanded that they shoulder their responsibilities and undertake the task of serving the umma. The task, he explained, consisted of two parts: the first, to rid the umma of its political shackles so as to achieve its freedom and restore its lost independence and sovereignty; and the second to rebuild the umma anew in order to pursue its path among nations and compete with others for the attainment of social perfection. Hence, Hasan Al-Banna's main concern was to mobilize the public against colonialism and its adverse effects on society. He called for the re- establishment of Islamic governance on three foundations: the ruler's accountability to Allah and to the public, the unity of the umma within a framework of brotherhood, and respect for the will of the umma and its right to check its rulers who are obliged to respect its will and opinions. In his analysis of the causes of European progress, he prognosticated the eventual collapse of Western civilization due to immorality, usury and political divisions.

In his message Bayn al-Ams wa'l-Yawm (Between Yesterday and Today), he cites (political) parties as one of the factors that would lead to European decline. Although he stood for parliamentary elections twice, and while stressing that the parliamentary and constitutional system is in essence compatible with the Islamic system of government, he was adamant in his opposition to political parties. He regarded them as a potential threat to Islamic unity, which he deemed was essential for the re-establishment of the khilafa. 'They (political parties) are this homeland's greatest misdeed, the root of social corruption whose fire is scalding us. They are not genuine parties in the sense by which parties in any other country of the world are known.

They are no more than a series of dissension caused by personal disagreements among a number of the children of this umma. Whose circumstances necessitated one day that they should speak in its name and demand its national rights... There is no more room for half solutions and there is no escape from the inevitability of the dissolution of all these parties. The forces of the umma ought to be joined in one party that would have to work for the restoration of its independence and freedom, and that would lay down the foundations for general domestic reform.' Between the two World Wars, thinkers affiliated with the liberal trend campaigned, like their 19th-century predecessors for total Westernization. Embracing secularism, they called for formulating modern constitutions and legal systems that, just as the Europeans had done, exclude religion and restrict its ryle to the private domain. They hoisted the slogan of 'separating state and religion' and blamed Islam for the backwardness of the Arabs.

The abolishment of the khilafa in 1924 aroused a debate among thinkers of the time over its importance. Ali Abd Ar-Raziq (1888-1966), an Al-Azhar graduate who later studied at Oxford, contributed to the debate with a book that turned out to be among the most controversial works in modern Islamic history. Abd Ar-Raziq's theory claimed there were no such things as Islamic political principles. He denied the existence of a political order in Islam and claimed that the Prophet never established one and that it was not part of his mission to found a state.

As Arab societies responded to the challenge of

colonialism and rose to restore their free Deen and struggle for their independence, Westernized elites took over the leadership of national movements that originally had Islamic inclinations. Despotic single-party regimes or absolute monarchies replaced the colonial authorities in most of the Arab countries. Throughout the post-independence era, Islam, its culture and its heritage came under savage onslaught in the name of modernization. The Al-Azhar of Egypt was turned into a secular university, the Tunisian Az-Zaytouna Institute was closed down, awqaf (endowment) institutions were nationalized, Shari'a courts were either dissolved or marginalized and political parties and groups were banned or outlawed. The Ikhwan, who had already established branches or strong links in many Arab and Muslim countries, were hit hard by Nassir in Egypt soon after he came to power in 1952. Following the execution of several of their leaders and the imprisonment of hundreds of their followers in 1954, they were driven underground. The challenge had once again changed shape. It was no more the challenge and struggle for independence and freedom, but rather the struggle to resist and defend the umma against what was perceived as a pernicious onslaught against Islam and the cultural identity of the umma not only by foreign colonial powers but also by post-independence regimes. From then until the early seventies, members of the Islamic movement were influenced mainly by the works of Mawdudi and Nadwi and by the writings of Sayyid Qutb.

Sayyid Qutb (1906-66), who was imprisoned for ten years in 1954 and then executed in 1966, became the leading ideologue of the Muslim Brotherhood from the mid-fifties. His book Milestones, which was written in response to Nassir's persecution of the Ikhwan, acquired a wide acceptance throughout the Arab world after his execution and following the defeat of the Arabs in the 1967 War with Israel. In it, he put forward the thesis of jahiliyya (ignorance, barbarity or idolatry), from which Islam came to deliver the world. Qutb divided social systems into two categories: the order of Islam and the order of jahiliyya, which was decadent and ignorant, the type which had existed in Arabia before the Prophet Muhammad received the Word of God, when men revered not God but other men disguised as deities. Muslim society, according to him, was itself divided into two realms, that of Islam and that of jahiliyya. This was clearly expressed by Qutb in Milestones as follows: 'Jahiliyya is now present not only in the capitalist West and the Communist East; it has also infected the world of Islam.

All that is around us is jahiliyya. Peoples' imaginings, their beliefs, customs, and traditions, the sources of their culture, their art and literature, their laws and statutes, much even of what we take to be Islamic culture, Islamic authorities, Islamic philosophy, and Islamic thought: all this too is of the making of this jahiliyya.' Drawing from the theory of Mawdudi (1903-79) that as Islam has reverted to a state of jahiliyya, true Muslims find themselves in a state of war against the apostates, Sayyid Qutb concluded that true Muslims, the tali'a (vanguards), are and must be set apart within the ambient infidel society as a sort of 'counter-society'. In his trial statement, Sayyid Qutb declared: 'We are the ummah of the believers, living within a jahili society. Nothing relates us to state or to society and we owe no allegiance to either. As a community of believers we should see ourselves in a state of war with the state and the society.'

However, as far as democracy is concerned Qutb seemed to develop his own theory. In this he went much farther than Mawdudi, rejecting the concept altogether, denouncing it as alien, incompatible and jahili. The term hakimiyya (sovereignty), which Qutb constantly referred to while arguing against man-made political systems, was originally coined by Mawdudi, who used it to distinguish between Islamic and jahili (barbaric) societies. Mawdudi had argued that in a jahili situation, the edifice of politics rises on the foundations of al-hakimiyya al-bashariya (human sovereignty) whether such sovereignty rests in the hands of an individual, a family or a class or is the sovereignty of the public. 'Legislating in this kind of reign', Mawdudi explained, 'is entirely in the hands of man. All laws are made and replaced according to desires and to experimental interests.

So is the case with political plans, which are only drawn or altered as dictated by the passion for utility and the provision of interests. In such a reign, no word is given precedence and no affair is awarded prevalence except if such were the functions of those who are most cunning, most resourceful and most capable of fabricating lies; those who have reached the pinnacle of deceit, cruelty and guilefulness; and those who have siezed full control and are recognised as leaders in their community where, in their "laws", falsehood becomes truth just because its proponents have power and have the ability to terrorise, and where, in their courts of law, truth becomes falsehood just because it has no supporter or defender.' In spite of all of this, Mawdudi still believed that Islam, by virtue of the institution of shura, was democratic.

In spite of his reservations about the Western liberal democratic practice, he called for a chance to be given to democracy, one which would allow it to adapt and succeed in Muslim countries. Considering the task of reforming the system of government and administration to be part of the Muslim faith, Mawdudi suggested that the means of achieving such a reform would be to 'displace those who are corrupt and misguided from power and to replace them with those who are fit and righteous.' As to how this change could be achieved, Mawdudi stressed:

There is no other way in a democratic system except to participate in the battle of elections, that is by educating the public opinion in the country and changing the people's standard in electing their representatives. We should also reform the election mechanism and cleanse it from theft, deceit and forgery. By doing so, we would be in a position to hand power to righteous men, who are eager to develop the country on the pure basis of Islam.

When asked about the flaws in liberal democracy, he explained to his students that notwithstanding the flaws in any particular form of democracy, the principle that the masses have the right to choose, and to bring to account and replace their government, should always prevail. When asked which method for running the affairs of the people is principally correct, Mawdudi retorted: 'Should those who are in charge of the affatirs of the people and who run them on their behalf be appointed by the free will of the people so that they only administer and govern through consultation, and after having obtained the consent of the people, and so that they only remain in power so long as they enjoy the confidence of the public?

Or should one person, or a group of persons, impose themselves upon the people, take charge of their affairs and run such affairs according to their own whims, and whose appointment or dismissal, or whose running of the people's affairs, are beyond the will or control of those who are being run by them?'

He further explained that any flaws in democratic practice were due to three main reasons. The first, the assumption that the masses are the source of total power and absolute sovereignty, while in effect, and in any attempt to set up an absolute democracy in the world, the masses come under the control of, and suffer the hegemony, of very few individuals. Mawdudi suggested that Islam had a solution for this problem. 'Islam', he stressed, 'rectifies this flaw at the outset by imposing a siege on democracy derived from a basic law dictated by the Creator, Master and True Sovereign of this universe. This is a law that both the public and those in charge of administering its affairs are obliged to abide by. Thus, the question of absolute independence, which eventually causes democracy to fail, does not arise.'

The second and third reasons, Mawdudi argued, pertain to the standard of education and the degree of awareness of the electorate, or what he refers to as the masses. Here too, Islam provides an answer with its emphasis on educating the Muslims, '... preparing them morally and calling on each of them to have a sense of responsibility'.

For democracy to yield its fruits and proceed successfully, Mawdudi argued, that much would depend on the existence of a strong and vigilant public opinion. 'Such a public opinion', he explained, 'comes [in] to being when the community comprises righteous individuals who are entered in a social system that is established on [a] sound basis, [one] that is so vivid that evil and those who invite to it do not grow whereas good and those who invite to it do grow.'

Reaffirming that Islam may provide all the necessary rules and teachings for such guarantees to be maintained; Mawdudi expressed his conviction that once these guarantees are secured the apparatus of democracy might function successfully. 'It might also be possible', he added, 'that whenever a flaw appears somewhere in this apparatus, mending it would be provided for by a better apparatus. The mechanism of self-correcting, together with progress and development, would suffice for democracy to be given an opportunity and be experimented with, for it is possible through experimentation to develop any deficient apparatus until it become[s], step by step, perfectly sound.'

On the other hand, Qutb seems to have been completely opposed to any reconciliation with democracy. In the beginning, he was opposed to the idea of calling Islam democratic and even campaigned for a just dictatorship that would grant political liberties to the virtuous alone. In his tafsir (interpretation) of Sura al-Shura he said: 'Democracy is, as a form of government, already bankrupt in the West; why should it be imported to the Middle East?' Sayyid Qutb and his disciples, including Sa'id Hawwa of Syria and Dr. Abdulqadir Abu Faris of Jordan, in their treatment of the issue of democracy took an anti-Western position. Their discourses exhibit a lack of interest in the origin, nature or conditions of democracy or of its compatibility or incompatibility with Islamic values. In all discussions, the abstract democratic concept is confused with the attitude or policies of Western democracies toward the Arab world and Muslim issues. Their rejection of democracy was, understandably, a reaction.

Sa'id Hawwa initially wrote: 'Democracy is a Greek term which signifies sovereignty of the people; the people being the source of legitimacy. In other words it is the people that legislate and rule. In Islam the people do not govern themselves by laws they make on their own as in democracy. Rather, the people are governed by a regime and a set of laws imposed by God.' However, Hawwa seemed to adopt a more moderate position later in life, in fact just before his death, one much more reflective of the changing attitude of the mainstream Islamic movement. He wrote: back to top

We see that democracy in the Muslim World will eventually produce victory for Islam. Thus, we warn ourselves and our brothers against fighting practical democracy. In fact, we see that asking for more democracy is the practical way to the success of Islam on Islam's territory. Our enemies have realised this fact, and that is why they have assassinated democracy and established dictatorships and other alternatives. Many of the followers of Islam have been unable to see the positive things democracy provides to us; they only looked at the issue from a purely theoretical and ideological perspective, and failed to look at it from the perspective of reality, namely that the majority rules, that the values of such a majority dominate and that in whichever country a Muslim majority exists Islam will prevail. Even when the Muslims are a minority, democracy is mostly in their interest.

In what amounted to a coup against his own previous stand and those of his mentor, Sa'id Hawwa seemed to campaign for, and encourage Islamists to adopt, the democratic alternative. He regretted that the Islamists have failed to benefit from the democratic circumstances that existed in many countries in the Muslim world, insisting that 'democracy in the Muslim World is the most appropriate climate for the success of Islam in the future.' Acknowledging the dilemma, he went on to say: 'The Islamists have fought democracy in the Muslim World because democracy in the Western concept has the right to make things halal (permissible) or haram (prohibited). It is a well established rule in Islam that no ijtihad (opinion) is allowed where a nass (sacred text) already exists. However, the problem here is that in the phase of conflict between Islam and other [ideologies] in the Islamic territory, we should know which system is better in order for the battle to be won by Islam.'

Hawwa's years of exile from the early 1980s until his death in the Jordanian capital, Amman, in 1988 represented an important transitional period in the thinking of the Mashriqi (eastern) Islamic school of thought away from the rejectionist thought of the earlier decade. The dramatic events of the early 1980s in Syria, particularly the military confrontation between the regime and some Islamist factions, as a consequence of which the government declared an all-out war against all forms of Islamic activity coupled with the destruction of the city of Hama and the wiping out of the organized edifice of the Muslim Brotherhood in the country, had profound and long-term effects on Islamic movements throughout the region. Ironically, it was the leaders and intellectuals of the severely bruised Syrian Islamic Movement that led the trend. The violent means of change had proven disastrous and the radical reform approach was a complete failure.

It was thanks to Hawwa himself, and those who shared his insight, that this transition took place. Criticizing those Islamic writers who stood adamantly against the democratic process, he wrote: 'Undoubtedly, democracy is the most favourable environment in the Muslim world for the battle to be won by Islam. Nevertheless, some people have been found in the Muslim world to fight democracy. The alternative has been military dictatorships and [single] party dictatorships that kept all the ills and prejudices of the Western democracy against Islam and the Islamists and denied Islam and the Islamists the freedom of passage. Democracy, wherever it exists in the Muslim world, means that eventually Islam and the Islamists will win and achieve their objective[s].' Then as if reminding his readers, who at the time were mostly members and supporters of the Muslim Brotherhood in the countries of the Middle East, Hawwa hailed the decision once made by the founder of the movement, Hasan Al-Banna, to participate in parliamentary elections. This was, as admitted by many pro-democracy Islamists, a very significant event in the history of the Islamic movement that for much of the 1960s and the 1970s nobody seemed, or probably wanted, to remember.

Hawwa wrote: 'Al-Banna was wise when he wanted to participate in the parliamentary life, and Al-Hudaybi was wise when he called for the revival of the parliamentary life in Egypt.' Then as if to distinguish between two different trends within the ranks of Islamism, Hawwa declared: 'Participating in the elections to benefit from the democratic life has become a common denominator among the genuine Islamic movements, and thus we ought to be brave and frank in declaring that we do not fear [the emergence of] democracy in the Muslim world but fear for it.' Hawwa went so far as to remind the Islamists that they would be committing suicide by rejecting democracy: 'Because they fought democracy and viewed it through its [literal] meaning rather than its implications, the Islamists have killed themselves.

Consequently, they have been governed by the worst regimes that have imposed on them what they had feared from democracy; they have been denied the freedom democracy grants to them.' Then he asked: 'How could the Islamists fear democracy, the fear of which only leads to usurping them their freedom and to the rule of the minority? They should instead fear for democracy. The human experience has thus far shown that there can be no alternative to democracy other than revolutions, minority conspiracies and violence. All of this is a much greater risk than giving everybody the freedom to choose so that the majority elects those whom it deems fit and capable.' It is, however, clear that Hawwa did not think of democracy as an end in itself, but as a means to what he believed to be the noblest end, namely the implementation of Islam. 'Experience has proven that, in the Islamic ummah, democracy is the lesser of the two evils and the more moderate of the two damages prior to reaching the state of Islamic government.'

In the meantime, a different school of thought was developing in the Arab Maghreb drawing its inspiration from the 19th-century reform movement of Khairuddin at-Tunisi and the ideas of 'Abduh (who had twice visited Tunis and had a number of associates there), Bin Badis, Ath-Tha'alibi, Al-Taher al-Haddad, 'Allal Al-Fasi and others. Malik Bennabi, however, is credited with having laid the foundations of this modern Maghreb school of thought. An Algerian thinker of French culture, Bennabi (1905-73) believed that the coming of Europe had enabled the Muslims to escape from their decadence - caused by the emergence of a type of mind incapable of thought and afflicted with moral paralysis - by breaking up their rigid social order and freeing them from belief in occult forces and fantasies. From the early 1950s until his death, he wrote and lectured on what he believed to be the grand issues: namely, civilization, culture, concepts, orientalism and democracy. In a lecture entitled 'Democracy in Islam' delivered in French at the Maghreb Students Club in 1960 - attended then by Rachid Al-Ghannouchi and later on co-translated into Arabic by him - Bennabi attempted to answer the question 'Is there democracy in Islam?' He pointed out that defining the concepts of 'Islam' and 'democracy' in a conventional manner would lead to the conclusion that, with respect to time and location, the connection between the two is non-existent.

He suggested that deconstructing the concepts in isolation from their historical connotations and re-defining democracy in its broadest terms, without linguistic derivatives and free from any ideological implications, would lead to a different conclusion.

'Democracy', he said, 'ought to be looked at from three angles: democracy as a sentiment toward the ego, democracy as a sentiment toward the other, and democracy as the combination of the socio-political conditions necessary for the formation and development of such sentiments in the individual.' He went on to say: 'Contrary to the depiction of the romantic philosophy of the era of Jean-Jacques Rousseau, these conditions are not created by nature, nor are they the requisites of natural law, but are the upshot of a specific culture, the crowning of the progress of the humanities and a new appraisal of the value of man; his appraisal of himself and his appraisal of others. Thus, the democratic sentiment is the product of this progress over the centuries and of this twin appreciation of the value of man.'

Citing the French historian Guizot, in his book Europe from the End of the Roman Empire to the French Revolution, Bennabi stressed that various stages of progress led to the emergence of democracy in Europe and to the growth of the democratic sentiment in the European countries. He said: 'The great historian explains to us how remote and simple the origins of Western democracy had been before the democratic sentiment slowly formed prior to bursting with the declaration of human rights and citizen rights; the declaration which expressed the new appraisal of man and the legendary and political crowning of the French Revolution. Thus, the European democratic sentiment began to express itself - though not yet ridden of the obscurity that accompanies an object while in the state of making or evolving - through the two grand historical movements, the movement of reform and the movement of renaissance.' Bennabi considers the two movements to be the first expression of the value of the European human in the domain of the soul and in the domain of the mind. He stresses that this is the essence of the Western democratic sentiment when ridden of the fetters of history and politics - since the obscurity is caused by a package composed of phenomena and characteristics peculiar to Western history and which are not found in the history of other races and peoples - and when things are expressed in the terms of psychology and sociology. In other words, the democratic sentiment in Europe was, according to Bennabi, the product and natural outcome of the reform and renaissance movements. 'This', he stresses, 'is its correct historical meaning, and therefore it cannot simply be severed from the history of Europe so as to be applied to other nations.' However, he reiterates that whether in Europe or anywhere else, the general rule with regard to the nature of the democratic sentiment is that it is the outcome of a specific social continuity. 'In psychological terms', he adds, 'it is the middle position between two ends that are opposed to each other; the end that expresses the psyche of the oppressed slave on the one hand and the end that expresses the psyche of the oppressive master on the other. The free man, or the new man, in whom the values and conditions of democracy are embodied is the positive co-ordinate that is the sum of two negatives that individually negate all such values and conditions: the negative of servitude and the negative of enslavement.'

As for the question of the existence of democracy within Islam, Bennabi argues that this is dependent on the provision of what he earlier refers to as the general conditions of the democratic sentiment. He then puts forward a set of questions: Does Islam provide and guarantee these objective and subjective conditions, in the sense that it creates a sentiment toward the 'ego' and toward the 'other' that is compatible with the democratic sentiment? And does it create the appropriate social circumstances for the development of such a sentiment? Does Islam truly reduce the quantity and intensity of the negative motives and of the anti-democratic tendencies that characterize the conduct of the oppressed and the conduct of the oppressor? He suggests that any project aimed at founding a democracy should be considered an educational enterprise for the whole community, administered through the implementation of a comprehensive curriculum that encompasses psychological, ethical, social and political aspects. 'Democracy', he asserts, 'is not - as is superficially understood by the common usage of its etymology - a mere political process; a process whereby powers are handed over to the masses... But is the generation of a sentiment, and of objective and subjective responses and standards, that collectively lay the foundations upon which democracy, prior to being stated in any constitution, stands in the conscience of the people. The constitution is usually nothing but the formal outcome of the democratic enterprise once transformed into a political reality indicated by a text that is inspired by customs and traditions, and dictated by a sentiment generated in a given circumstance. Such a text will have no meaning if not preceded by the customs and traditions that inspire it, or in other words the historical justifications that necessitate it.'

He then warns that the answer to the question 'Is there democracy within Islam?' is not necessarily pertinent to a fiqh (jurisprudence) rule deduced from the Sunna or the Qur'an, but is one which is related to the essence of Islam as a whole. 'In this sense', he argues, 'Islam should be viewed not as a constitution that proclaims the sovereignty of a given community, or that states the rights or liberties of a certain people, but as a democratic enterprise that is the product of an exercise, through which the position of a Muslim *vis-a-vis* his or her encompassing society is defined, along the path toward accomplishing democratic values and norms provided a Muslim's temporal activity is tied to the general principles endorsed by Islam in the form of a seed sown in the Islamic conscience, and in the form of a general sentiment, and of motives, that constitute the Islamic equilibrium within every member of the community.'

Speaking of models of democracy - 'Western' in Europe, 'popular' in the East and 'new' in China - that differ from one another in the way they express their new symbolic evaluation of man, Bennabi sees that an Islamic model of democracy is attainable. Whereas in the other models the main objective is to endow man with political rights, enjoyed by the 'citizen' in Western countries, or social securities, enjoyed by the 'comrade' in Eastern countries, 'Islam', is distinguishable, according to Bennabi, because it 'endows man with a value that surpasses every political or social value'. He explains that the declaration in the Qur'anic verse 70 of Chapter 17, (We have honoured the children of Adam), endows man with more than just rights or securities. 'This verse was revealed as if to lay the foundations for a democratic model that is above every other model, where the divine element within man is taken into consideration and not just the human or social aspects as in the other models. Thus, a kind of sanctity is endowed upon man raising his value above whatever value other models give to him.'

However, Bennabi is keen to distinguish between what Islam has the potential to offer and the prevalent state of the Muslims. He concludes that democracy exists within Islam, not during the era when Islamic traditions petrify and lose their brilliancy such as nowadays, but during the era of their making and when society is developing, such as during the first 40 years of Islamic history.

Bennabi's analysis was revolutionary during his time, when Islamists in much of the Arab world, especially in the Middle East, were influenced by Qutb's thoughts and made an enemy out of democracy without ever understanding it. It was primarily thanks to his disciples such as Rachid Ghannouchi and other North African thinkers that mainstream Islamic movements gradually, though sometimes reluctantly, relinquished old positions on this matter. Malik Bennabi, who according to Ghannouchi, 'undoubtedly represents an element of the Islamic culture of rationalism and particularly a revival of Ibn Khaldun's historical culture of rationalism', had a profound influence on the Tunisian Islamic group. The two men's first encounter came when, on his way back from Paris to Tunis, Ghannouchi travelled by land through Spain, Morocco and Algeria where he visited Bennabi before entering Tunisia. He had read his books in Damascus when he, as he put it, returned to Islam. Having read Sayyid Qutb during his student years in Syria and France, and having been greatly influenced by his thoughts during that initial period of self-searching, he listened attentively to Bennabi as he strongly criticized Qutb. The latter had actually referred to Bennabi in one of his writings without mentioning his name: 'An Algerian writer who writes on Islam believes that Islam is one thing and civilisation is another.' Bennabi was seemingly offended by Qutb's remark which he believed was demeaning.

After listening to the critique, Ghannouchi concluded that Bennabi had deeper knowledge and a better understanding of civilization than Qutb. Bennabi believed that 'whereas civilisation is the transformation of any good idea into a reality, Islam is a set of guidelines, a way of life, or a project, that creates a civilisation only when put into practice; when its adherents carry it and move through the world positively influencing man, material and time. Therefore, a Muslim may be uncivilised just as a non-Muslim may be civilised.' On the other hand, Qutb insisted that civility is a synonym of Islam; that a Muslim is civilized and a non-Muslim is not. 'This belief', Ghannouchi comments, 'would inevitably lead to takfir' (that is charging someone with unbelief), and goes on to say, 'Qutb seemed to have borrowed the belief of the Al-Khawarij that a person is not a Muslim unless he or she is sinless and applied it to the question of civility; that is a person is not a Muslim unless he is perfectly civilised, and therefore all those backward Muslims are infidels!'

Islam and Civil Society

When regard is made to the nature of the link between Islam and civil society, we may easily note that Islam is essentially a 'civil' religion. Unlike Christianity, which fell into the hands of the Catholic Church, Islam did not encourage the establishment of rigid, centralising, authoritarian or totalitarian states. The primary purpose of Islam is to show the human person what is right and what is wrong and to guide him/her into the true path. The task of guidance is not accorded to a rigid and centralising state. It is the revelation, which constitutes the primary reference for anyone to accept Islam and find the true path. The revelation, according to Islam, can be recognised through reason and conscience. Islam has taught the humankind the right and the wrong and left the choice to the free will of the individual. In a way, every human being possesses the freedom to decide for himself/herself.

Acting upon this point, Islam enjoins Muslims to rule the society on the principles of justice, consultation and peace. The Quran does not anticipate the building of totalitarian political structures and the imposition of a single way of life. On the contrary, the non-Muslims are accepted as a different category. There are certain clues within the Quran itself to indicate that both the *ahlel kitap* (people of the book, i.e. Christians and Jews) and idol-worshippers should peacefully live side by side with Muslims.

The verse 'to them is their religion and to you is yours' provides an important instance of this understanding. But we should not lose sight of the cardinal precondition for peaceful cohabitation, which is avoidance of betrayal to Muslims. The society, which came into existence in Medina at the time of the Prophet Muhammad, was founded on 'Medina Contract', which was unprecedented in its recognition of the principle of 'social differentiation'. Hence the ideal model of society envisioned by Islam is not an ideological society, which is both monolithic and monotonous.

Likewise, the form of governance, which Islam encourages, is neither authoritarian nor totalitarian in character. It is known that there were periods in Muslim history when authoritarian or totalitarian methods were pursued by rulers. However, this practice stems neither from the principles of the Quran nor from the deeds of the Prophet Muhammad. The two basic principles found in the Quran that relate to governance are 'consultation' and 'justice'. These principles are surely in conformity with the preferred type of society perceived from the perspective of civil society. We note that these criteria were also observed in the practices, as the guiding principles at the time of the Prophet Muhammad. Although he was the recipient of revelation, the Prophet always made his societal decisions on consultation and acted on the dominant views of his companions in preference to his own, although his views would later prove correct. That is what happened in the war at Uhud when the Prophet chose to apply the military tactic, which his companions had suggested although he had a different plan.

In short, Islam is disposed to 'social differentiation' as well as to 'social participation'. In other words, Islam contains within its own epistemology the idea of opposition by individuals against the views imposed by the state who may even make the state to accept them; such examples were not infrequent in the early years of Islam. The historical documents reveal that the first caliphs (succeeding the Prophet) were always disposed to social participation and gave due consideration to the grassroots opinion.

Rather than through a centralised authority, Islam anticipates the expansion of religion through religious scholars.

The 'use of force' as a means of spreading religion has never been accepted as a legitimate method in Islam. On the contrary, Islam seeks 'persuasion' in the transmission of the message. Accordingly, the main frame of reference for Islam is, unlike the totalitarian states, which address themselves to the 'masses', the individual himself/herself. The emphasis of Islam is not on the mass of peoples, classes or particular social groups, but on each and every individual. As the human person is the main addressee of the message, Islam seeks persuasion through science (Islamic learning). Not unexpectedly, therefore, the Quran has a higher regard for scholars than rulers.

The emphasis of Islam on the 'human person' has close affinity with the 'individual' in democracies. To a significant extent, the principles of democracy, such as the individual, social group, civil existence, private life, free enterprise, political participation, elections, human rights, the rule of law, limited state, agree with those of Islam such as the centrality of the human person, community (*camaat*), intimate sphere of life, free trade conditions, consultation in decision-making, justice, human rights, fairness and law. The principles, which are indispensable for democracy, are surely the products of particular social and historical conditions. To try to find the traces within Islam of social practices, which would entirely conform with them, would not be a reasonable approach.

Since every society has its own historical background, naturally, every society develops its own basic principles. This implies that we should not try to find within Islam the democratic principles as they are practised in Western societies. Given that democracy is organically linked to the rights and freedoms of individuals, the subject of our inquiry must be limited to an examination of whether Islam is disposed to such principles as they exist in the West. As a matter of fact, basic human rights such as life, freedom and property, which are enforced in democratic societies, are likewise guaranteed under Islamic theology.

What has been argued by now in this paper relates to the thesis that the basic principles of Islam are disposed to the existence of civil society. When regard is made of the social practice of Islam, we can identify different historical phases. Islam started off as a civil movement in the person of the Prophet Muhammad.

The civilian character of Islam survived until the establishment of centralised states in different parts of the Muslim geography. We observe that a rich mix of different understandings and approaches, profound religious perspectives, and various interpretative approaches developed during the 'civilian' phase of Islam. It was before the institutionalisation of centralised authorities that we witness the presence of the most vivid and dynamic forms of sectarian differentiation, philosophical revival, Sufi tradition, and various Islamic currents of thought. In other words, Islamic vitality belongs to the period when 'civil' Islam predominated. It is at this time that imaginative interpretation of Islamic law (*ictihad*) was common occurrence, which enabled the translation of Islam into the practical needs of social life. In this epoch of 'civil' Islam, Islam managed to lay down principles, which addressed themselves to the life of individuals and permeated the core values of social life. Concepts such as reason (*akl*), revelation (*vahy*), inspiration (*ilham*) and sovereignty (*valayet*) which concerned every individual, and others like politics, consultation and justice which concerned only rulers, easily gained different meanings (from the later strict definitions) in this period. This was a time when Farabi's project of a 'virtuous society' based on political participation could be formulated. This same period was also ripe with a multitude of ideas, which suggested that reason was as important, continuous and lively a source as revelation in the construction of social life.

In conclusion, we understand that, both in terms of the wealth of experience and wealth at the level of social values and symbols, Islam took firm roots in society during its 'civil' phase. Islam thus reached the 'civilisational' stage, and its particular modality of life became a centre of attraction for other societies. The extent of richness, which Islam gained during its 'civil' episode, enabled its expansion into other societies and cultures.

The civil stage of Islam eventually lost its ascendancy to the 'political' phase of Islam, which resulted in rigid and centralising institutionalisation. With the rise of the *political* cosmos, we observe the incorporation of the religious sphere into the domain of centralised states, like other spheres of social life. The realm of religious life and institutions, not unlike other spheres, were completely dominated by centralised states. As a result, the society's ability to take initiative faded while centralisation took the upper hand. A wide rift began to open between centre and periphery as a result of centralisation, and this laid the foundations of a transcendental state, which had little ties with society. The Ottoman Turkish experience is a lively example of the kind of transformation in the history of Islam mentioned above and thus merits some analysis here.

When looked at from the perspective of civil society, we witness three distinct stages which characterise the Ottoman history. During the first of these stages which lasted until the 16th century, we observe sound examples of civil society. A distinctly Ottoman model manifested itself at this time. The state was the type of organisation governed by those who sought to keep the idea of Jihad (*holy war*) alive. These organisations, rather than establishing monopoly over social life, sought to expand the Ottoman dominions by conquering new territories. The principal values and dynamics of social life were determined by the elements of civil society. The theological schools (*medrese*) and religious orders (*tarikat*) appeared as significant religious institutions. The Islamic foundations, which sponsored theological schools mostly flourished independently of the state in this first stage. It was the theological schools, which organised social education free of state involvement, and the main actors in this process were religious scholars (*ulema*). Likewise, religious orders established themselves as autonomous institutions independent of the state. The state did not interfere with education, and was only partially involved in the economic realm. During the same period, the guilds (*lonca*), which were the basic economic units in cities, performed their functions entirely free of state involvement and those who administered the guilds were elected by the artisans themselves. Acting as the patron of different religions, the Ottomans granted some kind of autonomy to every religious group under the *millet* system. Every religious group was accorded the freedom to choose its own leader to administer the community affairs.

The period preceding the 16th century witnessed the climax of Ottoman power as well as the golden age of civil society. Behind the peak of Ottoman grandeur lay the existence of a state which directed its energy toward the outside world and a society which took the initiative in organising social relations. This was a time when 'social differentiation', 'tolerance' and 'freedom' were guaranteed. An interesting proof of this 'tolerance' is the freedom of propagation accorded to an atheist sect called *surrinizm* which even had some adherents from the palace.

From the perspective of civil society, the second stage materialised from the 16th century onwards. This was the stage when the business of the state took precedence over that of the people. During this stage, which lasted until the 19th century, elements of civil society such as theological schools, pious foundations, religious orders, guilds, the *millet* system and farmers gradually came under the domineering influence of the centre and, compelled to pursue their activities in accordance with the priorities of the state, in time lost their autonomy.

In this second stage when the centralist bureaucratic state consolidated itself, civil society began retreating and the atmosphere of difference and tolerance began to vanish. A peculiar feature of this period was the excessive increase in the number of edicts issues by the Sultans, which sought to imprint social life with prohibitions.

The third stage from the perspective of civil society began in the 19th century and lasted until the 1920s when Turkey was proclaimed a republic. This stage carried within itself a major paradox as far as civil society was concerned. On the one hand, civil society became slightly more active with the spread of modernity, on the other, the centralist structure, after gaining in strength, began to assert absolute domination over civil society and was eventually in a position to absorb it. By virtue of these peculiarities of the centralist structure, civil society became more active at the turn of the 20th century, although it was controlled by the state. Hence civil society was significantly enriched by new elements, which were introduced in addition to conventional elements. Such modern elements included political parties, the media, different currents of thought, associations, economic groups, banking sector, trade, legal and administrative reforms all of which played a cardinal role in the development and expansion of civil society during the Ottoman rule.

This brief recapitulation of the Ottoman history may also be regarded as a summary of the evolution of the Islamic world. The Ottoman experience in the 20th century was astonishingly parallel to that which was experienced by other Islamic societies elsewhere. The summary of this experience is this: The reactions evoked by the colonisation of the Islamic world at the end of the 19th and beginning of the 20th century by Western powers, *inter alia,* resulted in the emergence of rigid, authoritarian and centralist states in the Islamic world. The 'political' stage of the Islamic history which roughly began in the 12th century was reinvigorated yet again in this century vie authoritarian nation-states. The greatest single obstacle, which has hindered the growth of civil society in the Islamic world, is the single-party politics or authoritarian oligarchic regimes which have remained in the hands of particular families. Such regimes not only disable the invigoration of civil society and, by implication, of democracy, but also constrain the political influence and freedom of activity enjoyed by Muslim masses.

Given that the republican era in Turkey has provided an interesting and important example for the Islamic world in the 20th century. The republican regime, proclaimed in 1923, inherited from the Ottoman Empire, on the one hand, a centralist tradition and, on the other, a fair number of civil society institutions. However, Turkey was effectively ruled by a single party regime during the period of 1923-1950 pursued the policies of forcible westernisation. Civil society institutions were completely destroyed by the single party rule, which was bent on changing and transforming the entire society along western values. As the regime chose to take socialist values rather than liberal values as a point of reference in its pursuit of westernisation, it was not late before a rigid state structure was built. Neither modern nor traditional elements of civil society stood any chance of survival in 1923-1950. While no political parties other than the ruling Republican Peoples Party (*Cumhuriyet Halk Partisi*) was permitted, no association, no social movement, or even a member of the press with a different orientation existed in this period. As the state totally permeated the economic and social realms, the civil society was crippled to an extent unprecedented in the history of the Turks.

The introduction of multiparty politics in 1950 opened the route for a revival of civil society in Turkey. The most extensive resurgence of civil society in Turkey coincides to the period of 1980-1993. This was the time when Turgut Özal, as the leading political figure in Turkey, began to inject democratic liberal values into Turkish politics. In spite of all the democratic trappings of the Turkish political system since the 1950, this process was not buttressed by a liberal democratic culture given that the area of economics and politics was under the shadow of the state. From the early 1980s, Özal began to reinforce the democratic process by encouraging the expansion of a liberal and civic culture. As part of this objective, he tried to limit the influence of the bureaucracy, lay the foundations of a free market economy, diminish the role of the state over the economy by means of privatisation, ensure greater acceptance by Turkey of Western democratic values, and devised policies which accorded greater social freedoms.

This process resulted in considerable convergence between Islam and democracy in the person of Islamic groups. While various Islamic groups began, on the one hand, to register their influence in the public sphere through the use of democratic mechanisms, they elaborated formulas to establish accommodation between Islam and democracy on the other. As the indispensable conditions of this peaceful coexistence, the Islamic groups almost pressurised the state into accepting an impartial role for the state, passing new legislation to consolidate the free market economy and engaging more extensively into international trade. Today Islamic groups in Turkey have come to a position where they occupy a distinguished place in the educational, intellectual, political as well as economic fields. It is the civil society institutions established by Islamic groups, which have set the most essential, firmly rooted and vibrant examples of such institutions in the post-1980s. It is likewise these groups, which have asked the state to adopt the rule of law and democracy.

In conclusion, it may be asserted that the Turkish experience is not separate from those experienced in other parts of the Islamic world. The civil society has never flourished under the shadow of centralist, rigid, and authoritarian states anywhere in the world, and this is also the case with Muslim societies. Where such states still run supreme, Islam manifests itself as a source of reaction, since Muslim masses live under oppression, rather than synthesis. Under conditions of peace and freedom, Muslims are likely to search for synthesis and, on this basis, utilise Islam as an essential source of motivation in this world. This means that, under democratic conditions, Islam may constitute a significant frame of reference in the democratic struggle for civil society and for individual rights and freedoms. In short, for Islam to become a source of tolerance, peace, freedom, justice, differentiation and development, there has to be law-abiding democratic states with limited functions. Undoubtedly, Islam will, in the hands of such states, bring peace, prosperity and happiness to the entire world in general, and to the Islamic world in particular.

The relationship between Islam and democracy in the contemporary world is complex. The Muslim world is not ideologically monolithic. It presents a broad spectrum of perspectives ranging from the extremes of those who deny a connection between Islam and democracy to those who argue that Islam requires a democratic system. In between the extremes, in a number of countries where Muslims are a majority, many Muslims believe that Islam is a support for democracy even though their particular political system is not explicitly defined as Islamic.

Throughout the Muslim world in the twentieth century, many groups that identify themselves explicitly as Islamic attempted to participate directly in the democratic processes as regimes were overthrown in Eastern Europe, Africa, and elsewhere. In Iran such groups controlled and defined the system as a whole; in other areas, the explicitly Islamic groups were participating in systems that were more secular in structure.

The participation of self-identified islamically oriented groups in elections and in democratic processes in general, aroused considerable controversy. People who believe that secular approaches and a separation of religion and politics are an essential part of democracy argue that Islamist groups only advocate democracy as a tactic to gain political power. They say Islamist groups support "one man, one vote, one time." In Algeria and Turkey, following electoral successes by parties thought to be religiously threatening to the existing political regimes, the Islamic political parties were restricted legally or suppressed.

The relationship between Islam and democracy is strongly debated among the people who identify with the Islamic resurgence in the late twentieth century and the beginning of the twenty-first. Some of these Islamists believe that "democracy" is a foreign concept that has been imposed by Westernizers and secular reformers upon Muslim societies. They often argue that the concept of popular sovereignty denies the fundamental Islamic affirmation of the sovereignty of God and is, therefore, a form of idolatry. People holding these views are less likely to be the ones participating in elections. Many limit themselves to participating in intellectual debates in the media, and others hold themselves aloof from the political dynamics of their societies, hoping that their own isolated community will in some way be an inspiration to the broader Muslim community.

Many prominent Islamic intellectuals and groups, however, argue that Islam and democracy are compatible. Some extend the argument to affirm that under the conditions of the contemporary world, democracy can be considered a requirement of Islam. In these discussions, Muslim scholars bring historically important concepts from within the Islamic tradition together with the basic concepts of democracy as understood in the modern world.

The process in the Muslim world is similar to that which has taken place within other major religious traditions. All of the great world faith traditions represent major bodies of ideas, visions, and concepts fundamental to understanding human life and destiny.

Many of these significant concepts have been used in different ways in different periods of history. The Christian tradition, for example, in pre-modern times provided a conceptual foundation for divine right monarchy; in contemporary times, it fosters the concept that Christianity and democracy are truly compatible. In all traditions, there are intellectual and ideological resources that can provide the justification for absolute monarchy or for democracy. The controversies arise regarding how basic concepts are to be understood and implemented. A relatively neutral starting point for Muslims is presented in a 1992 interview in the *London Observer* with the Tunisian Islamist leader and political exile, Rashid Ghanoushi: "If by democracy is meant the liberal model of government prevailing in the West, a system under which the people freely choose their representatives and leaders, in which there is an alternation of power, as well as all freedoms and human rights for the public, then Muslims will find nothing in their religion to oppose democracy, and it is not in their interests to do so." Many Muslims, including Ghanoushi himself, go beyond this and view democracy as an appropriate way to fulfill certain obligations of the faith in the contemporary world.

The Islamic tradition contains a number of key concepts that are presented by Muslims as the key to "Islamic democracy." Most would agree that it is important for Muslims not simply to copy what non-Muslims have done in creating democratic systems, emphasizing that there are different forms that legitimate democracy can take. Iran's President Mohammad Khatami, in a television interview in June before that country's presidential elections, noted that "the existing democracies do not necessarily follow one formula or aspect.

It is possible that a democracy may lead to a liberal system. It is possible that democracy may lead to a socialist system. Or it may be a democracy with the inclusion of religious norms in the government. We have accepted the third option." Khatami presents a view common among the advocates of Islamic democracy that "today world democracies are suffering from a major vacuum, which is the vacuum of spirituality," and that Islam can provide the framework for combining democracy with spirituality and religious government.

The synthesis of spirituality and government builds on a fundamental affirmation at the heart of Islam: the proclamation that "There is no divinity but The God" and the affirmation of the "oneness" of God. This concept, called tawhid, provides the foundation for the idea that one cannot separate different aspects of life into separate compartments. Ali Shariati, who made important contributions to the ideological development of the Islamic revolution in Iran, wrote in *On the Sociology of* Islam, that tawhid "in the sense of oneness of God is of course accepted by all mono-theists.But tauhid as a world view... means regarding the whole universe as a unity, instead of dividing it into this world and the here-after... spirit and body."

In this worldview, the separation of religion from politics creates a spiritual vacuum in the public arena and opens the way for political systems that have no sense of moral values.

From such a perspective, a secular state opens the way for the abuse of power. The experiences of Muslim societies with military regimes that are secularist in ideological origin, such as the Baath Arab Socialist regime of Saddam Hussein in Iraq, reinforce this mistrust of separating religious values from politics.

Advocates of Islamic democracy argue that the Oneness of God requires some form of democratic system; conservatives contend that the idea of the sovereignty of the people contradicts the sovereignty of God; often the alternative then becomes some form of a monarchical system. The response to this is an affirmation of tawhid, as expressed by a Sudanese intellectual, Abdelwahab El-Affendi, in the Islam *21*: "No Muslim questions the sovereignty of God or the rule of Shari'ah [the Islamic legal path]. However, most Muslims do (and did) have misgivings about any claims by one person that he is sovereign. The sovereignty of one man contradicts the sovereignty of God, for all men are equal in front of God.... Blind obedience to one-man rule is contrary to Islam." In this way, it is argued that the doctrine of tawhid virtually requires a democratic system because humans are all created equal and any system that denies that equality is not Islamic. There are a number of specific concepts that Muslims cite when they explain the relationship between Islam and democracy. In the Qur'an, the righteous are described as those people who, among other things, manage their affairs through "mutual consultation" or shura (42:38 Qur'an).

This is expanded through traditions of the Prophet and the sayings and actions of the early leaders of the Muslim community to mean that it is obligatory for Muslims in managing their political affairs to engage in mutual consultation. Contemporary Muslim thinkers ranging from relatively conservative Islamists to more liberal modernists to Shi'ite activists emphasize the importance of consultation. There would be little disagreement with the view of Ayatollah Baqir al-Sadr, the Iraqi Shi'ite leader who was executed by Saddam Hussein in 1980, who said in *Islamic Political System*, that the people "have a general right to dispose of their affairs on the basis of the principle of consultation." What this meant for the constitutional system of the Islamic Republic of Iran, which was influenced by al-Sadr's thought, was affirmed by President Khatami in last June's interview: the "people play a fundamental role in bringing a government to power, in supervising the government and possibly the replacement of the government without any tension and problems."

Another basic concept in the development of Islamic democracy is "caliph." In contemporary discussions, traditional political usage of the term caliph has been redefined. Historically the term caliph was used as the title of the monarchs who ruled the medieval Muslim empire. When medieval Muslim political philosophers spoke of the institutions of caliph rule, the caliphate, they were analyzing the political institution of the successors to the Prophet Muhammad as the leader of the Muslim community. However, this concept of the caliphate was something that developed after the death of the Prophet.

In the Qur'an, the Arabic words for caliph (khalifah) and caliphate (khilafah) have a different meaning. These terms in the Qur'an have the more general meaning of steward and stewardship or trustee and trusteeship. In this way, Adam, as the first human, is identified as God's caliph or steward on earth. Muhammad is instructed to remind humans that God made them the caliphs (stewards or trustees) of the earth. In this way, in the Qur'an, the term caliphate refers to the broad responsibilities of humans to be the stewards of God's creation.

By the late twentieth century, long after the last vestiges of the political caliphate had been abolished by the reforms of Ataturk in Turkey in 1924, Muslim intellectuals began to see the importance of the concept of all humans as "caliphs" or God's stewards. As the intellectual dimensions of the late twentieth-century Islamic resurgence became more clearly defined, Ismail al-Faruqi, a scholar of Palestinian origins, outlined an ambitious project in a small book, Islamization of Knowledge. The concept of the caliphate involved responsibilities for all humans, in all dimensions of life, but especially the political: "Rightly, Muslims understand khilafah as directly political....

Islam requires that every Muslim be politicized (i.e., awakened, organized, and mobilized)."

The implications of this reassertion of a more explicitly Qur'anic meaning of human stewardship for Islamic democracy were spelled out by the South Asian Islamist leader, Abu al-Ala Mawdudi in *The Islamic Way of Life*: "The authority of the caliphate is bestowed on the entire group of people, the community as a whole.... Such a society carries the responsibility of the caliphate as a whole and each one of its individual[s] shares the Divine Caliphate. This is the point where democracy begins in Islam. Every person in an Islamic society enjoys the rights and powers of the caliphate of God and in this respect all individuals are equal."

In theory and concept, Islamic democracy is, at the beginning of the twenty-first century, quite well developed and persuasive. In actual practice the results have been less encouraging. Authoritarian rulers such as Ja'far Numayri in Sudan and Zia al-Haqq in Pakistan initiated formal programs of Islamization of the law and political system in the 1980s with results that were not encouraging for democracy. A military coup brought a combination of military and civilian Islamists to rule in Sudan in 1989 and despite the proclaimed goal of creating an Islamic democracy, the regime's human rights record in terms of treatment of non-Muslim minorities and Muslim opposition groups is deplorable.

International human rights groups have also been critical of the treatment of non-Muslim minorities in Iran, where the Shah was overthrown in 1979. During its first decade, the Islamic Republic set narrow limitations on political participation. However, the end of the nineties saw the unprecedented presidential election victory of Mohammad Khatami, who had not been favored by the conservative religious establishment. He was reelected by an overwhelming majority again in 2001. Although there are continuing grounds for criticizing Iran in terms of its repression of opposition and minorities, increasing numbers of women and youth are voting in elections. Instead of "one man, one vote, one time," the "one man" is being joined by "one woman" as a voting force.

Beyond the formally proclaimed Islamic political systems, there has also been an increasing role for democracy with an Islamic tone. In many countries Muslims who are not activist Islamists have participated in electoral processes and brought a growing sense of the need for morality and Islamic awareness in the political arena. In an era when politics in many countries is becoming "desecularized," leaders of Islamic organizations play important roles in electoral political systems that are not explicitly identified as Islamic. When the military regime of Suharto in Indonesia was brought to an end, the person who became president in 1999 as a result of the first open elections was Abd al-Rahman Wahid, the leader of Nahdat ul-Ulama, perhaps the largest Islamic organization in the world. He did not campaign on a platform of Islamizing the political system, even though he participated in the democratic system as a clearly identifiable Islamic leader.

When he was removed as president this year, it was by a process of orderly replacement, and neither his followers nor his opponents engaged in religious warfare.

Similarly, islamically oriented political parties have operated successfully in the secular electoral politics of Turkey, with the leader of one such party, Necmettin Erbakan, serving as prime minister briefly in 1996-1997. Although in succession, the islamically oriented Turkish parties have been suppressed and many of their leaders jailed, the response of the people in the parties has simply been to form new parties and try again within the political system rather than withdrawing into a violent underground opposition.

The Turkish experience reflects the fact that many Muslims, whether living in formally secular or formally Islamic states, see democracy as their main hope and vehicle of effective political participation. One important dimension of this participation is that despite conservative Muslim opposition to the idea of rule by a woman, the three largest Muslim states in the world - Indonesia, Bangladesh, and Pakistan - have had or now have elected women as their heads of government. None of these women was explicitly Islamist and one was directly opposed by an Islamist party.

There is a small but growing literature that attempts to identify empirically differences between the extent of democracy (and characteristics often identified with democracy) in majority Islamic and in majority non-Islamic nations. In this section, we briefly outline key contributions that helped to direct our own empirical analysis.

An early impulse for research on the relationship between Islam and democracy emanated from Samuel Huntington's 'clash of civilization' hypothesis articulated in a controversial *Foreign Affairs* article in 1993. Huntington argues, among other things, that 'Western ideas of individualism, liberalism, constitutionalism, human rights, equality, liberty, the rule of law, democracy, free markets, the separation of church and state, often have little resonance in Islamic, Confucian, Japanese, Hindu, Buddhist or Orthodox cultures'.

This 'clash of civilization' hypothesis has been taken widely to be prophetic in the post-September 11, 2001 environment, yet, in non-Western, *non-Islamic* countries, democracy and freedom, according to available data, are quite widespread. Surely, it is hard to identify inter-civilization 'clashes' in today's world other than those involving Islam.

In 1999, Robert Barro accepted the narrow definition of democracy adopted from Huntington: 'The central procedure of democracy is the selection of leaders through competitive elections by the people they govern.' On this basis, Barro deployed a political rights measure of democracy developed by Freedom House as the basis for a panel study of over 100 countries from 1960 to 1995. A panel study of over 100 countries from 1960 to 1995 found that improvements in the standard of living predicted increases in democracy as measured by this selective indicator of electoral rights.

Specifically, the propensity for democracy rises with per capita GDP, with primary schooling, and with a smaller gap between male and female attainment. By allowing for the effect of such economic variables, the interplay between democracy and religious affiliation is weakened. Barro also tests for the impact of religion on democracy and finds a 'significantly negative coefficient of the Muslim variable' even when the measures of standard of living and the other explanatory variables are held constant. Barro's estimated coefficient implies that the long-run level of electoral rights is lower by two Freedom House categories in a Muslim country as compared with the benchmark of a Catholic country. A similar such relationship is discerned when Barro replaces the dependant variable (political rights) with Freedom House's measure of civil liberties. Barro's results are broadly supported by Manus Midlarsky whose 1998 study concludes that Islam is negatively associated with all available indexes of democracy.

Perhaps the most forceful numbers-based exposition on Islam's democracy deficit is Adrian Karatnycky's 2002 paper published in the *Journal of Democracy* based on the 2001 Freedom House Survey. Karatnycky identifies 'a dramatic gap' in democracy between Islamic countries and the rest of the world:

> Since the early 1970s, when the 'third wave" of democratization began, the Islamic world – and its Arab core in particular – has seen little significant improvement in political openness, respect for human rights, or transparency...In the 47 countries with an Islamic majority, only 11 (23 percent) have democratically elected governments, while 110 of the 145 non-Islamic states (76 percent) are electoral democracies. This means that a non-Islamic state is nearly three times more likely to be democratic than an Islamic state. Furthermore, none of the 16 Arab states is a democracy.

Karatnycky identified an even more dramatic gap in freedom between majority-Islamic countries and the rest of the world. In 2001, there was only one Islamic country, Mali, registered as a free country by Freedom House, while 18 were Partly Free, and 28 were Not Free. Among the non-Islamic countries, by contrast, 85 were Free, 39 were Partly Free, and 21 were Not Free.

This differential was part of a long-term trend. Between 1981 and 2001, in the non-Islamic world, the number of Free countries increased by 35, the number of Partly Free countries increased by 8 and the number of Not Free countries declined by 21. In the Islamic world, the number of free countries remained stuck at one, the number of Partly Free countries declined by two and the number of Not Free countries increased by ten.

Karatnycki also confirmed that the democracy gap persisted in every region where there were Islamic countries, including the post-communist world. Notably, no Islamic-majority democracy had a majority-Arab population, and all Islamic-majority electoral democracies were located on the geographical and cultural edges of the Islamic world. Nevertheless, Karatnycki concluded that Islam was not inherently incompatible with democracy. If the large Muslim populations of India, Bangladesh, Indonesia, Nigeria and Turkey as well as the Islamic populations of North America and Western Europe, were accounted for, a majority of the world's Muslims actually lived under conditions of democracy (albeit less unambiguously, in our view, of freedom).

One possibility is that Islam may simply serve as a proxy for oil and gas natural resources. What Karatnycky calls the "Arab core" of the Islamic world is rich in such resources; and these commodities have conferred vast riches on narrow ruling elites in a number of Middle Eastern countries.Such elites may utilize their wealth to repress democratic tendencies for financial rather than religious reasons. This possibility is explored in some depth by Michael Ross in a 2001 paper published in *World Politics*.

Michael Ross studies the question, whether or not oil hinders democracy. Using pooled time-series cross-national data from 113 countries over the period 1971-1997, he tests three hypotheses, namely (1) oil resources hinder democracy, (2) that this negative influence does not extend beyond the Middle East and (3) that non-mineral wealth also impedes democracy.

He finds the oil-impedes democracy claim to be both valid and statistically significant. Moreover, oil does relatively greater damage to democracy in poor states than in rich ones. He finds that this negative influence is not restricted to the Middle East. Oil wealth has impeded democracy in Indonesia, Malaysia, Mexico and Nigeria. It may well have done so in oil rich states in Central Asia.

He also finds that non-fuel mineral wealth somewhat impedes democracy. While the major oil exporters are concentrated in the Middle East, major mineral exporters are scattered across Africa, Asia and the Americas and has deterred democracy in such countries as Angola, Chile, the Democratic Republic of Congo, Cambodia and Peru.

Ross concludes that three causal mechanisms link oil with autocracy, namely:

1. A *rentier* effect through which governments use low tax rates and high spending to dampen pressures for democracy,
2. A repression effect through which governments build up their internal forces to ward off democratic pressures, and a modernization effect, through which the failure of the general population to move into the industrial and service sectors renders them less likely to push for democracy. These links empirically are much more evident in the case of oil than in the case of non-oil mineral wealth. Interestingly, from our perspective, Ross deploys Islam as an independent variable in his regres-sions. The coefficient on that variable is consistently significant, and with a negative sign.

Yet, there is dissent within the literature. Przeworski suggests that the best way to evaluate the determinants of democracy is to focus on "regime dynamics", the patterns through which regimes, classified in binary fashion as either democracies or as dictatorships, emerge and fall. He offers a surprising result:

No democracy ever, including the period before World War

II, fell in a country with a per capita income higher than that of Argentina in 1976, $6,055. This is a startling fact, given that since 1946 alone forty-seven democracies collapsed in poorer countries. In contrast, thirty- spent 1046 years in wealthier countries and not one died. Affluent countries survived wars, riots, scandals, economic and governmental crises, hell or high water...Above $6,055... democracy lasts forever.

On the basis of a data set that runs from 1950 to 1999, encompassing 135 countries (but excluding major oil producers) Przeworski concludes that it is difficult, if not impossible, to determine how democracies emerge, but easy to explain their survival, once established, in terms of per capital income. It was difficult or even impossible, at a general level, to determine how autocracies emerge or survive. Once established, there is little difference with respect to democracies and dictatorships with respect to the total growth in GDP.

Using the same methodology, Przeworski rejected the notion that religious variables - notably Islam - exercised influence on the emergence of democracy. He inferred that the only observed effect of religion is that democracies are more likely to emerge in Catholic-majority countries. This inference, in our view is suspect. Przeworski's data runs only from 1950 to 1999. Most Protestant countries were democratic before 1950 and stayed so. Few Islamic countries became democracies (broadly defined) either before or after 1950.

Another counter-argument against the hypothesis that an Islamic democracy deficit exists is raised by Pippa Norris and Ronald Inglehart whose 2003 paper deploys data from the World Values Survey to demonstrate that Muslim populations are more supportive of democracy on average than are non-Muslim populations. Norris and Inglehart take this striking empirical result to demonstrate that Huntington's 'clash of civilizations' hypothesis is refuted.

Operational Definitions

Democracy and Autocracy

Democracy is a contentious term, with many different

meanings attributed to it. The concept emanates from Ancient Greece, where *demos kratia* meant 'people authority', in the sense of government by the majority vote of male citizens, an extremely elite group. Women, slaves, other subordinated groups, and all aliens were completely excluded from this privilege. This limited ideal was nearly achieved (but fairly quickly lost) by Athens in the fifth century B.C.. From such early times, democracy became recognized as rule by the people as opposed to rule by one individual (autocracy) or rule by the few (oligarchy).

In more modern times, democracy is defined as a system of government by all eligible members of a country, typically through representatives elected usually, but not always, by some kind of majority vote, with each individual exercising an equal vote in a secret ballot. Democracies are defined, from this perspective, by process and not by title. Many so-called people's republics and democratic republics in reality are autocracies (for example, China, and the Congo). Evidently, there are many forms of democracy with varying degrees of democratic process at any point of time. Equally, there are many forms of autocracy, of varying degrees of autocratic process at any point in time. In this empirical study, we rely for data on the Dataset provided by the *Polity IV Project.* This data set comprised 161 countries in 2004, some of which had experienced recent regime change. In 2002, a new variable was added to the *Polity IV* data series: POLITY2, to facilitate the use of the Polity regime measure for time-series analysis.

Democracy, for purposes of this dataset, is conceived as three essential, interdependent elements. One is the presence of institutions and procedures through which citizens can express effective preferences about alternative policies and leaders. Second is the existence of institu-tionalized constraints on the exercise of power by the executive. Third is the guarantee of civil liberties to all citizens in their daily lives and in acts of political participation. However the dataset does not include coded data on specific aspects of civil liberties such as the rule of law, systems of checks and balances and freedom of the press, which are viewed as means to, or specific manifestations of, these general principles.

This (inevitably subjective) operational Democracy indicator is graded on an additive eleven-point scale (0 - 10) (with the quality of a defined democracy rising from a minimum of 0 to a maximum of 10) derived from coding of:

1. The competitiveness of political participation,
2. The openness and competitiveness of executive recruitment and
3. Constraints on the chief executive. A mature and internally coherent democracy is operationally defined as one in which political participation is fully competitive, executive recruitment is elective and constraints on the chief executive are substantial.

The *Polity IV Project* codes autocracy, in a similar operational fashion, in terms of the presence of a distinctive set of political characteristics. In mature form, autocracies sharply restrict or suppress competitive political partici-pation. Their chide executives are chosen, through a regulated process, from within the political elite and, once in office, they exercise power with few institutional constraints. On this basis, an operative *autocracy indicator* is constructed additively from coding:

1. The competitiveness of political participation,
2. The openness of political participation,
3. The openness and competitiveness of executive recruitment and
4. Constraints on the chief executive. The scale runs from 1 (minimal) to 10 (maximum) autocracies.

Standards of Political Rights and Civil Liberties

Any scale of measurement from democracy to autocracy, including that of *Project IV,* must be subjective. In order to broaden our own empirical analysis of the Muslim democracy deficit in section 4, therefore, we draw also upon the extensive data base provided by the *Freedom in the World Survey* published by Freedom House. The survey provides annual numerical ratings separately for the state of political rights and for civil liberties in each of 193 countries and 15 select territories. Each scale runs from 1 (maximum rights) to 7 (minimum rights). These ratings (inevitably) are subjective.

The ratings process is based on a checklist of 10 political rights questions and 15 civil rights questions. The political rights questions are grouped into three sub-categories:

1. Electoral process,
2. Political pluralism and participation and
3. Functioning of government.

The civil liberties questions are grouped into four sub-categories:

- Freedom of expression and belief,
- Associational and organizational rights,
- Rule of law and
- Personal autonomy and individual rights. Raw points are awarded to each sub-category assessment on a scale of 0 (worst) to 4 (best). These raw scores are then aggregated into a 1-7 overall rating for each country in terms of political rights and of civil rights.

Some Simple Arithmetic on Islam and Democracy

The Extent and Nature of Islam's Overall Democracy Deficit

Muslim countries are less democratic than non-Muslim countries. For the year 2004, the Polity IV data set ranked 153 countries on a scale of democratic governance ranging from -10 (most autocratic) to 10 (most democratic). For non-Muslim countries, the average Polity IV score was 5.24. For Muslim countries, the average score was -2.16. Not a single majority-Muslim country was assigned Polity IV's highest scores of 9 and 10, while 47 out of 115 non-majority-Muslim countries were assigned one of those scores.

Freedom House publishes data which ranks Political Rights and Civil Liberties on a scale from 1 (most free) to 7 (least free). In majority-Muslim countries, the average score for political rights in 2004 was 5.24, for civil liberties 4.90. In non-majority-Muslim countries, political rights averaged 3.13, and civil liberties 3.04, so that both scores are about two points lower (i.e., freer) in non-Muslim than in Muslim countries. Not a single Muslim country achieved Freedom House's top score of 1 for either civil liberties or political rights. Only two countries, Mali and Senegal, scored a 2 in political rights, while only one country, Mali, scored a 2 for civil liberties.

Are Muslim countries less democratic because they are Muslim, or is the Islamic world's democracy deficit explained by some factor, which merely happens to be correlated with Islam? In particular, the lack of democracy in the Muslim world is often attributed to (a) poverty, and (b) oil. It is true that Muslim countries are generally poorer than non-Muslim countries, even if we exclude the European Union and the English-speaking nations. While the median country in the EU and/or the English-speaking world had a real GDP per capita in 2002 of $24,282, and the median non-Muslim country outside the EU and English-speaking world had $4,173, the same statistic for the median Muslim country was a bit less at $3,707. Poorer countries, of course, tend to enjoy less democracy. It is also true that Muslim countries are, on average, more dependent on oil exports, though of course this varies widely. The share of oil in total exports in Muslim countries is significantly higher than in non-Muslim countries, and this relationship remains if GDP is controlled for. Oil share of exports also has a negative impact on the Polity IV democracy score.

The Dynamics of Islam's Democracy Deficit

Islam has existed for over a thousand years, so if the democracy deficit we observe in the Islamic world is a consequence of Islam, we might expect it to be long-standing. Of course, it is true that democracy has rarely if ever existed in the Islamic world historically, but the same is true of other regions until relatively recently.

In 1950, the statistical impact of Islam on the Polity IV score was actually positive, though not significant. Only in 1965 did Islam begin to have a negative and significant effect on the Polity IV score. For three decades afterwards the coefficient on Islam continued to become more strongly negative. At the same time, the coefficient on log GDP per capita as a determinant of the Polity IV score, though remaining significant at the 1% level, trended downwards, so that by 2000 it was one-third lower than in 1950. Democracy has spread through many poorer countries, but has penetrated the Islamic world much less than other regions.

The Missing Income-Democracy Correlation

In most of the world, there is a strong positive correlation between wealth and democracy, but this does not apply in the Islamic world. In fact, whereas in non-Muslim countries wealth is associated with more democracy, in Muslim countries wealth is actually associated with *less* democracy.

An obvious explanation of the lack of democracy in wealthy Muslim countries is that these countries are mostly oil states, and natural resources provide rulers with a source of wealth that makes them less accountable to their subjects. And it turns out that when oil's share of exports is controlled for the negative correlation between wealth and democracy/ freedom loses significance.

Yet the puzzle remains that the correlation between income and democracy is *missing* which is observed in the rest of the world. Over time, most countries experience economic growth. In the past few years, economic growth has been especially strong in developing countries in every region of the world. Since GDP is correlated with democracy, economic growth gives us grounds for optimism that the world will continue to become more democratic as well. Unfortunately, the missing, or even inverse, income-democracy correlation prevents this rosy forecast from being applicable to the Islamic world.

The Democracy Deficit in the Historic Islamic Heartland

Islam appeared in the Arabian Peninsula in the 7th century, then expanded in a surge of explosive conquests, after which the lands ruled by Islam stretched from Central Asia and modern Pakistan all the way to Spain. We shall classify the countries whose territory, or a substantial part of it, was part of the Islamic empire by 750 A.D., and which have not since been conquered and settled by non-Muslim peoples (e.g. Spain and Israel) as Islam's "historic heartland."

Regressions show that when a dummy variable is entered for a country's location in Islam's historic heartland, this becomes overwhelmingly significant in explaining the Polity IV score and the two Freedom House indicators, while the Muslim share of population indicator's coefficient keeps its sign and remains large enough to be suggestive, but loses statistical significance.

Regressions restrict the sample to Muslim countries, and show that within the Islamic world location in the historic heartland is a significant determinant of democracy, political rights, and civil liberties. Regressions use a global sample excluding the historic heartland, and show that majority-Muslim countries in the "periphery" are actually not significantly less free or democratic than non-majority-Muslim countries, though, again, the coefficients retain their signs and remain large enough to be suggestive.

The fact that Islam's democracy (and freedom) deficit is especially severe in the historic heartland of Islam may be evidence that Islam is, somehow, the cause of that deficit, for it is there that Islam has the deepest historical roots and has had the most time to shape and to transform the culture, and may thereby have gained the strongest influence.

This raises an important question: Are majority Muslim countries that are democratic "less" Muslim than Muslim countries that are not? There are ten sizeable Muslim countries[7] that have Polity IV scores greater than 0: Albania, Algeria, Bangladesh, Indonesia, Malaysia, Mali, Niger, Senegal, Sierra Leone, and Turkey. Of these, Malaysia and Sierra Leone are only 60% Muslim, Albania 70%. Bangladesh and Indonesia have large Muslim majorities, 83% and 86%, respectively, but they are notably late converts to Islam. Indonesian Islam in particular has always been unusually moderate and syncretist.

To a significant degree, the striking variations in the practice and interpretation of Islam-*in a much less austere form than that practiced in the Middle East*-in various parts of Indonesia reflect its complex history. Introduced piecemeal by various traders and wandering mystics from India, Islam first gained a foothold between the twelfth and fifteenth centuries in coastal regions of Sumatra, northern Java, and Kalimantan. Islam probably came to these regions in the form of mystical Sufi tradition. Sufism easily gained local acceptance and became synthesized with local customs.

Four of the Muslim-majority democracies—Senegal, Sierra Leone, Niger, and Mali—are in sub-Saharan Africa. For whatever reason, Sub-Saharan Africa is the one region in the world where the Islamic democratic deficit is *not* observed. Muslim countries in sub-Saharan are significantly more democratic than Muslim countries elsewhere, whether we use the Polity IV score or the Freedom House measure of political rights (though not civil liberties). And among sub-Saharan African countries, Islam has no significant effect on democracy or civil liberties. This may be related to the fact that democracy in Islamic countries is correlated with poverty, contrary to the pattern in non-Muslim countries.

Algeria is a 99% Muslim country in the historic heartland of Islam. But its Polity IV score in 2004 was only 2, having jumped from -3 the previous year, and before that, it was negative for Algeria's entire history since independence. Algeria was the scene of an abortive democratic revolution in 1989, which is suggestive of an explanation for democratic deficit in the Islamic world: Muslims may just vote for the wrong people. At the peak of the "Third Wave" of democratization, as the communist dominoes were toppling in Eastern Europe, popular pressure induced the ruling Front de Liberation National regime in Algeria to hold democratic elections and 62 percent of the vote went to an obscure political start-up, the Islamic Salvation Front. Could an Islamist party lead a democracy? As it turned out, they never got the chance: the FLN rejected the election results and plunged the country into civil war. The Economist describes the most recent election, in March 2007, as follows:

"Fifteen years ago the FIS, which is now banned, offered a real alternative to the regime. Today there are plenty of parties but less real choice. As the recent campaign got under way, many Algerians were more interested in the presidential election across the Mediterranean, in France. In Algeria, the National Liberation Front, the country's sole legitimate party from independence in 1962 until a political opening in 1989 easily won the day, with its allies in second and third place. Two parties with strong traditions of opposition were almost entirely excluded: the Islamists of el-Islah, which had been the largest opposition party in the last parliament, were reduced to three seats after the government blocked their former leader from standing for reasons that were never clearly explained; and the Socialist Forces Front, a liberal party based in the Berber region of Kabylia, decided, for the second time in a row, to boycott the proceedings.

That leaves Turkey. Turkey is 99.8% Muslim. It is not, strictly speaking, part of the "historic heartland" as we have defined it here, because the territory of modern Turkey was not under Islamic rule in 750 A.D., as the Byzantine empire successfully stopped the advance of the early Arab conquerors, and was gradually conquered only in the course of the later Middle Ages by the Seljuk and Ottoman Turks, with then-Constantinople (now Istanbul) finally falling in 1453. However, Ottoman Turkey was hardly the "periphery" of the Islamic world. For centuries, the sultans of the Turkish Empire held the title of "caliph," and were regarded by Muslims worldwide as leaders of the entire Islamic *umma*, and Turkey was an integral part of Middle Eastern Islam. Today, unlike Algeria, Turkey has a strong democratic tradition. Since 1950, Turkey's Polity IV score has always been positive except during two brief episodes (1971-72 and 1980-82) when the military seized power. Turks are the only Muslims who have enjoyed credible, competitive elections and made their laws through parliamentary politics for most of the twentieth century.

But what has Turkey done to achieve this? A critical element of Turkish democratic success appears to have been a rigid secularism and exclusion of Islam from politics. The army has acted as a guarantor of secularism even, to some extent, at democracy's expense. The current ruling party, for example, was repeatedly banned by the army for being too Islamist, even when they were winning elections.

The Extent of Muslim Support for Democracy

A simple explanation for the lack of democracy in the Muslim world would be that there is little *demand* for democracy in the Muslim world. Maybe, for cultural reasons, Muslims just have less desire for self-government than non-Muslims. The missing income-democracy correlation in the Muslim world is suggestive of this explanation. When other peoples become richer, they demand more of the things they want, and are more willing and able to engage in the political mobilization required to get and sustain democracy. Muslims, not regarding democracy as desirable, do not use greater wealth to secure it. This story turns out to be false. *The World Values Survey* provides a data set of hundreds of thousands of observations from countries all over the world, and the results indicate that not only are people in Muslim countries no *less* supportive of democracy, they even appear to be *more* pro-democratic.

Further survey questions tried to evoke negative attitudes towards democracy by suggesting some flaws of the democratic system. Once again, people in Muslim countries appear to be more pro-democratic than people in non-Muslim countries. For example, on the economy: 73% of people in

Muslim countries, as compared with 64% in non-Muslim countries, disagree with the claim that democracy is bad for the economy .

The results do not confirm the "grass is greener" hypothesis: in general, people living in more democratic countries appear to be, if anything, more favorable to democracy. But the pro-democratic slant of public opinion in Muslim countries is confirmed, as the coefficient on Muslim share of population is consistently positive.

The Attitudes of Muslims toward Freedom and Order

The main finding, which emerges very strongly, is that an explanation of Islam's democratic deficit as a function of negative cultural attitudes to democracy must be rejected. Pippa Norris and Ronald Inglehart summ-arized this evidence in a 2001 *Foreign Policy* article as a confirmation of President Bush's views:

"The peoples of the Islamic nations want and deserve the same freedoms and opportunities as people in every nation," President Bush declared in a commencement speech at West Point last summer. He's right. Any claim of a "clash of civilizations" based on fundamentally different political goals held by Western and Muslim societies represent an oversimplification of the evidence. Support for the goal of democracy is surprisingly widespread among Muslim publics, even among those living in authoritarian societies. But Norris and Inglehart do not answer a question that is obviously raised by the evidence they describe: If there is so much demand for democracy among Muslims, why do they not secure more of it? Of course, rulers are often reluctant to surrender power to the electorate. But it is not clear why this factor should specially affect *Muslim* countries. Are there other attitudes characteristic of Muslims that are not conducive to democracy? In parti-cular, are Muslim attitudes less favorable to *freedom* than in other parts of the world?

If so, these attitudes may prevent the development of democracy, because an essential aspect of democracy is the right of minorities to speak their minds and organize, in hopes of becoming majorities, and democracy cannot be sustained if these rights are not respected.

There are two World Values Survey questions that ask respondents for the relative valuation of:

a. Freedom versus equality, and
b. Government order versus freedom. Unfortunately, the first of these questions was asked only in Turkey, the second, only in Turkey, Azerbaijan, Albania and Bangladesh.

The results are striking. Relative to respondents in non-Muslim countries, Turks clearly place more value on equality relative to freedom. And Turks, Azeris, Albanians and Bangladeshis place far more value on government order relative to freedom than respondents in non-Muslim countries. Whether these results can be generalized to the rest of the Muslim world cannot be confidently inferred from this data.

Islam's Religious Freedom Deficit

What is clear is that there is less religious freedom in the Muslim world than elsewhere.

Democratic countries have more religious freedom, and Muslim countries are less democratic, so it is not surprising that Muslim countries have less religious freedom. But the causal link lies deeper than that. For even when the level of democracy is controlled for, Muslim countries have less religious freedom.

Our data about religious freedom is taken from a data set derived from State Department Reports. The main dependent variable is the answer to the question "In the [State Department] Report [on religious freedom], how is freedom of religion described?" Other questions ask:

a. Whether the government 'generally respects' freedom of religion,

b. Whether foreign missionaries are allowed to operate,

c. Whether there are limits on proselytizing, preaching or conversion,

d. Social attitudes towards other religions, and

e. Attitudes towards other or non-traditional religions.

Religious freedom is related to democracy. Democratic countries have more religious freedom than non democratic countries. There is no sign of a relationship between religious freedom and GDP, so this variable is omitted from most of the regressions. The key finding is that not only is the Muslim share of population associated with less religious freedom directly, but this coefficient retains its statistical significance, for our main dependent variable, even when the Polity IV score is controlled for. When other measures of religious freedom are used, the coefficient on Islam sometimes appears significant and sometimes not. It is very large and highly significant as a determinant of restrictions on conversion and proselytizing.

We saw earlier that there was something different about the historic heartland of Islam, possibly because Islam has had more time to permeate the culture there. This raises the question: Is the religious freedom deficit a feature of the Muslim world generally, or is the historic heartland driving these results? We can test this by regressing religious freedom against indicators of Islam while excluding the historic heartland. The coefficients generally retain sign but lose significance, with one exception: restrictions on proselytizing and conversion are still associated strongly, and with statistical significance at the 1% level, with Islam.

One reason that Muslim countries have less religious freedom may be that their peoples just care about religion more than non-Muslim-majority countries. Simple arithmetic has shown:

a. That there is a deficit of democracy in the Islamic world, which is not explained by poverty or oil but seems to have something to do with Islam itself;

b. That this democracy deficit is larger in the Islamic heartland than elsewhere in Muslim-majority countries,

c. That this democracy deficit does not reflect a lack of demand for democracy, indeed if anything public opinion in Muslim countries is more pro-democratic than elsewhere; and

d. That the Muslim world has less religious freedom than other parts of the world.

5

Islamic Democracy and the Christian Model

Religion's role in any political society has been questioned and the topic of heated debate from both the left and right. Many have been cautioned about historical fallacies and tragedies such as the Crusades and more recently, the Holocaust and September 11, all done in the name of a religion. Yet many do contend that religion does provide a moral doctrine which can assist governments, and ultimately society, in becoming more ethical. The world's two largest religions, Christianity and Islam, have been in the spotlight with regards to their relationship to democracy. Christian Democracy was a recent historical phenomenon occurring in Europe and took full force after World War II. Although not surviving with the same force today, it most certainly cannot be called a failure.

Islamic democracy, however, is interesting because although it is the subject of constant study, it has yet to truly co-exist with the essence of democracy as we know it today. This has made many wonder if it is even possible whether they are fundamentally destined to collide, or whether they can co-exist. Upon examining Christian Democracy, Islamic Democracy, and the similarities and differences between the two, it can be concluded that although no tangible proof has yet to come, Islam and Democracy can co-exist. However, in order for it to do so, it must follow very similarly to the model of Christian democracy in Europe.

The best example of the relationship between Christianity and Democracy as a success is the Christian Democratic movements during the last few centuries. Although it is difficult to define a common opinion of different Christian democratic parties, especially from its origins in the eighteenth centuries to modern times, Michael Fogarty believes that there are three essential characteristics which are similar in all programs of Christian democracy. He asserts that all Christian democracies are:

1. Comprehensive and balanced, a catholic (with a small 'c') synthesis of views from all quarters of the political universe on the whole range of problems with which government is concerned;
2. Based consciously and, usually, explicitly on the Christian revelation and the tradition and teaching of the Churches;
3. Empirical, built up in the light of history and current experience rather than of any systematic, *a priori*, theory"..

Although the beginnings of Christian Democratic parties started taking an active role in European politics post World War II, the Christian Democratic movement originated during the eighteenth and nineteenth centuries, particularly in France. Remnants of Christian Democracy still exist all throughout Europe, in the form of Great Britain's Movement for Christian Democracy and other political parties who, in their constitutions, believe that Christianity is central to a country's political, economic and social affairs. Movements for Christian democratic parties arose in France after the Republic had been the enemy of the Church since the Civil Constitution of the Clergy (Fogarty 4). Under the *ancien régime,* the Church and Monarchy had been so closely linked that when the latter was deprived of its privileges, the former was inevitably attacked as well.

The more recent success of Christian democracy has been reliant on the support it garnered from the Catholic Church. The Catholic Church and its relationship to Christian democracy involves both ideological and institutional ties that have varied across time and place. The Catholic Church heavily questioned the position of democracy before World War II, and even found the positions of Mussolini and Hitler more appealing and more in line with the doctrines of the Church. Finally, after World War II, the Vatican began to accept the doctrines of parliamentary democracy. Their sharing of social doctrine has also been responsible for the relationship between the Church and Christian Democracy. According to Mitchell, a commitment to the poor, a concern for the integrity of the family, and a critique of the materialist assumptions under girding ideology provided common ground for Christian democrats. Thus, we see the rise and success of Christian Democratic parties in Europe as more of a gradual process than something that happened overnight, and also one founded on basic moral doctrine.

Christian Democratic parties in France identified most with the Mouvement Republicain Populaire (MRP). While referring rarely to Christianity by name, the MRP always based their doctrinal arguments on a Christian interpretation of the value of the individual. This was the essence of the MRP's doctrine. Democracy, the family, the school, the trade union—even the Church—were important only in so far as they made it possible for the individual to develop his capacities to the maximum. In other words, the MRP saw democracy, and ultimately the Christian Democratic parties, more as a means rather than as the goal. The MRP doctrine was therefore very individualistic, not in the nineteenth century liberal sense, but in a Christian sense. By de-emphasizing religious institutions in the political state, the MRP was able to take care of the society as whole.

The aspect of faith in Christian democracy is obviously one of crucial importance. In his *Cet Inconnu*, Borne describes an act of faith as something that "has no meaning unless it leads to action. Faith must generate thought and political engagement. Because we believe that freedom and justice are ultimately reconcilable, we must try to bring this about. Political engagement entails a passion for freedom and a passion for justice". The correlation between action and faith, then, is very interesting. A separation of church and state really is only necessary when the Church begins to dictate and influence government unfairly towards those who don't follow the Church's doctrine. Yet if the Church influences the state in a way that helps the state to become more moral and just, this can only be seen as beneficial to the society as a whole. Here Borne explains that these actions *must* fall in line with ideas of freedom and justice, two crucial aspects of democracy. This is another reason why Christian democratic parties were able to exist in European society: their primary agenda was to benefit society with ideas of freedom and justice through acts of faith.

The main question, however, remains about the role that revelation and texts, namely the Gospels and the New Testament, had to play in Christian democratic movements. According to Fogarty, "in the main stream of Christian thought it has always been clear that revelation completes natural knowledge but does not replace it. To have a full picture of the world, one which will allow Christians to take hold of their surroundings and shape them according to their principles, the broad and long views of revelation must be filled in with the detail of purely human science, experience, and intuition". This is crucial to the Christian democratic argument, for it falls in line with much modern democratic thinking in using reason and intuition in order to make political decisions. It almost seems as though Fogarty interprets the place of revelation as taking a back seat to reason. In essence, many times this is necessary in order to prevent irrational decisions that can be ultimately very costly for those in society who do not adhere to the Christian faith.

In comparison, the Islamic experience and experiments with Democracy have not been so pleasant. This has led many to wonder whether or not fundamentally Islam and democracy as we know it are incompatible. In actuality, however, despite attempts by moderate Muslims in the West to bring Middle Eastern countries and self-proclaimed "Islamic states" towards a democratic ideal, Islamic democracy has yet to exist in the modern world. Even in states such as

Algeria that had what Noah Feldman coined a "democratic flirtation," democracy does not last for long because of Western fear that Islamist control will eventually lead Westerners to believe that elections that were not "fair" would be better than no elections at all.

In order to test the Islamic experience with democracy, Samuel P. Huntington conducted a test in which he defined a democracy as two consecutive and peaceful changes in government through free and fair elections. However, upon testing Middle Eastern countries that deem themselves as "Islamic states" or where the official religion of the country is Islam, the only country that passed Huntington's test of democracy was Turkey. Even within Turkey, as Bernard Lewis points out, though it seems the Middle Eastern country with the most promise for democracy, it cannot truly be proclaimed to have the essence of democracy within itself. Lewis is also quick to point out that all throughout history, from the time of the Prophet Muhammad's death in 632 C.E. until modern times; the most predominant form of political systems found within so-called Islamic states is autocracy. Most recently, the Islamic Republic of Afghanistan has formed its new constitution, though disparagingly democratic, has the essence of Islam contained within it.

Modern attempts at Islamic democratization can be traced back to the 1909 Young Turk Revolution (Lewis). Ottoman Sultan Mehmed V spoke about the commitment of his administration to begin using constitution and consultation as major principles in the reconstruction of government. Thus, the Turkish constitutional monarchy was established. However, the Turkish constitution still contained remnants of Islamic law (Sharia), though it proclaimed to use both reason and tradition to govern. This soon becomes a trend within many Islamic reformers of the twentieth centuries: the essential Sharia needed to be complemented with reason and tradition.

Three essential modern case examples can be used to examine Islamic experiments with democracy. First, Iran is the only republic state in the Middle East, thus deeming it by many to be the closest in the Middle East (other than the state of Israel) to democracy.

Secondly, an analysis of the case of Turkey is important because it is the only country that Samuel Huntington has deemed democratic. Lastly, the newly founded Republic of Afghanistan deserves an examination because it is the latest example of Islamic "flirtation" with democracy. It remains to be seen whether Iraq can be included within this examination.

The Islamic Republic of Iran implied that through a republic, some sort of democracy would co-exist with Islam in this state. Although declared as a republic, Iran intrinsically carries with itself a history that would show that Islamic democracy is perhaps not altogether a real possibility. In 1979, Ayatollah Khomeini, an Iranian cleric, overthrew the then-leader Mohammed Pahlavi in order to introduce himself as what he called "The Supreme Leader." For a decade, Khomeini introduced Islamic laws and doctrines into Iranian law, and his main agenda was to rid Iran of the pro-Western orientation that the shahs were heading towards. Upon the Khomeini's death, the Iranian constitution still has given the Supreme Leader a large amount of power. Thus, because of the heavy political influence that the Supreme Leader has, we see our first example of democracy failing to arise in the Middle East.

Feldman notes that Turkey is "both the home of the most forward-looking group of Islamic democrats in the world, and the country in which Islamic democracy is most widely dismissed as a contradiction" (102). In the early twentieth century, at the fall of the Ottoman Empire, the Grand National Turkish Assembly declared Turkey to be a Republic and deeming Mustafa Kemal to be first president of this republic. Thus, we see Turkey making a transition towards democracy (it is the first country in the Middle East to do so). Kemal's agenda was quite simple: he encouraged the Turkish peoples to use their Turkish descent as their basis for identity, rather than their religion. However, after his reign, the Islamists attempted successfully to bring a vision of Islam back into the state. However, coup after coup forced Islamic political leaders to resign or leave office all throughout the twentieth century. Thus, again, we have a failure for Islam and democracy to co-exist.

Lastly, Afghanistan after the overthrow of the Taliban has made its own attempt to become more of a democratic state. It follows in the step of Iran by regarding itself as the Islamic Republic of Afghanistan. Upon overthrowing the Taliban, interim President Hamid Karzai is in power until the scheduled elections in 2004. Afghanistan has already presented a draft constitution. However, there are many skeptics about the possibility of democracy rising in Afghanistan. Robert Barro believes that a country that has as low income levels and education levels as Afghanistan does, democracy can almost never be sustained. The draft Constitution also inevitably contains remnants of Islamic doctrine. For example, Islam is decreed as the nation's official religion. The first part of the preamble also states that the people of Afghanistan all "have firm faith in God Almighty and [believe] in the Sacred Religion of Islam" (Constitution). Thus, we see the implementation of Islam into the "democratic" Constitution.

In comparing the successes of Christian democracy to the failures of Islamic democratization, one can only highlight one more major difference that allowed Christian democracy to survive more easily: moderation. Christian democracy, though relying on what Jacques Maritain termed "evangelical inspiration," still offered a third path after World War II, as a way of compromising the leftist and rightist views. Muslims in the Middle East have yet to give up what they perceive as their "religious values" in order to pursue something for the greater good. In fact, according to Feldman, these values do not contradict one another; rather, they complement and enhance one another. Thus, we lose any sense of moderation or compromise, which inevitably do not allow for democracy to exist in the Middle East.

This idea of moderation can be seen in several ways while the Christian democratic parties in Europe to modern day struggle for Islam to surrender to modernity. Firstly, the MRP's interpretation of doctrine is crucial. For Islamists, their primary objective seems to be able to prove Islam as not only a religious and social force, but also a political force as well. Thus, they lose part of the moral doctrine in Islam that entails ideas of compassion, justice and equality. On the other hand, the MRP was able to look at the bigger picture in determining their doctrine. Secondly, the interpretation of an "act of faith" was also important to the Christian democratic doctrine. As explained earlier, the Christian democratic acts of faith were those that were done for the sake of freedom and justice. Lewis points out that acts of faith regarded within Muslim political states now involve suicide bombings and other undemocratic forms of expressing popular protest.

There would seem to be no hope: all the evidence points towards a direction where no hope for democracy (and ultimately peace) can reign in the Middle East. Many doctrines in Islam will undoubtedly complement, and perhaps even promote, the democratization of the Islamic Middle East. If we learn a lesson from history, it would be that However, inherently, with the Islamic tradition there has been nothing that would contradict Islam and democracy without further looking at the historical context within each of those traditions.

Already, trends are quickly forming towards democracy in Muslim states. Although Barro argues that the lack of education and income level will inevitably assist Islamists to gain unfair control over Afghanistan, what is reflected in the Constitution seems to be a genuine and sincere effort towards democracy.

For example, the Constitution guarantees the rights of women by ensuring that the upper legislative house will have a population of women of at least 16.5%. Also, the Constitution guarantees non-Muslims to right to worship (within a certain wide realm) other religions besides Islam. Perhaps most importantly is the essential promise in the draft

Constitution that indeed, this republic will be "based on the people's will and democracy." Whether or not these actions will become reality is something that will be discovered within the next few years, but no one can doubt that this is a great step forward for a nation that up until then had been plagued with injustice.

Many academics and scholars who believe that there is a fundamental "clash of civilizations" between Islamic civilization and democratic, Western civilization, especially after September 11, seemed to be able to foretell the future quite accurately. Namely, Huntington and Lewis have advanced their theories about the predictability of September 11, and future terrorist attacks on America. Part of the reason for the success of these theories is that some Muslims themselves believe that Islamic and Western values such as democracy are essentially at odds. Muslims thus become resistant to Western ideals at any cost, even if they do not contradict Islamic values. Thus, those who believe that Islam and the West are in opposition of one another have the tendency to make decisions for Islamic civilizations, and forget that Muslims can make such decisions on their own. Imposing Western dominance in these areas would thus lead some to feel threatened of their independence, which is yet another crucial reason why democratization in the Middle East may have always been a very violent process. Instead of focusing on such a pessimistic attitude, therefore, it is perhaps in the best interest for the West to simply be there as a source of support to regain stability in the Middle East, and no more.

Democratization must also be looked at as a gradual process and something that cannot be fully achieved overnight. As we saw with the Christian model, it took from the French Revolution of 1848 until the end of World War II for the Catholic Church and acceptance of Mussolini's and Hitler's doctrines that the Church finally grew to acknowledge Christian democracy. While it would seem like the opposite of true, as I have demonstrated, Muslim efforts are constant in democratizing their countries. There still stand a good number of Muslims who are pro-democracy.

It must also be considered that the ideas being promoted are essentially those of an Islamic democracy, not Islamist democracy. Intrinsically, by faith, Islam does bring about a moral doctrine which can, if practiced correctly, ultimately be very beneficial to the society. It is easy to confuse this with the doctrine of the Islamists, who can easily more identify with those who don't even see democracy as a desirable political system. However, it is also the failure to understand that Islamist democracy is still a democracy that may attribute to the inability for these states to remain consistently democratic. Western interference, then, seems like the best solution for ensuring that the states remain peaceful. However, as history has shown with French interference in Algeria during its democratic experiments, ultimately this intervention proves to be more bloody than diplomatic.

The cycle of history has seemingly come full circle. In the early twentieth century, sparked for a desire for change, Muslim reformists in countries such as Iran and Turkey sought for that very crucial change in government. Now, more than ever, Muslims are longing for the democratic promise that will not allow dictatorship regimes to rule supreme. Islam in principle embodies the entire essence of democracy.

The Christian model provides lessons that Muslims may learn in order to successfully bring about democracy in the Middle East. It certainly will be a gradual process, much like it was for the Christians throughout the nineteenth and twentieth centuries. However, undoubtedly, it is one that the Muslims have been waiting far too long to not enjoy when the promise finally arises.

Peace and Democracy in Islamic Faith and Muslim Community

Real Situation in the World and Muslim World

Humanity, having made so much progress in so many different aspects, has failed to show the same degree of success in building a peaceful world. The period after the Age of Reason in the 17th century has been defined as the period of the 'articulating mind', that is, the Age of Enlightenment. The 19th century, on the other hand is generally known as the Age of Revolutions. In response to the question 'What have we been able to achieve in our century, the 20th Century?' Baumann answers: "In this century we have learned this - Modernity is not merely about increasing production, or faster travel, or becoming more affluent or living more freely. It is also about speedier and more effective killing and scientifically planned and implemented massacre".

Islamic teachings have shaped the history and political culture of hundreds of millions of people over fourteen centuries, and have embraced a vast range of nations, cultures, sects, and schools of thought.

The Muslim world is a vast region that consists of more than one and half billion people and stretches some 10,000 miles from Morocco to Indonesia. It is an immensely diverse region politically, composed of countries that fall into all of the categories- from dictatorships such as Iraq at the time of Saddam; to semi-authoritarian countries like Egypt or Tunisia; to electoral or emerging democracies such as Turkey, Mali, Indonesia, and Bangladesh; to war-torn countries like Iraq, Algeria, Sudan, Somalia, and Afghani-stan. Fully one-eighth of the world's Muslim population lives as a minority in India.

While recognizing this diversity, there are two principal reasons for highlighting the importance of democracy in the Muslim world. First, there is a significant "democracy gap" between the Muslim world as a whole and the rest of the world. Only 11 of the 47 countries with a Muslim majority (23 percent) have democratically elected governments, as compared with 110 of the 145 non-Muslim countries (76 percent); and none of the 16 Arab states is an electoral democracy.

Second, it is also within the Muslim world that democracy is under political and ideological challenge from Islamic movements. Such movements may not be broadly representative of the population in the countries where they exist, but their influence is considerable.

Democracy faces four inter-related challenges. The first is to liberalize the political system, ending repression and human rights violations, permitting freedom of expression and association, and introducing genuine party contestation. The second is to modernize the state and the economy, so that meaningful steps can be taken to reduce poverty, ignorance, and inequality and to provide young people with opportunity and hope. The third is to control corruption and establish a genuine rule of law. And the fourth is to end the political abuse of religion and to reconcile Islam - the framework in much of the Muslim world for political and social activism - with modern concepts of pluralism, citizenship, and individual rights.

Reconciliation of Peace and Democracy in Muslim Communities

The question of Islam's compatibility with liberal democracy can be viewed from varying perspectives. Too often the notion of democracy is confused with Western culture and society.

We should analyze the concept of reconciliation depends on definition of democracy. Current controversies among both Muslims and Westerners about the relationship between Islam as a revealed scriptural religion and democracy as a specific form of modern government imply that Islam promotes a specific format for politics and government.

For this reason we will draw your attention to some facts: First of all, we can't easily say that the Islam and democracy is identical, because while democracy is a political system, Islam is a religion, which involves all aspect of materialistic and spiritual dimension of mankind. However there are some fundamental principles of Islam and democracy are similar:

Firstly, the idea or notion of freedom of the people to choose the rulers they want. Islam teaches principles of freedom, human dignity, equality, and governance by contract, popular sovereignty, and the rule of law that are compatible. The two pieces to the puzzle of forming a functioning democracy are the essential notions of equality and freedom in society, without which a people cannot truly govern them.

The Qur'an says what means (O humankind, we created you from a male and a female, and We made you races and tribes for you to get to know each other) These verses and many more make human equality in society and before God an essential teaching of the Qur'an and a core characteristic of an Islamic ethos. As such, any Islamic political system would necessitate the respect for equality and diversity of all men and women.

We are all born free, which makes freedom our destiny. This is reflected strongly in the Qur'an's understanding of human free will, which distinguishes man from the rest of God's creation. The notion of free will necessitates freedom of choice, and this is why the Qur'an so emphatically states (There is no compulsion in religion).

Secondly, the idea that is similar is that of participation in the decision-making process in some form or the other. The Qur'an insists on mutual consultation in deciding communal affairs which includes choosing leaders to represent and govern on the community's behalf.

Interestingly, a model exists in Islamic history for Muslims in using mutual consultation as a process of selecting a new leader. When Prophet Muhammad was on his deathbed, many of his Companions urged him to name a successor who would lead the community, but the Prophet refused to do so-a clear indication that he wanted the next leader to be chosen through mutual consultation rather than be imposed upon the community.

Thirdly similarity between democracy and Islam is the notion of the removal of some governments, which fail to meet the expectations of the people. However, electing leaders to govern is not enough. Holding those who govern accountable is also an essential principle of democracy if government by the people is to work.

First, the Qur'anic teaching of mutual consultation does not end in selecting leaders but forms an essential part of governance in which leaders must conduct their affairs in a non-dictatorial manner. *Second,* leaders are not left to govern based on their own whims and desires; rather their governance must be in accordance with the teachings of the Qur'an and Sunnah. *Third,* the Qur'an mandates that leaders pay back their trusts to those entitled to it meaning that leaders are responsible to the citizens of the land.

According to most of Muslims present-day democracy and civilization:

- Accepts 'force' as the point of support in human social life. But the mark of force is aggression.
- It takes as its aim 'benefits', but since the benefits are not sufficient to meet every need, their mark is that everyone tussles and jostles over them.
- It knows the principle of its life to be 'conflict'. The mark of the principle of conflict is contention.
- It considers the bond between communities to be 'racialism and negative nationalism'. But the mark of racialism is aggression, since it thrives on devouring others.
- Its aim is to provide certain 'amusements' for gratifying the appetites of the soul and increasing man's needs.

Thus, it is because of these principles of civilization's that despite all its virtues, it has afforded a sort of superficial happiness and peace for only twenty per cent and cast eighty per cent into distress and poverty.

For conciliation of peace and democracy, Islam advocates five principles as basics:

- Our point of support should become truth instead of force, and the constant mark of truth is justice and balance. Security and well-being result from these, and villainy disappears.
- Our aim should become virtue instead of self-interest, and the mark of virtue is love and mutual attraction.

Happiness results from these, and enmity disappears.

- Our principle in life should become co-operation instead of conflict and killing, and its mark is unity and solidarity, and the community is strengthened.
- Our service should become the form of guidance and direction instead of lust and passion. And the mark of guidance is progress and prosperity in way befitting humanity;
- We should reject racialism and negative nationalism and look for some common connections among human beings...like religion and moral connections".

The cause that fell us down to the lowest level of democracy and prevented us from peace is poverty whose results are the immorality and abuse. Just as the source of mankind's revolutions is one phrase, so too one phrase is the origin of all immorality.

First Phrase: "So long as I'm full, what is it to me if others die of hunger?"

Second Phrase: "You work so that I can eat."

Yes, the upper and lower groups in human society, that is, the rich and the poor, live at peace when in equilibrium. The basis of that equilibrium is compassion and kindness in the upper groups, and respect and obedience in the lower groups. Now, the first phrase has urged the upper groups to oppression, immorality, and mercilessness. And like the second phrase has driven the lower classes to hatred, envy, and to contend the upper groups, and has negated man's tranquility for several centuries, so too this century, as the result of the struggle between capital and labour, it has been the cause of the momentous events of World well-known by all.

Human beings have been created differently with regard to their livelihoods. As a consequence of the difference, God Almighty invites the rich to assist the poor, so that through the hunger experienced in fasting, the rich can truly understand the pains and hunger which the poor suffer. The bridge that maintains peace and order in social life is Zakat.

In humanity, the life of social life is born out of mutual assistance. The cure and remedy for the calamities that stem from uprisings, revolts, and conflicts that prevent the advancement of mankind is mutual assistance.

We can summarize that in first step, Islam treats of peace in the *eschatological* sense, as the ultimate goal of human life, almost synonymous with salvation. A second way in which the Islam looks at peace might be called the *psychological* sense, as tranquility and peace of mind, an inner confidence born of faith that enables the religious believer to face adversity without anxiety or despair. Particularly when one is facing the approach of death, the believer can attain a peace of mind which will enable the person to overcome spiritual turmoil and fear. A third aspect of peace is *universal* peace. It reflects the widespread conviction of the time that humankind can sink no lower in criminality towards its own kind and expresses the hope for a time of peace and prosperity for all mankind. According to Sayings for our Prophet, the virtues of civilization will prevail, the face of the earth cleaned of filth, and universal peace be secured.

It should be declared from the highest positions of the Islamic world to the entire world with the loudest voice that: "We as Muslims condemn the use of terror and weapons of mass destruction under all conditions; we view the murder of an innocent as the greatest cruelty and as a crime committed against humanity; and we consider those who attempt to use terror and weapons of mass destruction as the lowest and the cruelest of all people. We as Muslims are destroying all weapons of mass destruction - including nuclear weapons - under our possession, and we are terminating all research, development, and manufacturing activities of all such weapons. We also declare to the whole world that, even when we are bombarded with such weapons, we will never respond in kind."

For the most part, misguidance and evil are negative, destructive, and pertain to non-existence. While in the great majority of cases, guidance and good are positive, constructive, repairing, and pertain to existence. Everyone knows that one man can destroy in one day a building made by twenty men in twenty days. Yes, although human life continues through the existence of all the basic members and conditions of life, and is particular to the All-Glorious Creator's power, through severing a member, a tyrant may make the person manifest death, which is non-being in relation to life. The saying 'Destruction is easy' has for this reason become proverbial."

Five principles are necessary, essential, at this strange time in order to save peace in the social life of this country and nation from anarchy: respect, compassion, refraining from what are prohibited (haram), security, the giving up of lawlessness and being obedient to authority.

Indeed, mankind is very unjust, very ignorant as follows: "Here is the terrifying ability of injustice in the nature of man. It means this: Unlike animals, the senses and tendencies of people are not limited. The tendency to commit injustice and the love for self can go very far. Yes, if self-concern, self-adoration, conceitedness, and pride and stubbornness, which are the ugly sides of selfishness and ego, join that tendency, the person can invent such greatest major sins that, the humanity could not find a name for it as yet. As it is evidence for the necessity of the hell, its punishment can only be the hell.

Eliminating the concern for injustices is only possible by establishing that strength is in righteousness - not the reverse. This can be done by enforcing fair rules that conform to general wisdom and the human conscience. Using such rules as the base in human affairs provides general peace and order in a society, and satisfies the sense of justice. This, in turn, increases the enthusiasm and passion, which is the key for advancement, and eliminates hopelessness, which is the biggest obstacle to advancement.

Conclusion

I believe and Islam considers the whole humanity as one family. All have common ground in being the worshippers of Allah and the sons of Adam. That is why the Prophet, has put it clear in front of the Muslim congregation at the Farewell Pilgrimage saying: "O people, Your Lord is One and your father is one. All of you are traced back to Adam, and Adam was created from dust. No privileges of a certain person over the other save by righteous deeds."

Islam commands that "one believer should not be vexed with another believer for more than three days," and that so long as there is no reconciliation, both sides perpetually suffer the torments of fear and revenge." Islam advices us like that: 'Look at the defect in your own soul that you do not see or do not wish to see.

Deduct a share for that. As for the small share which then remains, if you respond with forgiveness, pardon, and magnanimity, in such a way as to conquer your enemy swiftly and safely, then you will have escaped all sin and harm.' Thus, self-awareness should lead to repentance, repentance to forgiveness, forgiveness to reconciliation and the seeds for a lasting peace are laid.

For just as one of man's hands cannot compete with the other, neither can one of his eyes criticize the other, nor his tongue object to his ear, nor his heart see his spirit's faults. Each of his members completes the deficiencies of the others, veils their faults, assists their needs, and helps them out in their duties. Otherwise man's life would be extinguished, his spirit flee, and his body be dispersed.

And so, O members of World Family! You and I are members of a collective personality such as that, worthy of the title of 'perfect man.' We are like the components of a factory's machinery. We should work to bring people together; otherwise the world factory demolish entirely and mankind body be dispersed.

Human Rights and Women's Rights: Challenges and Contestations

We can all agree that in the modern world today, the new universal morality is one of democracy, human rights, and women's rights. Where is the place of Islam in this dominant ethical paradigm of the modern world? The principles of democracy, human rights and women's rights can pose a formidable challenge to an Islam as conceptualised by the traditionalist ulama and the political Islamists who demand for the establishment of an Islamic state and shariah law. They believe that in Islam, God is the only sovereign and ultimate source of law. Any man-made law is therefore considered an illegitimate innovation (bid'ah).

In a democracy, sovereignty of course lies with the people and the people are the source of law. Thus in the debate in many Muslim societies on the compatibility of Islam and democracy, the issues of divine sovereignty vs. human sovereignty, divine law vs. human legislation have become issues of contention.

In the traditional conception of Islamic law, all rights are subject to classification in terms of religion and gender. There are different rights for Muslim men, Muslim women and non-Muslims and minorities, rather than equal rights for all. This of course contradicts the principles of human rights which recognize that all human beings are born equal, they enjoy equality before the law and all rights are due to them by virtue of their humanity.

I want to take you through one area of contestation and contradiction between Islam and human rights and women's rights, in the context of multi-ethnic and multi-religious Malaysia with a Constitution that grants equality and non-discrimination on the basis of gender. This is the area of law.

Muslim Personal Status Law

In the name of women's rights and the principle of non-discrimination in a democratic state, several laws in Malaysia have been amended to end discrimination against women. Since the 1970s, amendments to the Law Reform and Marriages Act, the Guardianship of Infants Act and the Distribution Act have enabled non-Muslim women in Malaysia to enjoy equal right to marriage and divorce, guardianship of children and inheritance. But not for Muslim women, because in the name of Islam, Muslim women in Malaysia continue to be discriminated against in marriage, divorce, guardianship and inheritance. For e.g.:

- A man can divorce his wife at will, but a woman has to go to court and obtain a judicial divorce on very specific grounds that need to be proven.
- A woman is supposed to obey her husband and her failure to comply with the "lawful" wishes of her husband constitutes "nushuz" and she can lose her right to maintenance.
- A man has a right to four wives, but a woman can only have a monogamous marriage (not that women want the right to 4 husbands. On the contrary women are demanding that a Muslim man is allowed only 1 wife).
- A woman is not entitled to the guardianship of her children.
- A woman can get physical custody of her children only up to the age seven for a son or nine for a daughter. Custody then reverts to the father. Even while the woman has custody of the children, the father as the lawful guardian maintains control over matters where the consent of the guardian is required, e.g. permission to obtain a passport, to register or change schools, to undergo surgery, ownership and disposal of the children's property.
- A daughter inherits half what the son gets. A woman's right to inherit from her husband's estate is also half of the husband's portion of inheritance upon the death of his wife.

Shariah Criminal Law

Under the Hudud law, the punishments prescribed for criminal offences of theft, robbery, illicit sex and false accusation include amputations, cross-amputations, floggings and stoning to death. These punishments can easily be regarded as "cruel, inhumane or degrading treatment or punishment" according to international human rights standards.

The Hudud law also does not admit the testimony of women and non-Muslims, a clear denial of the principle of equality before the law. For murder and bodily injury, women and non-Muslims are accorded less monetary compensation (diyah) than Muslim men.

Freedom of religion is a fundamental tenet of Islam and yet the dominant orthodox view in Islam prescribes the death penalty for apostasy. This is usually provided for under the Hudud law, although the Qur'an does not prescribe such a punishment. Even in Muslim societies which do not prescribe the death penalty, Muslims do not enjoy equal right to freedom of religion as restrictions are placed that make it very difficult or near to impossible for those who wish to leave Islam for whatever reason. This therefore infringes principles of freedom of religion and freedom of expression.

Strategies for Reform

In many Muslim countries today, women's groups are at the forefront in pushing for reform of Islamic laws that infringe the principles of equality and justice. The strategies taken are different. There are those that are engaged in the struggle by using universal human rights standards, in particular United Nations instruments. There are others who have chosen to fight this battle by working from within the Islamic framework.

Many Muslim human rights and women's rights activists reject this latter approach as they believe that religion has no place in public life, and the struggle for rights within Muslim societies must be guided by the authority of international human rights standards. Many Muslim feminists also believe that religion is inherently patriarchal and unjust and to work within the religious framework is a losing battle because for every alternative interpretation that women can offer to justify equality and justice, the ulama can offer 100 others to challenge that interpretation. Moreover, within a society where the word of the ulama is considered the "gospel truth", human rights activists challenging the ulama on their "home turf" would never enjoy the same legitimacy and authority and therefore their arguments within the Islamic discourse would have no impact.

Sisters in Islam of course have chosen to struggle for equality and justice from within the Islamic framework. We do this because as believers we want to find liberation, truth and justice from within our own faith. We feel strongly we have a right to reclaim our religion, to redefine it, to participate and contribute to an understanding of Islam, how it is codified and implemented - in ways that take into consideration the realities and experience of women's lives today.

We are helped in the struggle by a growing body of scholarship which promotes progressive ideas and values of equality, justice, and democratic principles within an Islamic framework. This scholarship from reformist Muslim scholars challenges the Islamic agenda of the traditionalist and the fundamentalist activists and their misogynistic, intolerant, extremist brand of Islam. This reformist scholarship which recognises equality between men and women in Islam, which argues for the imperative of ijtihad (re-interpretation of the Qur'an in the context of changing times and circumstances), which addresses the dynamics between what is universal for all times and what is particular to seventh century Arabia, which looks at the socio-historical context of revelation, which articulates the need to differentiate between what is divine revelation and what is human understanding of the word of God, has enabled more and more progressive Muslim activists all over the world to realise the validity and possibility of working within the Islamic framework, to fight for justice and equality.

It is my firm belief that Islam is compatible with democracy, human rights and women's rights and Islam upholds the principles of justice, equality, freedom and dignity. The internal transformation that is needed to achieve these values has already begun as Muslim scholars and activists engage in the public space to advocate the process of re-interpretation of the texts and develop principles and methodologies within the Islamic discourse in order to deal with the challenges posed by changing times and circumstances.

The most exciting development in the Muslim world is the challenge posed by feminists and women's groups and our demand for justice and equality within religion, culture and family. It is of course a tough job. For challenging orthodoxy and the privileged status of men, we are accused of being anti-Islam, anti-shariah, and anti-God. Our credentials and credibility to speak on Islam is questioned. We are accused of undermining the authority of the ulama, of confusing the ummah and causing disunity.

But we believe that if Islam is used as a source of law and public policy, then it must open itself to public debate and engagement as how it is interpreted and codified into law affects the lives of all citizens. Public law must be opened to public debate. If we can question and debate the economic, political and social issues that affect the country, why is it when it comes to policies made in the name of Islam we are supposed to shut up?

Religion can no longer remain the exclusive preserve of the ulama. The public role of religion as a source of law and public policy in Muslim countries necessarily renders open the public space for debates and disagreements. Even though the contestation that takes place can be intimidating and menacing, for e.g. the kind of mob mobilisation, demonisation and use of hate speech to silence the voices of dissent that we saw last year, I feel in the end it is this public engagement and contestation that will propel change as it brings about new understandings and production of knowledge in Islam. This in the end will be good for democracy in Malaysia.

As more and more Muslims become aware of their rights in the religion, and learn and understand the religion for themselves, there is growing awareness of the rich heritage of diversity and differences within Islam and that it is this pluralistic tradition that actually has enabled Islam to thrive and spread its influence to all cultures and regions of the world. With this understanding, also comes the understanding that it is human agency that determines which texts are relevant and how they should be interpreted to serve the best interest of the community. Therefore the role of human experience and intellect in the pursuit of the divine will lead to the production of Islamic knowledge and Islamic laws that cannot then be regarded as divine. While the source is divine as it is the revealed word of God, human understanding of the word of God is a human construct that is fallible and changeable in accordance with changing times and circumstances. It is this God-given human agency that must be used to serve the cause of justice and equality in the 21st century.

We need to pose a challenge to those at the vanguard of the Islamic movement and their demand for an Islamic state with shariah rule: Why would citizens of a nation-state, support the concept of an Islamic state which asserts different rights for Muslim men, Muslim women and non-Muslims and minorities, rather than equal rights for all? Why would those whose equal status and rights are recognised by a democratic system support the creation of such a discriminatory Islamic state? If an Islamic state means an authoritarian theocratic political system committed to enforcing doctrinal and legal rulings that privilege Muslim men, and silencing or even eliminating those who challenge its authority and its understanding of Islam, then why would those whose fundamental liberties are protected by a democratic state support an Islamic state?

It is not for nothing that the recently concluded PAS general assembly used the theme, Defending Democracy, Upholding Justice and demands were made to appoint more women to their decision-making positions and to stand for elections. If religion is to be relevant in a modern world dominated by an ethical paradigm of human rights and women's rights within a democratic state, then those who want to establish an Islamic state must bring about an understanding of Islam that address the challenges of the 21st century.

As women, as activists we play an important role to reclaim the Islam that liberated women 1400 years ago, the Islam of justice, compassion and mercy, the Islam that upholds human freedom and dignity. That was our rich heritage lost. We need to reclaim that heritage and all must participate in this project.

But there already exists in the Qur'an the ethical message of justice and equality that women find liberating and empowering and can be used to contest the dominant patriarchal voice in religion.

For women and women's groups like Sisters in Islam it is the ethical vision of Islam which advocates the absolute moral and spiritual equality of women and men found in verses such as Surah 33:35 (on common and identical spiritual and moral obligations placed on all individuals regardless of sex); Surah 3:195 which declares that men and woman are members, one of another; 2:187 which describes Muslim men and women as each other's garments; 9:71, the final verse on the relationship between men and women which talks about them being each other's *'awliyya* -protecting friends and guardians - and the obligations for both men and women, to enjoin what is just and forbid what is evil, to observe regular prayers, *zakat* (tithe) and obedience to Allah and his Messenger and they will be equally rewarded.

These verses are unequivocally egalitarian in spirit and substance and reflect the Qur'anic view on the relationship between men and women.

This egalitarian vision also extends to human biology. The verses on creation of men and women, talk about the characteristic of pairs in creation (51:49, 53:45, 78:8, 50:7, 22:5, 36:36). Since everything created must be in pairs, the male and female must both be necessary, must exist by the definition of createdness. Neither one comes before the other or from the other. One is not superior to the other, or a derivative of the other. This means that in Allah's creation of human beings, no priority or superiority is accorded to either man or woman.

This is a revolutionary and powerful challenge that takes place in the public sphere at the national and international levels in many parts of the Muslim world. Basically women have had enough of the use of religion to perpetuate patriarchy and have decided to study the religion for ourselves, to claim our right to define what it means to us given the realities of our lives in the 21st century.

Muslim Women In The Indian Media

When we seek to define what it means to be a Muslim woman in India, one is almost immediately confronted with the gross inadequacy of the term, as it forcibly erases the multiple cultural and social identities that a Muslim woman encapsulates. She is a woman, Muslim, and in the Indian context, a minority, with a diverse regional identity. Like any other Indian woman, she is constituted differently across class, religion and region, and has to constantly negotiate her space and freedom in terms of security and conflict, defining herself through a constant dialogue with patriarchal society. At the same time, there is also certain specificity about her situation, for perhaps more than any other Indian woman, a Muslim woman's self-perception must engage with popular representations about her religion and the way these locate her within the community. These popular perceptions often privilege one of the Muslim woman's multiple selves as definitional of her.

The need to understand the representation of Muslim women in the India media arises from the fact that they combine in themselves the images of the Muslim community both in India and in the Islamic world - they are the victims of Islamic fundamentalism and also its most important signifier. In the western media Islamic resurgence is seen as the chief perpetuator of atrocities against women with Islam and Muslim men representing the return of the barbaric medieval Arab. In the Indian context Muslim women remain firmly grounded in minority politics with the media perceiving their role to be only within the community. In its representation of Muslim women, the Indian media's textual practices seem to be in tune with the "given order" of the society in which it is embedded - it reinforces dominant norms and understandings of Islam and Muslim women in India. Media studies argue that the structure of news reporting and notions of news value may entail that a minority or non-elite groups within any community may have to engage in 'negative' behaviour before they are noticed by the media - they can make it to the news only when they are presented as a problem. The Muslim community seems to make it to the News only on controversial issues, with Muslim women and Muslim Personal Law being an integral part of this negative coverage. Consequently biased media coverage legitimises dominant misunderstandings of Muslim and Islam in Indian society.

It was evident that in the period at hand (1985-2001), media coverage of the Muslim minority community invariably assumed its complete insulation from larger processes and trends in Indian society, and diagnosed its members to be suffering from one shared problem -Islam. The period of the 1990's was a period of diverse political and social changes. Communal Politics acquired a volatile face and a definite identity, majority and minority conflicts increased, and Muslim women came to represent only their community. Media reportage reflected the same trend irrespective of the issue being on Muslim Personal Law, or the demolition of the Babri Masjid or the emergence of "Islamic terrorism". India seemed to hurtle along a dismal trajectory of secular degeneration with unthinking support from the media. The media, as well as its representations of reality, has been as affected as individuals by the rightward ideological shift, and its power and influence has ensured that many of the media's ideological constructs have now become embedded as immutable truths in the minds of its consumers.

This trend emerging with Shah Bano controversy in 1985 forms a definite image during the 90's and credibility with the turn of the century. The overall negative coverage of the 90's reduces the acceptability of brief interludes of positive identification. The media in the last decade has worked effectively as a legitimiser of popular misconceptions about

Muslims and Muslim women.

The identity of the Muslim woman as portrayed in the media remains firmly rooted within the community and even when the coverage is positive she finds no other face but than that of a "Muslim woman". From the study it is evident that, be it the issue of child brides of Hyderabad, or the issue of triple Talaq, or the forced veiling of Kashmiri women, media attention has accorded priority only to the religious and national political ramifications of these issues. In fact issues related to Muslim women only received media attention when they involved a legal and religious controversy. A study of the last 15 years also reflects that Muslim women only appeared in the news when there was a religious controversy and then also mainly as a subject to be debated on.

Even where the media sought to support the struggles of Muslim women for their rights, it nevertheless blacked them and their opinions out. When issues with clear socio-economic dimensions arose, media representations ensured that they acquired a religious dimension, by which Muslim women's struggles were believed to address only the men and religious leaders of their community.

The lack of recognition by the media of cultural and social differences within the Muslim community critically determines how women are represented. The trajectory of the last two decades is reflective of how media images combine with political and social trends to shape and reinforce public opinion. The image of the barbaric Muslim man finds equal acceptability, as the sympathetic image of the poor Muslim woman.

"Fatwas" or issuing of a religious decree is what has always caught media attention, and at times media provides larger legitimacy to these decrees. Ranging from the International issues of the Ban on The Satanic Verses, to the issue of Forced Veiling of Kashmiri Women, media has often provided the publicity, giving legitimacy and power to an agency which otherwise has no political or legal credibility in the larger social world. Fatima Mernissi talking about media constructs gives the example of the growing power of the fanatical Imam who does not share the humility of his predecessor. He survives today largely due to media images. "This vulnerability is completely absent from the modern media image of the imam. Two needs are superimposed on that image. First there is the need of the Western journalist, who wants to inform his audience as quickly as possible and to give a simple, clear description of what is happening in our part of the world; and there is the need of the political leader who claims the title of imam, who wants to be filmed and interviewed, and who has a precise message to sell. If these two needs are not kept carefully distinct, we will not understand anything about that "despotic and fanatic Islam," a media construct that is easily conveyed but that neglects many important historical and symbolic mechanisms.

It is this image propagated by the fundamentalists that the media sees, and makes the mistake of determining it as the only image. The lack of difference between Muslims, women and communities is what allows the fundamentalist logic to prevail. The media by propagating these images lends legitimacy to the rhetoric of the fundamentalist. Muslim women are a section which are caught in this bind of a minority, religion and gender identity. She gets often marginalised by society and thus also gets to some extent marginalised by the media.

6

Islamic Law on Democracy

Around the middle of the nineteenth century, new ways of thought began to emerge in the Middle East, primarily as a result of contact with European industry, communications, and political ideas and institutions. While they were not breaking with the Islamic past, there was a modern element in the thought of some Muslim thinkers and officials—who argued that Muslims could increase their strength by adopting selectively Western institutions and practices that were compatible with sharîah (Islamic law).

Some writers of this period maintained that the principles of social action are rational and that they change as society changes. The Egyptian reformer Muhammad Abduh (1848 – 1905) sought to strengthen the moral roots of Islamic society by returning to the past, recognizing and accepting the need for change and linking that change to the teachings of Islam. Disseminating his ideas through the periodical al-Manâr (The Beacon), Abduh asserted that Islam could form the moral basis of a modern, progressive society while moving in the direction of new ideas about social and political organization.

Other modernist thinkers argued further that human society constitutes its own judge and master, and its own interest should reign supreme. Some reformists of the period, such as the Egyptian Qâsim Amîn (1863 - 1908), went so far as to affirm the benefit of the active participation of all citizens, including women, in matters of public concern.

From about 1900 until the early 1950s, two lines of thought regarding the proper bases of government coexisted in the Middle East. Supporters of the first advocated the principles of secularism and constitutional democracy, including representative government based on broad political participation. Following the dissolution of the Ottoman state, this principle was advanced by leaders of political groups and national liberation movements; it seemed to have reached its logical end with the establishment of quasi-constitutional systems in a number of Arab countries on the model of Western style democracies. Experimentation with democracy was not, however, a happy experience. Rigged elections, puppet governments, arbitrary arrests, and rubber stamp parliaments raised serious doubts about the ability of the Arabs to create and tolerate democratic institutions and practices.

Following a second line of thought were those who believed that Islamic law and institutions should be the basis of political and social organization. For most of this school, the ideal was to live in the inherited Islamic framework and to preserve the continuity of the Islamic tradition. This contrasts in many ways with the thinking of the advocates of democratic reform, most of whom accepted Islam as a body of principles but believed that secular norms of nationalism and liberal democracy were best suited to the reorganization and regulation of Arab society and politics.

Following the 1948 Palestine war and especially with the advent of revolutionary regimes in key Arab states (Egypt, Syria, and Iraq), the balance of political thought tilted decisively in favor of the radicalism of the revolutionary state. The new ways of thought and action were embodied in a form of nationalism that expressed social reform in the idiom of Arab socialism and that expressed foreign policy in the language of anti-colonialism and positive neutrality. In the 1950s and 1960s, many secularists as well as Islamists were engaged in attempts to prove that Islam and socialism were compatible, and that the pursuit of Arab unity was more important than the pursuit of democracy and pluralism. In North Africa and in the Arab East, the principle of Arab unity held first place, on the grounds that socialism, freedom, and the liberation of Palestine could not be achieved without it.

This was a position clearly articulated by the representatives of Arab nationalism – Egyptian president Gamal Abdel Nasser, and such Baþthist activists and intellectuals as the Syrian Michel Aflaq, the Palestinian Abd Allâh, and the Jordanian Munîf.

In the 1970s and 1980s, the unrest generated by war and civil strife in some Arab countries, the failure of Arab governments to stand up to Israel, the rising discontent with socioeconomic performance, and the unchecked growth of the power of the state brought about a change in the scale of political life: there was a broader agenda of grievances and a larger public for new ideas and rhetoric. The movement for the revival of Islam as the only valid basis for social and political life was perhaps the most significant aspect of this change.

With the rise of Islamic political movements in the 1970s and 1980s, writers and activists formulated diverse ideas about social and political organization. We shall deal in a general way with three of them – the rejectionist, moderate, and liberal Islamic perspectives – because they are broadly representative of certain attitudes and positions with respect to the notion of democracy. However, we should neither impose a false unity on the ideas of a particular category nor view the categories as mutually exclusive, particularly because the works of many of the writers have evolved over several decades. The term "fundamentalist" is likewise too narrow to be applicable to any of the intellectual trends discussed here. In fact, advocates of each of the views were influenced by the modernizing impulse and the call for ijtihâd (independent reasoning) of Muhammad Abduh, who encouraged Muslims to establish their government by reasoning from Islamic principles in the interest of the Islamic community. What distinguishes the three perspectives is not only their assessment of democracy, but the scope permitted to, and the basis of, their ijtihâd.

Rejectionist Islamic View

(Syria/Egypt 1865 – 1935) edited al-Manâr from 1898 until his death. Like Abduh, Rashîd - Rida encouraged Muslims to emulate the scientific and technological achievements of the West but discouraged the imitation of foreign ideas and practices. He maintained that the backwardness in Muslim countries arose from the neglect of the true principles of Islam.

The Egyptian thinker Sayyid Qutb (1906 – 1966), who was a leading member of the Society of Muslim Brothers and whose writings became very popular after his execution by the Egyptian authorities, shared Rashîd Rida's concern with emulation of the foreign. Qutb condemned the Arab nation state systems as un-Islamic and as part of what he calls the modern jâhilîyah, a term that originally denoted the period prior to the emergence of Islam in the seventh century but which, for Qumb, corresponds to the prevailing aspects of modern life, including Western institutions and beliefs inconsistent with Islam.

Qumb believed that the comprehensiveness and universality of Islam made it good for all peoples, regardless of place and time. Qumb asserts that the Islamic political order is an eternal system that rests on three fundamental bases: "justice on the part of rulers, obedience on the part of the ruled, and consultation between ruler and ruled" (Qumb 2000, 119–120). For Qumb, a just political and social order based on the Qur'ân and the sunnah (tradition) will lead to the implemen-tation of the sharîah and will thus achieve the main political goal of Islamists, which is the establishment of the Islamic state. The main value is not democracy but the implementation of the sharîah, and the only political system of any type that can claim Islamic legitimacy is one that enforces the sharîah.

An even sharper distinction between democracy and "consultation between ruler and ruled" is drawn by Sayyid Abû al-Alâ Mawdûdî (India/Pakistan, 1903 – 1979), who believed that the notion of popular sovereignty that lies at the basis of democracy violates the principle of hâkimîyah (the absolute sovereignty of God over the world) and is tantamount to shirk bi-allâh (the sacrilegious attribution of partners to God).

Mawdûdî terms the proper Islamic system of government a "theo-democracy," distinct from European theocracies because, rather than rule by a clerical class that enforces its decisions upon the people in the name of God, the entire Muslim population is to run the state in accor-dance with the sharîah, which rules over all aspects of life.

While this perspective remained common throughout the 1970s and 1980s among various groups calling for the establishment of an Islamic state, the number of thinkers adopting an outright rejectionist stance toward democracy—generally the most radical Islamists—has diminished in recent years. Many Islamist groups, including most factions of the Muslim Brotherhood, have moderated their stance on democracy.

Nonetheless, much contemporary scholarship has questioned whether this or that Islamic thinker who has claimed the mantle of democracy merely exploits the popularity of the term for political opportunity or cloaks more radical stances in moderate language.

The Moderate Islamic View

Three concepts are central to the moderate Islamic understanding of democracy: shûrâ (consultation), al-macla%ah (public interest), and adl (justice). There are disagreements among Muslim scholars with regard to shûrâ, but in essence they all agree, on the basis of the Qur'â, that God instructed the Prophet to consult with his advisers, even those whose advice had led to defeat in battle, and that good Muslims should consult with each other in conducting their affairs. While Qumb, Mawdûdî, and others have rejected the equation of shûrâ and democracy, others consider this principle of mutual consultation to be a basis for the election of representative leaders and government institutions, as in the case of Western democracies. Fatwâs (scholarly opinions), it is further argued, have allowed and will continue to allow different systems of government to legitimize their authority in the name of Islam.

Al-maclaqah means doing what is good for the people and avoiding what is injurious. Critical here is the extent to which the people can be involved in determining what is good and what is not good for them. Theoretically speaking, this can be resolved by means of mutual consultation through the representative organs of the state, but regardless of the extent of consultation, just rule is a sine qua non for the promotion of the public interest. Islamic political leaders are considered to be just insofar as they follow policies that are consistent with the public interest as defined through shûrâ and insofar as they do not inflict unnecessary hardship on their people.

Representing this perspective is Sasan al-Turâbî (b.1932), a leading Islamic thinker and the primary ideologist of the Sudanese Islamic National Front, the main pillar of the Sudanese government; he argues that any political or social system must be based on tawaîd, the unification of all Muslims as a fulfillment of the rabbânîyah (lordship) of God. Shûrâ and tawaîd should go hand in hand. Shûrâ is needed to interpret sharîah and to deal with constitutional, legal, social, and economic matters. Al-Turâbî distinguishes between shûrâ and Western-style democracy: shûrâ represents the ultimate sovereignty of God as embodied in the Qur'ân, while democracy connotes the ultimate sovereignty of the people.

According to al-Turâbî, liberal democratic systems have two flaws. First, they are based on factional interests and therefore cannot promote real political equality, unity, and freedom. Because wealth, and therefore power, are concentrated in the hands of a few, ultimate authority is vested in a small elite. Second, the liberal democracies are based on human reason, and regardless of how people may try to perfect the political and social order, reason still suffer from the limitations that God has imposed on humans.

For al-Turâbî, Islam thus has a unique advantage in postulating the divinely ordained connection between political shûrâ and tawaîd. This connection prevents tyranny because it resolves ideological conflicts and unifies Muslim actions. It also leads to a aqd al-bayah (contract of allegiance) between the people and their ruler. The origin of this aqd is ijmâ (consensus) through political shûrâ. Al-Turâbî believes that by following this course Muslims will be able to create a democratic system free from the flaws of liberal democracies. This system will be able to deliver the Islamic ummah from jâhilîyah and will provide through shûrâ a means of participation and adaptation, as well as a mechanism for the realization of true political equality.

The Tunisian thinker Râshid al-Ghannûshî (b. 1941) has considered how present-day Muslims might best pursue the political ideals of shûrâ, al-maclaqah, and adl. Acknowledging that Islamic government exists only as an idea, unrealized in contemporary circumstances, al-Ghannûshî encourages Muslims to participate in existing non-Islamic governments as a nonviolent means of laying the foundation for a truly Islamic social order.

He defends this strategy as necessitated by the exceptional circumstances of the present, where Muslims are unable to establish Islamic rule directly and where the choice is not between Islamic and non-Islamic rule, but between dictatorship and democracy.

Further, this approach is rendered permissible by the Islamic principle of maclaqah: Muslims must actively pursue the (even partial) implementation of Islamic laws and values in order to serve mankind. In those countries in which Muslims form the majority, Islamic movements will benefit from working with other groups to topple dictatorships that stand in the way of the realization of respect for human rights, security, and freedom of expression, essential bases for preparing the way for the longer-term goal of establishing an Islamic government. In those countries where Muslims are minorities, they should work to transform the values of their society in order to secure their freedom of worship and belief.

The development of a moderate Islamic discourse has influenced some of the most prominent Islamist thinkers. Yûsuf

Qara âwî (Egypt/Qatar, b.1926), who in a 1977 work placed democracy at the top of a list of "imported solutions" to be rejected, revealed a change in stance in a widely circulated 1990 work, in which he argued that the main objective of the Islamist movement is to oppose political despotism and the usurpation of the people's rights and to stand for political freedom and true democracy. Qara âwî argues that Islam and democracy are different things. The former is a comprehensive system of values, while the latter is a means. Democracy, in Qara âwî's view, means that Muslims would be permitted to rule themselves according to their own beliefs in those countries in which they are majorities. Only in an atmosphere of freedom and democracy has Islam flourished. Qara âwî shares with Qumb and Mawdûdî the belief that the Islamic community is charged with ensuring that rulers govern within the limits of Islamic law, to which everyone is held accountable. However, while Qumb and Mawdûdî seem to assume a unified Islamic community and a narrow legislative space, Qara âwî believes that Islam's binding texts are few, leaving a wide space capable of accommodating multiple permissible interpretations of Islam. Further, whereas Qumb and Mawdûdî rely upon that which unites the Islamic community, Qara âwî trusts the Muslim masses to assert Islamism through majority rule.

The Liberal Islamic View

Like the moderate Islamic view, that of Islamic liberals is influenced by Abduh's emphasis on the role of reason in understanding religion and in dealing with the demands of modern life. According to the Islamic liberals, the challenge in coping with worldly matters is to enter social transactions and relations on a basis that allows for adaptation to changing conditions. The liberal Islamic view is, however, distinguished by its emphasis on the importance of a plurality of positions and the freedom of thought for the emergence and proper functioning of a democratic system. Liberal Islamic thinkers argue that the Qur'ân allows for political and religious diversity. The often-cited verse, "lâ ikrâh fî al-dîn" (there is no compulsion in religion, 2.256), is interpreted to mean the equality of Muslims and non-Muslims in civic rights and duties. There is inequality in matters of faith, but that is something that should be left to God. Human beings are not entitled to pass judgment on other people's religious beliefs.

Islamic thinkers like Egyptians Fahmî Huwaydî (b. 1937) and Târiq al-Bishrî (b. 1933) have constructed important justifications for the full citizenship of non-Muslims in an Islamic state. Based on Muhammad's ruling in the Charter of Medina regarding ahl al-kitâb (people of the book), they assert that Christian, Jews, and Zoroastrians are muw¡tinûn (citizens), not dhimmîyûn (protected subjects), and thus share rights and duties equal to Muslims. Other thinkers, like Mohammed Arkoun (Algeria/France, b. 1928) and Nacr $âmid Abû Zayd (Egypt/Netherlands, b. 1943), have attempted further to assert the value of plurality and freedom by extending the boundaries of acceptable interpretations of Islam through the incorporation of postmodern or literary modes of textual interpretation. These approaches are unified by a willingness to forego the literal interpretation of scriptures when it is believed to harm the interests of Muslims.

The Iranian thinker Abdolkarim Soroush (b. 1945) is exemplary in this regard. He argues that the reason, freedom, and democracy are universal, primary values that cannot be constrained by religious or political dictates. Going further than moderate Islamic thinkers, Islamic liberals affirm not just the possibility of the coexistence of religion and democracy but the necessity of the constant examination of religious understanding, which can only be done in a democratic context. What Soroush calls "religious democracy" does not require that democracy be religious, but that religious thought be democratic, tolerant, and just. Religion needs freedom and tolerance to flourish.

Soroush maintains that religious democracy is thus more demanding and substantive than secular democracy, because whereas the latter removes matters of faith and belief from the realm of politics, the former necessitates the constant engagement with and renewal of under-standings of faith and belief.

One finds within these three Islamic trends distinct, though not necessarily conflicting, elements of modernity and tradition that echo the thoughts of nineteenth-century Islamic writers. They show the point at which certain ideas about political organization have entered contemporary Arab intellectual discourse. They also illustrate intellectual attempts to restructure Islamic society and politics, on the basis of an inherited Islamic past that is believed to contrast with Western political traditions, on the basis of the selective appropriation of modern democratic thought made to conform to Islamic values and law, or on the basis of a theory of liberal norms that becomes the basis for a reinterpretation of Islamic thought.

Democracy Building an uphill Struggle in most Muslim Countries

The explanation of why so many Muslim countries are not democratic has more to do with historical, political, cultural, and economic factors than with religious ones. Nevertheless, many Muslim activists, using broad and sometimes crude notions of secularism and sovereignty, consider democracy to be the rule of humans as opposed to Islam, which is rule of God.

Scholars of Islam agree that the principle of shura, or consultative decision-making, is the source of democratic ethics in Islam. But a great deal more reflection is required to clarify the relationship of shura to democracy.

In establishing the compact of Medina, Prophet Muhammad demonstrated a democratic spirit quite unlike the authoritarian tendencies of many of those who claim to imitate him today. He chose to draw up a historically specific constitution based on the eternal and transcendent principles revealed to him but also sought the consent of all who would be affected by its implementation. Conservative Muslims tend to view the western world's advocacy of human rights as a modern agenda by which the West hopes to establish its hegemony over the Muslim world, whereas reformist Muslims tend to be more receptive to new ideas, practices, and institutions.

Reformists stress the need for continuity of basic Islamic traditions but believe that Islamic law (sharia) is historically conditioned and needs to be reinterpreted in light of the changing needs of modern society. Secular Muslims look to the experiences of the secular West as models in an effort to promote their countries' development.

Despite the degree to which human rights are suppressed in Muslim countries, two grassroots movements are struggling to change this situation. Women are beginning to effectively assert their rights, and in some countries young people are agitating against government oppression.

The United States has generally accepted the fiction that repression in the Muslim world is the best way to prevent Islamism from growing as a threat to the West and to U.S. interests. Those countries that have weak civil society structures and authoritarian regimes are fertile ground for terrorists. If western countries want to suppress terror then they must foster civil society and support movements that bolster democratic trends within these repressive political systems.

The United States should:

a. Increase substantially the amount of U.S. foreign assistance that is spent on promoting democracy in the Muslim world;

b. Provide governments and key interest groups in Muslim societies with incentives to engage in demo-cratic reforms;

c. Take seriously the existing framework of multilateral agreements and treaties that bear on democratization, such as those in the field of human rights; and

d. Promote regional accountability mechanisms.

An election banner in the spring 2000 Iranian elections reads: "Obtaining Women's Rights, Freedom of Thought, and Social Justice."

It is true, as some claim, that democracy is basically a western concept and ideology and therefore fundamentally at odds with the values and principles of Islam? If so, then the Muslim world, consisting of 55 countries populated by more than 1.4 billion people, is doomed to dictatorship and oppression. Moreover, Muslims would have to choose between their religion and democracy. In introducing the discussion, Radwan Masmoudi asserted that there is no inherent contradiction between Islam and democracy and that democratic ideals and principles are also Islam's ideals and principles. Thus, the explanation of why so many Muslim countries are not democratic lies in historical, political, cultural, and economic factors, not religious ones. "Not only must we understand these reasons, but we must also find out what needs to be done to correct this situation. What can we as Americans and especially as American Muslims do to promote democratization in Muslim countries?"

U.S. administrations have generally chosen to build strong ties with those regimes in Muslim countries that seem to support American interests, ignoring their records on human rights, accountability, and democracy. "We have been content to support dictators in the Muslim world, as long as they are allies and do what we want them to do. What are the implications of this policy for the Muslim world? Could this policy lead to the growth of political extremism, political violence, and anti-Americanism?" asked Masmoudi. If we want to change our policy and promote democratization in the Muslim world, can we do it without destabilizing the region and allowing extremist groups to come to power? Do we have to choose between democracy and stability? Or is there a way to promote democratization without causing havoc and anarchy?

While these issues have been asked for many years, they have taken on new significance since September 11. Particularly important is the question of whether the lack of democracy in Muslim states has provided fertile ground for the recruitment of supporters for al Qaeda and other extremist groups. Moreover, has the growth of Islamic extremism reduced the likelihood that democracy and Islam can co-exist?

7

The Problem of Democracy in the Muslim World

Democracy building remains an uphill struggle in most Muslim countries, asserted Laith Kubba. Progress in liberalizing societies, modernizing institutions, and developing infrastructures is generally slow and limited. Worldwide democratic trends have in most cases failed to transform authoritarian and patriarchal political cultures in Muslim countries. Military officers, westernized elites, and tribal/traditional leaders usually keep a monopoly over state power. The weakness of democracy in many Muslim countries is also evident in the many indicators used by western institutions to measure the extent of openness of states and societies. This is most evident in political violence, violations of human rights, and abuse of public office.

Most Muslim countries are at an impasse. Dysfunctional, corrupt, repressive states are neither willing nor capable of reform. Apathy and despair breed radicalism. The failure of secular politics in Muslim countries provides fertile ground for the rise of political Islam. Moderation of Islamic political movements is closely linked to inclusion in the political process, while radicalization is linked to repression and exclusion.

Most Muslim countries, like others in the developing world, are driven by deep needs and a passionate quest for modernity, development, and dignity, Kubba said. For the past several decades, their vision of a better future was anchored in a simple version of a strong central state with a top-down reform approach. That vision was thought to be more likely to succeed than democracy, which offered a complex, multi-institutional participatory system anchored in individualism and liberal values.

Failure of strong secular states to meet the increasing demands of newly educated societies led to soul searching for alternatives. Following the 1979 revolution in Iran, social and political groups became aware of the power of religion in mobilizing public support. Islam, whose ownership, interpretation, and use are open to all, continues to be dragged into the arena as a sharp instrument that may be used by the ruler and opposition alike, by the modernists and conservatives alike, and by groups on the left or right of the political spectrum. Various Islamic groups agree on favoring Islam over secularism but differ on their leanings toward democracy or authoritarianism.

Over the past two decades, as the communist development model failed and models of both secular and Islamic governance failed to deliver solutions to growing social and economic needs, Muslim intellectuals started to advocate democracy and human rights. They did so not only to achieve modernity, development, and dignity, but also to ensure a better practice of Islam.

In Kubba's view the key to understanding the root cause of the democracy predicament in Muslim countries does not lie in the text or in the tradition of Islam but in the context of modernity, politics, and culture. The rather arbitrary use of the term Islamic to describe states, regions, and even people adds to the confusion and blurs the real issues. Although a solution may require addressing Islam and its interpretations, the basic issue is not about Islam but about Muslims. It is not about religion but about modernity. Islam is only one element in the history and culture of the 55 Muslim nations in more than eight distinct regions. Their cultures are influenced to widely varying degrees by the traditions and values of Islam.

They are as diverse as the cultures of predominantly Christian nations from Latin America to the Philippines.

Despite the rather bleak situation at present, Kubba noted that there are grounds for hope. Education is having a significant impact. In addition, there are strong pressures toward liberalization, both because the media continuously provide alternative models from other countries and because states in the Muslim world can no longer function without fundamental structural reforms and without more effective partnerships being developed between the government and the governed. "Looking ahead, I am an optimist. We need to watch the discourse taking place among Muslim intellectuals by which they are bringing about authentic Islamic interpretation of how they should govern themselves in modern societies. I have a lot of faith that this debate will lead to democracy and to full recognition of human rights, but it will come with local language and interpretation and it will be approached from a totally different perspective than we are accustomed to in the West."

Compatibility of Islam and Democracy

In considering the compatibility of Islam and democracy, Muqtedar Khan noted, one must recognize that it is false to claim that there is no democracy in the Muslim world. At least 750 million Muslims live in democratic societies of one kind or another, including Indonesia, Bangladesh, India, Europe, North America, Israel, and even Iran. Moreover, there is little historical precedent for mullahs controlling political power. One exception is Iran since the revolution in 1979 and the other is the Taliban in Afghanistan. For the preceding 1500 years since the advent of Islam, secular political elites have controlled political power.

Two extremely different groups, one from the West and one from the Muslim world, have been arguing that Islam and democracy are incompatible. On the one hand, Khan pointed out, some western scholars and ideologues have tried to present Islam as anti-democratic and inherently authoritarian. By misrepresenting Islam in this way they seek to prove that Islam has a set of values inferior to western liberalism and is a barrier to the global progress of civilization. This misconception also promotes Israel's claim to be the sole democracy in the Middle East.

On the other hand, many Muslim activists, using broad and sometimes crude notions of secularism and sovereignty, consider democracy to be the rule of humans as opposed to Islam, which is rule of God. Those who reject democracy falsely assume that secularism and democracy are necessarily connected. But secularism is not a prerequisite for democracy; religion can play a significant role in democratic politics, as it does in the United States.

As Khan noted, Muslim scholars agree that the principle of shura is the source of democratic ethics in Islam. While there is considerable truth in this claim, one must also recognize the differences between shura and democracy before one can advance an Islamic conception of democracy based on shura. Shura is basically a consultative decision-making process that is considered either obligatory or desirable by different scholars. Those who choose to emphasize the Quranic verse "and consult with them on the matter" (3:159) consider shura as obligatory, but those who emphasize the verse praising "those who conduct their affairs by counsel" (43:38) consider shura as merely desirable. There is no doubt that shura is the Islamic way of making decisions, but is it obligatory? Does a government that does not implement a consultative process become illegitimate? We do not have decisive answers to those questions.

More and more Muslim intellectuals agree that consultative and consensual governance is best. Jurists, however, are more doubtful or ambivalent. Many jurists depend on non-consultative bodies for their livelihood and are in no hurry to deprive themselves of the privileges that non-consultative governments extend to them. But even if shura is considered supportive of democratic process, the two are not identical, Khan asserted. What is clear is that a great deal more reflection is required among leading Muslim thinkers about the nature of shura and its relationship to democracy, as well as other Islamic principles that relate to democratic practice.

As Khan pointed out, the rise of political Islam has made the concept of Islamic sovereignty central to Islamic political theory and that concept is often presented as a barrier to any form of democracy. The Quranic concept of sovereignty is universal (that is non-territorial), transcendental (beyond human agency), indivisible, inalienable, and truly absolute. God the sovereign is the primary law-giver, while agents such as the Islamic state and the Khalifa (God's agents on earth) enjoy marginal autonomy necessary to implement and enforce the laws of their sovereign. At the theoretical level, the difference between the modern and Islamic conceptions of sovereignty is clear. But operational implications tend to blur the distinction.

Democracies are seen by some Muslim activists as systems in which human whim is the source of law, whereas Islamic principles are transcendental and cannot be undermined by popular whim. But what many of them fail to understand is that democratic institutions are not just about law. They are also about prevention of tyranny by the state. Regardless of where sovereignty is placed theoretically, in practice it is the state which exercises it and not God. Even though God was supposedly sovereign in Taliban's Afghanistan, it was in fact the Taliban that was sovereign there; Mullah Omar ruled, not God. Sovereignty in fact is always human, whether in a democracy or an Islamic state. The issue is not whether people are sovereign, but how to limit the de facto sovereignty of people, since they reign under both systems. Democracy with its principles of limited government, public accountability, checks and balances, separation of powers and transparency does succeed in limiting human sovereignty. The Muslim world, plagued by despots, dictators, and self-regarding monarchs, badly needs the limitation of human sovereignty, Khan argued. Many Muslim activists also fail to recognize that Islamic governance is interpreted differently by different Islamic scholars, and hence is not nearly as immutable as they contend.

While sovereignty belongs to God, it has been delegated in the form of human agency. The political task is to reflect on how this God-given agency can be best employed in creating a society that will bring welfare and goodness to the population both now and in the future. God is sovereign in all affairs, but God has exercised sovereignty by delegating some of it in the form of human agency. God cannot become an excuse for installing and legitimizing governments that are not accountable to their citizens and responsive to their needs.

Khan described a precedent set by Prophet Muhammad that demonstrates how democratic practices and theories are compatible with an Islamic state. This is the compact of Medina, referred to by some scholars as Dustur al-Medina (the Constitution of Medina). After Muhammad migrated from Mecca to Yathrib in 622 CE, he established the first Islamic state. For 10 years he was not only the leader of the emerging Muslim ummah (community) in Arabia but also the political head of Medina. He ruled as political head as a result of the tripartite compact that was signed by the Muslim immigrants from Mecca, the indigenous Muslims of Medina, and, significantly, the Jews of Medina. Although the Medina compact cannot serve as a modern constitution, it can serve as a principle.

The compact of Medina also illustrates, Khan pointed out, the proper relationship between divine revelation and a constitution. Muhammad, if he so wished, could have merely indicated that the truth revealed by God would serve as the constitution and forced this revelation upon both the Muslim and non-Muslim residents of Medina. Demonstrating instead a democratic spirit quite unlike the authoritarian tendencies of many of those who claim to imitate him today, Muhammad chose to draw up a historically specific constitution based on the eternal and transcendent principles revealed to him but also sought the consent of all who would be affected by its implementation. Thus, the first Islamic state was based on a social contract, was constitutional in character, and had a ruler who ruled with the explicit written consent of all the citizens of the state. Today, Khan argued, Muslims need to emulate

Muhammad and draw up their own constitutions in a manner that is both appropriate for their specific circumstances as well as based on eternal principles.

The constitution of Medina established the importance of consent and cooperation for governance. According to this compact, Muslims and non-Muslims were equal citizens of the Islamic state, with identical rights and duties. Communities with different religious orientations enjoyed religious autonomy. The constitution of Medina established a pluralistic state—a community of communities. The principles of equality, consensual governance, and pluralism were central to the compact of Medina. Khan noted that it is amazing to see how Muhammad's interpretation of the Quran was so democratic, tolerant, and compassionate, while some contemporary interpretations, like that of the Taliban, are so harsh, authoritarian, and intolerant.

Muslim views on human rights can be grouped into three broad categories, according to Mahmood Monshipouri. The first group is Muslim conservatives. They tend to look to both the classical and medieval periods for inspiration. Conservatives adopt a communitarian view that sees the individual as part of the community, to which he or she owes certain obligations. Conservatives' emphasis on drawing boundaries around the community is expressed not only in stipulations about dress for women (hijab) and the repression of women's sexuality, but also in the proclamation of a different way of life and of a transformation of mind by bringing the faithful back to the proper practice of the faith and tradition.

These conservatives tend to view the western world's advocacy of human rights as a mechanism by which the West hopes to establish its hegemony over the Muslim world. They have vehemently objected to several articles of the Universal Declaration of Human Rights (UDHR), including Articles 16 and 18, which deal with equality of marriage rights and freedom to change one's religion or belief. They also object to the provisions on women's rights, questioning the equality of gender roles and obligations. Islam, they argue, prohibits the marriage of a Muslim woman to a non-Muslim man. Apostasy (ridda) is forbidden and is punishable by death.

Muslim conservatives challenge the idea of natural reason as an independent source of ethical knowledge. According to conservatives, following past traditions (taqlid) and returning to established norms in times of crisis are two cardinal rules of Islamic orthodoxy. Among the most prominent of the conservative leadership advocating these positions are such scholars as Sayyid Abu al-A'la al-Maududi (1903-79), Hassan al-Banna (1906-49), Sayyid Qutb (1906-66), and Ayatollah Ruhollah Khomeini (1902-89).

Muslim reformists or neo-modernists, in contrast, are more receptive to non-Islamic ideas, practices, and institutions, according to Monshipouri. They argue that material progress is necessary to bring about human and economic transformation within an Islamic framework. They stress the need for the continuity of basic Islamic principles but believe that Islamic law (sharia) is historically conditioned and needs to be reinterpreted in light of the changing needs of modern society.

A comparison between two reformist positions helps explain the contending perspectives within this camp. Some reformists have argued that what conservatives call divine law in reality only reflects the interpretation of a few specialists. Abdolkarim Soroush, an Iranian philosopher, has argued that "divine legislation in Islam is said to have been discovered by a few and those discoverers think that they have privileged access to the interpretation of this law" (Soroush and Charles Butterworth at the Middle East Institute, November 21, 2000, "Islamic Democracy and Islamic Governance," www.mideasti. org/ html/b-soroush. html).

Having questioned the monopoly over interpretation by one group or class, Soroush argues the need for a dialogical pluralism between those inside and outside of religious intellectual fields. Human rights, according to Soroush, lie outside religion and are not solely intra-religious arguments based on jurisprudence (fiqh). Rather, they belong to the domain of philosophical theology (kalam) and philosophy in general. Some values, he argues, cannot be derived from religion. Human rights are the case in point. The language of religion and religious law is essentially the language of duties, not rights.

Sheikh Rached al-Ghannouchi, leader of the Tunisian An-Nahda political party, articulates a different vision and rationale for reform. For Ghannouchi, the central question is how to free the Muslim community from backwardness and dependence on the "Other." Reconciling Islam and modernity, according to Ghannouchi, involves introduction of democracy and freedom, both of which are consistent with Islamic principles. The community not the individual remains the ultimate reality, and democracy and freedom of thought are tools that Muslims should use to achieve their community's goals and defend its interests.

The third group, according to Monshipouri, is the Muslim secularists. Secular Muslims look to the experiences of the secular West as guiding models in an effort to promote their country's development. Secularists often support policies and programs that are grounded in pragmatic considerations. Muslim secularists are reluctant to replace secular laws with sharia. To secularists, Islamic practices such as shura and bay'a (a binding agreement that holds rulers to certain standards and governs relations between rulers and the ruled) have failed to support individual political participation and to provide a basis for democratic accountability by governments. Secular rule is the prevailing pattern in the Muslim world; with the exception of Iran since 1979, Sudan since 1989, and Afghanistan under the Taliban, the Muslim world is ruled by secular regimes.

The Muslim world is indeed in uncertain transition, with its youth facing cultural disorientation and its political scene dominated by internal power struggles. The greatest threats to human rights in the Muslim world are not religious or theological but political. In a globalizing world, concern has been expressed about whether Muslims will lose the ability to control their own economies, power, and cultural assets. Many in the Muslim world, however, see hope in such a globalizing world. The youth, women's organizations, the press, intellectuals, and Islamic reformers all see great opportunities, especially if they become part of the global civil society.

The biggest question is how to adopt new ideas and policies while maintaining religious and cultural integrity. Monshipouri argues that to maintain such a balance, the Muslim world's elites, scholars, and activists must interpret Islamic values and social norms in a manner consistent with modern and internationally recognized human rights. The western world must treat Muslim masses as partners in the struggle against human rights abuses, while helping to empower reformist voices and civil society.

Despite the degree to which human rights are suppressed in Muslim countries, two grassroots movements are struggling to change this situation. The first is the women's movement and the second is the youth movement. Over the long term they can have enormous impact on human rights in these countries. Women are beginning to effectively assert their rights, and in some countries young people are agitating against governmental oppression and corruption.

Monshipouri concluded his presentation by making three points. First, the greatest threat to human rights in the Muslim world comes not from Islam but from economic, political, and educational forces. Second, human rights struggles in the Muslim world will be lost or won on the national level, not on the international level; it is up to Muslims themselves to decide how much respect to accord human rights. Third, those countries that have weak civil society structures and authoritarian regimes are fertile ground for terrorism. If western countries want to suppress terror then they have to foster civil society and support those movements that express dissenting voices within these repressive political systems. Western countries can also apply economic and political pressure on these authoritarian regimes to encourage fundamental change.

Neil Hicks noted that while the shortcomings in human rights and democratization of many U.S. allies in the region have been noted in official statements, particularly in the U.S. State Department's annual country reports on human rights practices, policy has tended toward the preservation of the status quo for fear of what might replace it. In the Arab world especially, authoritarian leaders have traded on their self-proclaimed status as bulwarks against Islamic extremism.

For the most part, the United States went along with the fiction that repression in the Muslim world was the best way to prevent Islamism from growing as a threat to the West and to U.S. vital interests. In the name of confronting radical Islam, Hicks said, basic rights and freedoms were virtually extingui-shed in Tunisia and severely curtailed in Egypt. In Turkey, Malaysia, and Algeria, authoritarian regimes employed anti-democratic measures to suppress Islamic movements that were gaining popular support.

The greatest casualties of this broad-brush repression were basic values of tolerance, political pluralism, and free speech that are essential to democracy. The institutions of democracy, like an independent judiciary, free political parties, civil society, and the separation of powers, were undermined. On realizing that the non-violent, democratic path to power or reform was blocked, some felt vindicated in embracing violence as the only way of bringing about change. Polarization, extremism, and political violence all flourished. It is worth mentioning that liberal, pluralistic forms of political Islam have been a particular casualty of this unpromising political climate. On the one hand, they have been subjected to repression by state authorities as undesirable expressions of political dissent. On the other, they have been marginalized by some within the political Islamic movement itself for being utopian and ineffectual.

At the same time as many U.S. allies in the region were stifling democracy (with only token criticism at best from the West), the United States strongly criticized its foes in the region as enemies of democracy and human rights. There is no doubt that the governments of Iran and Sudan and that of the Taliban in Afghanistan were richly deserving of such criticisms, but the violations of human rights perpetrated by these regimes in particular were added to the indictment against Islamism in general. The mostly unspoken accepted wisdom became that U.S. allies in Egypt, Jordan, or Tunisia may have their failings, but we have to choose between them and the Iranian mullahs, the Taliban, and Sudan's National Islamic Front, and that choice is easily made. Human rights also became a vehicle for criticizing other regional foes like Saddam Hussein in Iraq.

Hicks asserted that many people in the Muslim world and elsewhere quickly recognized a double standard in U.S. advocacy of human rights and democracy in the region. If the United States is so critical of Iran for not better protecting women's rights, then why is it silent about the abject situation of women in Saudi Arabia? If the Iraqi people deserve to choose their own leaders then what about the Egyptian people or the Tunisian people? In Afghanistan, the United States was willing to cooperate with the mujahedin, and to call them freedom fighters, during the conflict with the Soviet Union, even though their commitment to democracy was virtually non-existent, Hicks pointed out.

There has been a glaring contradiction between U.S. rhetoric supporting democracy and human rights, on the one hand, and a policy that held major violators of human rights like Pakistan and Saudi Arabia to be key strategic allies while at the same time condoning repression by other allies, like Egypt, on the other hand. The perception of double standards was exacerbated by the Israeli-Palestinian conflict, where many Muslim observers thought that Israel was allowed to disregard international law with impunity, whereas Muslim states like Iraq or Libya could be subjected to international sanctions or even armed intervention for their departures from international norms.

U.S. policy, Hicks continued, recognized the importance to regional stability and political development of resolving the

Israeli-Palestinian conflict. The first Bush administration and the Clinton administration expended considerable effort in promoting the Madrid process and then the Oslo process. However, even these well-intentioned initiatives, especially in the middle and later phases of the Oslo process, had negative repercussions for democratization in the region.

Supporting the "peace process" became an article of faith and the main goal of U.S. policy in the Arab world. Dissent from this orthodoxy was regarded as unhelpful by the United States. U.S. allies claimed that they were taking great political risks for peace by going against the views of their people, and this assertion was generally accepted. U.S. policy did not seem to question what was creating this public mood that was supposedly hostile to peace with Israel and whether more repression was the way to deal with it. In fact, many U.S. allies were fanning the flames of anti-Israeli sentiment and exploiting such feelings as a distraction from domestic problems and as another reason to keep the lid on political dissent.

Out of this morass of contradictions and double standards it is not surprising that some hostility toward U.S. policy developed, and some skepticism about the values the United States claimed to espouse. Indeed, some in the Muslim world expressed open hostility toward democracy and human rights as alien western values, and found an enthusiastic audience in doing so. Hicks asserted that this hostility is largely a reaction to the use to which such values had been put by cynical authoritarian governments and by the West, rather than a lack of identification with common values of justice and human dignity. Unfortunately, a kind of self-fulfilling stereotyping of Muslim attitudes to human rights and democracy has developed, partly as a result of the disaffection expressed by many in the Muslim world towards "democracy" and "human rights" as they have experienced them in practice.

What can be done? Hicks noted that promoting democracy abroad is not something new for the U.S. government, even if there has been less of it in the Muslim world than elsewhere. There are lessons to be drawn from Eastern Europe and Latin America, regions where democratic advances since the end of the Cold War are discernible, and from the former Soviet Union and parts of Africa, where signs of progress are often less apparent. Perhaps the most important lesson is that there is no single prescription that will ensure a transition to democracy. Local conditions vary enormously. In the vast and diverse Muslim world it will be necessary for the U.S. government to develop country-specific plans to promote democracy.

Recommendations

Increase substantially both the proportion and the amount of U.S. foreign assistance that is spent on promoting democracy in the Muslim world. It is important to note that simply spending more is not a solution by itself. We can learn from the example of U.S. foreign assistance to Egypt, which has remained at high levels even while foreign aid budgets elsewhere were evaporating.

In Egypt the United States has funded democratization projects and supplied hundreds of millions of dollars of other civilian assistance while, by any measure, democratic freedoms have contracted. To succeed the United States must demand accountability from the recipient governments. The question then becomes, is the United States willing to have a more adversarial relationship with regional leaders, and perhaps to see some of them overthrown, as part of the messy process of promoting democracy? These leaders, after all, are valued because they are seen as assisting in the protection of vital U.S. national interests.

Provide governments and other key interest groups in Muslim societies with incentives to encourage democratic reforms. A major commitment to foreign assistance to the Muslim world by the U.S. government would provide an attractive incentive to recipient governments to embark on the path to reform. Foreign assistance should be linked to clear progress in strengthening institutions of accountability. Here domestic interest groups independent of existing power elites take on a particular importance, because existing leaders typically have little interest in diluting their own privileges. When providing foreign assistance, the U.S. government must insist that there be a free press, that the judiciary be independent, and that civil society organizations operate free from governmental interference.

Incentives should come not in the form of aid alone, which inevitably has some patronizing connotations. Real partnerships, especially in the field of trade, but also in a host of other areas, including cultural and educational ones, are also important. The positive impact on democratic reforms of Turkey's accession process to the European Union is a good case in point. Because many sectors of Turkish society anticipate benefits from EU membership, there has been a considerable groundswell of support for the stringent reforms required by the European Commission. The process of change has been and is painful to many entrenched interests. Nevertheless, the business community has put pressure on the government to press forward with political as well as economic reforms. Business elites in other Muslim states, who recognize the benefits of participating in the global marketplace, and who also recognize that the price of entry is compliance with international standards, are a largely untapped resource for democratic change.

Take seriously the existing framework of multilateral agreements and treaties that bear on democratization, such as those in the field of human rights. Since there is skepticism over the U.S. government's motives in promoting democracy in the Muslim world, it is wise to disarm doubters by embracing multilateral approaches with like-minded governments wherever possible. Treaty bodies within UN human rights mechanisms—like the Human Rights Committee and the Committee Against Torture, which oversee state compliance with treaties like the International Covenant on Civil and Political Rights, and the Convention Against Torture and other Forms of Cruel, Inhuman, or Degrading Treatment or Punishment—are highly regarded for the integrity of the work of their members, who sit as independent experts. Their work is often favorably compared to the politicized machinations of the UN Human Rights Commission, for example. Yet these effective bodies are chronically under funded. Members operate with little or no research support and their findings are virtually unknown beyond the world of human rights specialists. It would surely be a sound investment for the U.S. government to lend its financial and political support to the work of these under-appreciated institutions.

Promote regional accountability mechanisms. The Muslim world is lacking in regional accountability mechanisms. The great virtue of such mechanisms is that they cannot be accused of being alien or inauthentic because they are of the region over which they exercise jurisdiction. Again, Turkey provides an example of the merits of such mechanisms. One of the reasons for Turkey's advantage over other Muslim states in its progress towards democratization is its longstanding participation in the human rights mechanisms of the Council of Europe, especially its acceptance of the right of individual citizens to petition the European Court of Human Rights and its agreement to be bound by the rulings of the court. The benefits go beyond the individual cases that have been heard before the court. Turkey's legal community and human rights organizations increasingly know and make use of the fact that there is a functioning mechanism for them to resort to in the face of state violations. The United States should make great efforts to promote effective regional mechanisms of accountability within existing regional institutions like the Organization of the Islamic Conference and the League of Arab States.

8

Islam and Modernity

Democracy and modernity go hand in hand. One can hardly be modern without being democratic. Whilst it is possible to argue that there are successful authoritarian models of modernization like China and Singapore, on deeper reflection it will be seen that democratic model is more congenial to modernization, particularly in the social sphere. Modern social sciences cannot flourish under authoritarian regimes even though natural sciences might.

But the lack of modernity in Muslim countries is not because of Islamic teaching per se but is due more to its medieval interpretation. Islam can come to terms with modernity. Its teachings are quite modernistic if one goes by the Qur'anic pronouncements. The Qur'an encourages pluralism in verses like 5:48, 6:109, and 60:8. All these verses are quite supportive of a pluralistic social structure. In fact early Islamic societies were far more pluralistic than any others throughout the medieval period. The Qur'an not only recognizes the validity of other faiths but also makes it incumbent for Muslims to respect equally all past prophets - and one who fails to do so is not true Muslim. Clear proof can be found in verses 4:150-152.

The intolerance in Muslim societies today is more political than religious. Islam need not be intolerant of any other religion including that of kufr (unbelief) if it agrees to coexist peacefully and harmoniously. Thus Islam and pluralism can go together and have always done so. In fact it was Europe in medieval times that as intolerant of non-Christians. Islam today must free itself from the grip of intolerant theologians close to authoritarian power structures - authoritarian power that is at the root of their intolerance.

The Organization of Islamic Conference (OIC) has fifty-six member states plus Palestine with ten other entities including the United Nations holding observer status. Out of the fifty-six, Syria, Iran, Libya, Pakistan, Iraq, Tunisia, Algeria, Somalia, Maldives, Burkina-Faso, Uganda, Sudan, Gambia, Uzbekistan, Azerbaijan, Cote d'Ivoire, Gabon, Mauritius, Lebanon, Guinea, Turkmenistan and Kazakhstan are categorized as 'Authoritarian Regimes'. That is a total of twenty-two or 40 percent of the OIC (Afghanistan has long been classified as a 'Totalitarian Regime').

Nearly 15 percent of OIC member states are 'Traditional Monarchies'. They are: Saudi Arabia, Bahrain, Kuwait, UAE, Brunei, Oman, Qatar and Morocco. Some nine OIC members pass as having 'Restricted Democratic Practices': Malaysia, Jordan, Egypt, Cameroon, Senegal, Comoros, Yemen, Chad and Tajikistan.

Only 15 OIC members are considered to be "Democratic": Indonesia, Turkey, Bangladesh, Sierra Leone, Guinea-Bissau, Niger, Mozambique, Mali, Kyrgyz, Togo, Benin, Guyana, Djibouti, Albania and Suriname. Any member state that fulfills just three objectively analyzed criteria (multi-candidate, multiparty, competitive elections) qualifies as a Democracy. Thus at least 70 percent of OIC members are Authoritarian Regimes, Totalitarian Regimes or have Restricted Democratic Practices.

Political Rights and Civil Liberties

Freedom House, a nonpartisan, nonprofit, broad-based, democracy-related research think-tank, has since 1978 published Freedom in the World, an annual comparative assessment of the state of political rights and civil liberties in 192 countries and 18 related and disputed territories. The methodology of these surveys is based on the Universal

Declaration of Human Rights with little or no culture-bound view of freedom. Each country is rated on a scale of 1 to 6 for political rights and civil liberties and given an overall rating: Free, Partly Free, or Not Free.

In the 2003 Freedom House survey at least thirty of the 56 OIC member states were classified as being 'Not Free'; 53 percent of the total membership. The 'Not Free' countries are: Pakistan, Saudi Arabia, Iran, Egypt, UAE, Syria, Iraq, Libya, Bahrain, Qatar, Oman, Afghanistan, Tunisia, Sudan, Gambia, Uzbekistan, Turkmenistan, Kazakhstan, Algeria, Maldives, Mauritius, Somalia, Lebanon, Guinea, Kyrgyz, Tajikistan, Chad, Yemen and Cameroon.

Bangladesh, Indonesia, Turkey, Malaysia, Morocco, Kuwait, Jordan, Burkina Faso, Uganda, Azerbaijan, Cote d'Ivoire, Gabon, Sierra Leone, Guinea-Bissau, Comoros, Senegal, Niger, Mozambique, Nigeria and Togo are 'Partially Free'. Only four OIC members were classified as 'Free'. They are: Mali, Benin, Guyana and Suriname.

Conclusion: At least 93 percent of OIC members are either 'Not Free' or only 'Partially Free'.

Economic Performance

More than 1.3 billion people, one-fifth of humanity, live in the OIC states. Within the OIC are Saudi Arabia, Iraq, Iran, UAE and Kuwait that between them possess 700 billion barrels of proven oil reserves. All the 1.3 billion put together have an annual GDP of less than $1.5 trillion.

There are only 290 million Americans and their annual GDP is $10.4 trillion. France is at $1.54 trillion, Germany $2 trillion, UK $1.52 trillion and Italy, long the sick man of Europe, $1.4 trillion. Kuwait, UAE and Brunei are the only OIC members where per capita income exceeds $10,000 a year. At least fifty OIC members have per capita incomes of under $5,000 a year. Forty-five OIC members have per capita incomes of under $1,000 a year.

Education

Of the 1.3 billion OIC Muslims more than 800 million continue to be absolutely illiterate. Of the 290 million Americans 227 are Nobel Laureates (India has 4). Of the 1.3 billion Muslims less than 300,000 qualify as 'scientists'. That converts to a ratio of 230 scientists per one million Muslims. The United States of America has 1.1 million scientists; Japan has 700,000. Among them, fifty-six OIC countries have an average of ten universities each for a total of less than 600 universities for 1.3 billion people. India has 8,407 universities, the US has 5,758.

The Arms Trade

The planet's poorest countries include Ethiopia, Sierra Leone, Afghanistan, Cambodia, Somalia, Nigeria, Pakistan and Mozambique. At least six of the poorest of the poor are OIC members.

The largest buyers of conventional weapons are Taiwan, Saudi Arabia, Turkey, S Korea, China, India, Greece, Egypt, Japan, UAE, Israel, Finland, Pakistan, Kuwait and Singapore. Of the fifteen top buyers of conventional weapons six are OIC members. The US, Russia, France, UK, Germany, Netherlands, Ukraine, Italy, China, Belarus, Spain, Israel, Canada, Australia and Sweden are the largest suppliers of weapons. Not one is part of OIC.

Is the Ummah Listening?

We are trapped in a vicious cycle of illiteracy, poverty and violence. We continue to blame non-Muslims for all our failures. Salman Rushdie is convinced that America's 'war on terrorism' is all about Islam. Rushdie says what we have is a "paranoid Islam, which blames outsiders, 'infidels' for all the ills of Muslim societies, and whose proposed remedy is the closing of those societies to the rival project of modernity.... this is presently the fastest growing version of Islam in the world."

Rushdie goes to add that "if Islam is to be reconciled with modernity... the restoration of religion to the sphere of the personal, its depoliticization, is the nettle that all Muslim societies must grasp in order to become modern. The only aspect of modernity interesting to the terrorists is technology, which they see as a weapon that can be turned on its makers.

If terrorism is to be defeated, the world of Islam must take on board the secularist-humanist principles on which the modern is based, and without which Muslim countries' freedom will remain a distant dream."

Islamic Reformation Awaited

An Islamic Reformation has yet to materialize, but without it the Muslim world is seriously handicapped, intellectually and materially, in facing the challenges of the present and future.

The current wave of fundamentalist Islam conveys a distorted image of the highly variegated Muslim heritage. From quite early times diverse and pluralistic approaches existed among Muslims for understanding their religion. Some schools approached the Quranic text as a multilayered discourse comprising literal as well as symbolic and esoteric messages. On the other hand, populist movements insisted that each word should be understood in the literal sense. The latter tendencies gave birth to anthropomorphist doctrines about God's detailed intervention in all matters and came to represent the fundamentalist strand.

Rationalism, as a movement of free thought, also made an early appearance and between the 9th and 13th centuries it constituted a robust intellectual activism with adherents in many parts of the Muslim world. The first statement in favor of rationalism was presented in the following words by Al-Kindi (801-66): "We should not be ashamed to acknowledge truth from whatever source it comes to us, even if it is brought to us by former generations and foreign powers and for him who seeks the truth there is nothing of higher value than truth itself".

The general assumption upon which Muslim philosophers built their rationalism was that if reason was applied correctly it could furnish reliable and certain knowledge about the universe but it was necessary to believe that some knowledge comes only through revelation. The Spanish-Arab philosopher Ibn Rushd (1126-98) emphasized the preeminence of human intelligence and philosophical reflection over the apparent meaning of Quranic verses. He asserted that in case of a contradiction between the truths discovered by philosophy and what the Quran appeared to state, the discoveries of the philosophers were to be relied upon and the Quranic verses interpreted metaphorically.

For various reasons the rationalist movement could not consolidate itself and the intellectual leadership passed into the hands of Imam Ghazzali (d. 1111). With the help of a simple formula that revelation was superior to reason, he established the lasting hold of scholasticism over Muslim intellectual activity. As a result dogmatism became permanently entrenched in Muslim intellectual discourses. It is therefore not surprising that the syllabi of the contemporary Islamic madrassas are based on scholasticism and dogmatism.

In societal terms the implications were that the Fuquha (jurists) and ulema seemed to have tacitly reached the conclusion that all matters deserving to be explained or regulated in law had been covered by Fiqh rulings; the world had reached its ultimate development which would last till such time that decline sets in and the whole universe declines into chaos, as predicted in the sacred sources, culminating in the Day of Reckoning or Qayamat. Belief in such teleology allowed medieval scholars of Islam to be complacent that in future all that was needed was to apply the rulings of Fiqh to specific circumstances. Such assumptions resulted in the doctrine, 'closing-of-the-gates-of-ijtihad'.

It was in the 18th century that the 'closing-of-the-gates-of-ijtihad' doctrine began to be questioned. The new reformers were the Wahabis of the Arabian Peninsula. They denounced the cult of sufi-saints, visits to shrines in the hope of intercession of dead masters on behalf of a supplicant and a host of elaborate ceremonies that had taken root in Muslim societies. Instead the Wahabis subscribed to a strictly Unitarian interpretation of Islam and sought to employ ijtihad to purify contemporaneous Islam of 'un-Islamic accretions'.

In one sense, the Wahabi reforms were not different from the Reformation that Luther and Calvin had successfully led in Europe. They too strove to restore pure, unadulterated Christianity, but it was purely fortuitous that the scientific discoveries of that time undermined the Aristotelian physics upon which the church had built its view of the universe. Such a confluence of religious reform and scientific change did not underpin the Wahabi attempts at reformation. Consequently it became a reactionary rather than a progressive intervention in Muslim affairs.

Muslim encounters with science and modernity came via the colonial intervention. Following Napoleon's landing at Alexandria in 1798 Muslim modernism began to take shape. However, under the influence of Jamaluddin Afghani it reaffirmed the supremacy of revelation over reason. He wrote a famous pamphlet denouncing 'materialism', the term he employed for describing science and the scientific method.

A more sophisticated position on reform was taken by Sir Syed Ahmed Khan. Deeply impressed by the achievements of English rule and English education, Sir Syed adopted a rationalist-scientific approach to phenomena by arguing that Islam was not only a religion based on reason as Afghani had asserted but also on nature. Hence the name of his intellectual movement, the Nechari (naturalist) School of Thought. Thus he not only supported a study of Western natural sciences but also economic methods and theory. In a bold reinterpretation of the Quran, Sir Syed came to the conclusion that the ban on usury was not applicable to modern banking and commercial practices. His followers however failed to sustain the Nechari School which slipped into oblivion soon after his death.

The intellectual leadership of the Muslim world passed on to Allama Iqbal who reverted to the scholastic position of Ghazzali and Afghani, asserting that reality was spiritual and therefore science, which could only deal with material data, was inadequate for fathoming true reality. His notion of 'spiritual democracy' charmed Muslim League leaders such as Prime Minister Liaqat Ali Khan who translated it into a constitutional principle by declaring God and not the people of Pakistan sovereign. Such formulations opened the market for Abul Ala Maududi's 'theo-democracy' and Ghulam Ahmad Pervaiz's 'Quranic democracy' and many other novel but bogus terms. Their disciples continue to churn out even more confused and contradictory notions of science, democracy and a modern economy of growth.

The government of Gen Ziaul Haq whose funda-mentalist leanings were proverbial caused the greatest harm to rationalism. Elsewhere in the Muslim world too fundamentalism became a prominent state ideology in the 1980s and this situation persists. The result is that an Islamic Reformation has yet to materialize, but without it the Muslim world is seriously handicapped, intellectually and materially, in facing the challenges of the present and future.

Rid Pakistan of Reactionary Laws

Each time the state tries to enforce Islam as a Deen it assumes totalistic or totalitarian characteristics. Both the religious establishment and the state should respect the freedom of the individual. President Pervez Musharraf's recent statement criticising 'honour killings' and his suggestion that the Blasphemy and Hudood laws should be debated at all levels in society is a step in the right direction. In his subsequent meeting with ulema and mashaikh, telecast by the national TV, he urged them to eradicate extremism from mosques and seminaries and cooperate with him in fighting terrorism. It was a most useful follow-up.

All sensible Pakistanis should support his move because it is in the best interest of Pakistan and Islam. A powerful rightwing lobby has begun to demonise Musharraf as a renegade but students of history know that no Muslim reformer has escaped the wrath of such elements. Indeed the war on terrorism will never be successful if it does not seek to eradicate the extremist mindset in all societies that thrives on outmoded, intolerant and repressive edicts.

Nobody is born a terrorist, a racist or a religious fanatic, although individual personality disturbances can be congenital and some people are prone to violent and extremist behaviour. Socialisation processes produce either a liberal and tolerant culture or a reactionary and intolerant one. In this regard, two institutions, besides the immediate family, play an important role in forming attitudes and opinions - the religious set-up and the state.

Let us address the religious set-up first. Unfortunately, since the Iranian revolution and the ensuing fierce competition between the Saudi and the Iranian state to establish their influence in the Muslim world, Muslims have been only exposed to two sectarian versions of extremism. The traditional Islamic polity based on Sunni moderation and the middle path has been sidelined. While the Shias have discarded their quietism in favour of political activism, the Sunnis have come increasingly under Khawarji fanatical influence represented by its modern permutation such as Wahhabism.

I grew up learning about Islam from my grandfather's conduct. He was a pious man who believed that the Prophet's (PBUH) message to humankind was to help the poor and needy. In his own simple way he practised an Islam that put a high premium on charity and helping the needy. We grew up hearing that the Caliph Umar would disguise himself and roam the streets of Madina to see if someone was in need of help? We never grew up thinking of Islam as a punishing or intolerant creed.

But just look around the Muslim world and can we find even one example of an Islamic state that practices a gentle and caring Islam? Wherever the expression 'Islamic state' is used to describe a polity, its record of barbaric punishments stands out conspicuously.

Consequently, the fact that the Muslim world today is in the stranglehold of extremism cannot be blamed on external sources alone. The USA, Israel, India and Russia are indeed guilty of crimes against innocent Muslims and that understandably generates an angry reaction, but the malaise has its roots within the world of Islam. Quite simply Islam has to go through a reformation. An Islamic reformation will need to accept the autonomy of the individual and his freedom to voluntarily choose to believe in Islam or any other religion or philosophy.

There is clear evidence that unscrupulous people in this country have used the blasphemy law to gain worldly ends. In any case, there is a need to look at the whole thing logically. There are always people in some societies who offend public sensibilities but they do not deserve to be given much attention. Also, it just requires one look at the sectarian sub-literature to see how low extremists on all sides of the divide can stoop. Millions of Muslims live in the West and our families are now settled here for good. We would find it totally unacceptable to be told that we could be charged for blasphemy in a court of law for not believing that Jesus was the Son of God.

The Western world realised that it should not be the business of the state to interfere in the personal beliefs of its citizens, only after inflicting the holocaust on Jews. That is a tragic way of finding the truth or gaining wisdom. We, immigrants, have benefited most from the new approach. Nobody can deny that Western democracies have not only created the most dynamic societies ever known to humankind, but also provided the freedom to every individual to follow his/her conscience in matters of religion.

Does it make any sense to say that Islam (officially) did not establish a church and each individual is personally responsible for ensuring his/her salvation and, then(unofficially), go on to make the state the guarantor of true Islam? The purpose of the state should be simply to take care of the worldly needs and rights of its citizens. Saying this does not mean that one is reducing the purpose of life to some material needs.

Worldly needs include the right to freedom of thought and expression as well as a reasonable standard of living.

Without an all-round enjoyment of material and intellectual freedoms a mature attitude towards God or truth cannot be established.

It is time to challenge the cliché that Islam is a complete code of life, a Deen (worldview) and not a madhab (ritualised religion). It has been employed for too long as a self-evident truth with the result that no serious discussion ever takes place to establish the full implications and ramifications of such rhetoric. Each time the state tries to enforce Islam as a Deen it assumes totalistic or totalitarian characteristics. Take any example – Iran, Saudi Arabia, Afghanistan under the Taliban, and the Zia period in Pakistani history. Therefore, both the religious establishment and the state should respect the freedom of the individual to find his own path to salvation.

Women's Right in Islam

According to the Sharia, despite declarations of the equality of the sexes before God, women are considered inferior to men, and have fewer rights and responsibilities. A woman counts as half a man in giving evidence in a court of law, or in matters of inheritance. Her position is less advantageous than a man's with regard to marriage and divorce. A husband has the moral and religious right and duty to beat his wives for disobedience or for perceived misconduct. A woman does not have the right to choose her husband, or her place of residence, to travel freely or have freedom in her choice of clothing. Women have little or no autonomy and are deemed to need the protection of their fathers, husbands or other male relatives throughout their lives. Any conduct that undermines the idea of male supremacy will fall foul of the Sharia.

The legal age of marriage varies from country to country, ranging from 9 in Iran to 13, 15 or 17 (in Tunisia). This follows from the marriage of Mohammed to Aisha, a 9-year-old girl, when the Prophet was 53. It should be noted, however, that the Prophet was allowed many actions by Allah that were denied to the other faithful, and not all Muslim scholars would accept the Aisha marriage as a precedent.

The various Sunni schools of law and that of the Shi'ites differ on a number of points important to women. In all schools, however, marriage is a contract according to which the husband should perform sexually and provide materially for the wife. The wife must have sex whenever the husband wishes. A man can easily divorce a woman by pronouncing that he is divorcing her three times. Polygamy with up to four wives is permitted, and in the Shi'ite sect, temporary marriage is allowed whereby a man can have access to an unlimited number of women. The practice is known as Mot'a or Sigheh. Men are also permitted concubines and female slaves.

In many Islamic countries a Muslim woman is not allowed to marry a non-Muslim man whereas Muslim men are allowed to marry non-Muslim women. With the object of protecting morality and preventing sexual anarchy, women are expected to cover their whole bodies bar their faces and their hands up to their wrists.

The Sharia is totally opposed to freedom of dress – for women. This is obviously a huge barrier to the personal development of women, not allowing them to develop sexually and as people. It is inhumane to imprison women behind veils when it is the men who according to Islamic law cannot be trusted to control themselves. On the pretext of protecting their honor women are kept locked up, isolated and unable to enjoy a full life or to develop their potential.

In order to protect their morality women can have no contact with men to whom they are not related without the presence of a male relative. The segregation of sexes in this way makes it very difficult for women to leave their houses and participate in society in any way at all. Under the Taliban many war widows were forced into starvation. Their crime? Had they prayed harder their husbands would have survived!

Many apologists for Islam, women among them, argue that women are happy in their roles in Islamic society, happy to be afforded the protection of their men folk and to be kept away from the gaze of other men. But this of course is a false argument. If some women want to stay at home under the protection of their men they can do so. But do the apologists for Islam have the right to tell all other women, including non-Muslims, how they should behave? Women deserve to be treated as autonomous human beings and for this reason alone misogynistic Political Islam and its imposition of the Sharia should be opposed.

The Liberation of Women in the Middle East

The position of women in the Middle East has aroused much recent interest. What are the facts about the subordination of Middle Eastern women? What role does Islamic ideology and practice play in the oppression of women in the region and other societies where Political Islam holds sway?

Few would argue that the status of women in the Middle East can be understood without reference to Islam. Although the legal-religious systems of no two Middle Eastern countries are identical, women are second-class citizens in all of them. But neither can the position of women in the region be understood without an appreciation of the economic and political contexts in which they live, and of the influence of Political Islam.

There are many schools of thought in the debate about the status of Middle Eastern women. One group denies that the great majority of women in the Middle East are any more oppressed than women elsewhere. A second group says that oppression is real but is not intrinsic extrinsic to Islam and the Quran, which they say, intended gender equality, but which has been undermined by Arabic patriarchy and foreign importations.

Among many intellectuals and many in the academic world, any attempt to point at Islam, even Political Islam, in connection with the oppression of women is stamped as "Orientalism". The defence of Islam in the face of western challenges has taken many forms, but ultimately aims to demonstrate the progressive nature of the Quran, Hadith and the Sharia, either by denying the low status of women in Middle Eastern societies or by attributing it to pre-Islamic traditions or to the conservative forces of contemporary Political Islam.

Many feminists and academic intellectuals apologize for the Islamists by saying that veiling; female genital mutilation and the savage oppression of women are not restricted to Middle Eastern societies. Some say that women who wear make up in the West are just as oppressed as those in the East wearing the veil, but it is a post-modernist kind of oppression. They say that women are inferior in all religions and it is not specific to Islam. They fail to compare conditions within Islamic states to those in the western nations, which introduced the idea of the secular state and restricted the power of Christianity over women's lives. This attitude is apparent in the following words of Nawal El Saadawi:

"I've noticed that many people including professors of religion and Islamic studies pick up one verse and say that in the Quran, God allowed men to beat women. They don't compare it to other verses. They also don't compare the Quran to the Bible. If you do, you will find the Bible more oppressive to women."

According to Nawal El Saadawi, women in the Middle East are oppressed not because they live under the rule of Political Islam or belong to the East, but as a result of the patriarchal class system that has dominated the world for thousands of years. In her view, the struggle for women's civil liberties, individual freedom and secularism have no significance. In this discourse, patriarchy as a blanket term is used to disguise the role of Political Islam in the oppression of women. Any and every aspect of women's subordination in the Middle East is inaccurately labelled as patriarchy. Of course, the economic system and political oppression play their part in the subordination of women. But if Islam has no effect on women's status, why is the position of women in the Middle East worse than in any other part of the world?

Resistance To Women's Rights

Historically, wherever Islam has held political sway it has

resisted women's rights, secularism, modernism and human values. Dramatic differences between Eastern and Western society emerged in the 19th and 20th centuries. In the Middle East, economic and social changes along with the impact of Western culture brought about forces favouring improvements in the condition of women. From the early 19th century the outcome of the process of change that Western influence set in motion was broadly positive, as the social institutions and mechanisms for the control and seclusion of women are for their exclusion from the major domains of activity in their society were gradually dismantled. But this rarely involved legal changes, rather such things as women's education. Western economic penetration of the Middle East and the exposure of Middle Eastern societies to western political thought and ideas did little to dismantle Islamic law and its backward social institutions oppressive to women.

Changes in the law pertaining to women have met with considerable resistance. Such changes were felt by nationalist, Islamic forces to be a final invasion in the last sphere they could control against the aggressive infidels, once sovereignty and much of the economy had been taken over by the West. When the French came to Egypt with Napoleon, the wearing of the veil increased as a reaction to their presence. The Islamists saw modern values such as women's rights as a western conspiracy accompanying the political and economic offensive, and turned to their own tradition as a cultural reaction. In the struggle to improve the condition of women, the first names associated with those struggles were male, but from the beginning women too were involved. In this period, women's rights, particularly the issue of the veil, emerged as a central subject for national debate. For the first time in the whole history of Islam, issues such as the veil, polygamy, divorce and segregation were openly discussed in Middle Eastern society.

Public and independent activity for women's rights became widespread in the twentieth century and modernization has improved women's position generally.

Although the success of reform was tied to economic and social changes, its immediate problems were often ideological, mainly what attitude to take to the holy Islamic law. But economic and social reality brought women in the Middle East more and more into the public sphere, and this was largely positive for women, particularly during the historical periods of nation building, secularisation and economic modernization in Turkey and Tunisia.

The main thrust of legal reforms where the law is not egalitarian has been to place restrictions on divorce; polygamy and age of marriage, often making use of Islamic precedents and often by making men justify divorce or polygamy to the courts. These changes are called Islamic and Islamic courts generally retain some power. Family law is the cornerstone of the oppression of women maintained by Political Islam and by many governments in the Middle East. That Islamic family law is preserved almost intact signals the existence of enormously powerful Islamic and traditional forces within Middle Eastern societies. Calls to reformist interpretations such as stressing the 'egalitarian spirit of the Quran', and reshaping the Sharia by reinterpreting the Quran were arguments that arose mainly because of a rapidly changing economy and society that was experiencing the influence of the West.

Political Islam

Political Islam is a major force that in recent decades has inflicted serious setbacks on women's lives in the region. It is a political movement that came to the fore against secular and progressive movements for liberation and egalitarianism, against cultural and intellectual advances, and against the oppressed who are fighting for justice, freedom and equality in the region. In the 1970s, the political Islamic movement grew stronger and became more widespread. In the 1980s, the movement was supported by Western governments both as a weapon in the Cold War and in the fight against progressive movements in the region. Key features of Political Islam include opposition to the freedom of women and to women's civil liberties, and to freedom of expression in the cultural and personal domains, the enforcement of brutal laws and traditions, not to mention killing, beheading, and genocide.

In Iran, the Sudan, Pakistan and Afghanistan under the Taliban, Islamist regimes proceeded to transform women's homes into prison houses, where the confinement of women, their exclusion from many fields of work and education and their brutal treatment became the law of the land. In addition, the misogynist rhetoric they have let loose in the social sphere implicitly sanctions male violence towards women.

Second Class Citizens

At present, women throughout the region are second-class citizens, being denied their full legal identities by being excluded from the rights, privileges, and security that all citizens of any country should enjoy. Unjust laws, discriminatory constitutions, and biased mentalities that do not recognise women as equal citizens, violate women's rights. A "national" of a country, a citizen, is defined as someone who is a native or naturalised member of a state. A national is entitled to the rights and a privilege allotted to a free individual, and is also entitled to protection from the state. However, in no country in the Middle East or Northern Africa are women granted full citizenship; in every country they are second-class citizens. In many cases, the laws and codes of the state work to reinforce gender inequality and exclusion from nationality.

The state is used to strengthen Islamic and tribal/familial control over women, making them even more dependents on these institutions. Unlike in the West, where the individual is the basic unit of the state, it is the family that is the basis of Arab states. This means that the state is primarily concerned with the protection of the family rather than the protection of individual family members. Within this framework, the rights of women are expressed solely in their roles as wives and mothers. State discrimination against women in the family is expressed through unjust family laws that deny women equal access to divorce and child custody.

Throughout the region, Arab women, should they choose to marry a foreigner, are denied the right to extend their citizenship to their husbands. Furthermore, only fathers, not mothers, can independently pass citizenship to their children. In many cases, where a woman has been widowed, divorced or abandoned, or if her husband is not a national in the country where they reside, her children have no access to citizenship, and are thus excluded from the rights of a citizen. These rights include access to education and healthcare, and to land ownership and inheritance. This inequality not only denies women their right as citizens; it also denies children their basic rights as human beings.

If the law is designed to protect women only within their role in the family, it will fail to protect women who are in need of protection from their families. By failing to protect women from violence such as domestic abuse, rape, marital rape, and honour killings, the state fails to provide the protection available to a full citizen. In fact, by ignoring issues of gender-based violence and by granting lenient punishments to the perpetrators of violence against women, the state actually reinforces women's exclusion from the rights of citizens.

Family laws based on the Sharia frequently require women to obtain a male relative's permission to undertake activities that should be theirs by right. This increases the dependency women have on their male family members in economic, social, and legal matters. For example, in many Arab countries adult women must obtain the permission of their fathers, brothers or husbands in order to obtain a passport, travel outside of their country, start a business, receive a bank loan, open a bank account, or get married. What is to be done?

Given this intrinsic animosity to equality between the sexes and to women's rights and their role in society, how can the condition of women in these societies be improved? The answer must be to get rid of Political Islam as a precondition to any improvements in the status of women in the Middle East. The social system is based on misogyny and backwardness, and Middle Eastern women will have no cause to regret its passing.

The 21st Century must be the century that rids itself of Political Islam. I believe that this will begin in Iran. The most hopeful signs and the most remarkable stimulus for change continue to come directly from Iranian women both in Iran and in exile. In Iran, women presented the first and the most effective challenge to the Islamist regime by courageously questioning the right of Islamic authority to define the conditions of their lives.

And, as ever, the answer to the question of liberating women in the Middle East is secularism, and the establishment of egalitarian political systems in the region. Secularism has been and continues to be a prerequisite for women's liberation in the middle East. Our objectives must be:

The complete separation of religion from the state. The elimination of all religiously inspired, repressive laws.

Religion to be recognised as the private affair of the individual. Any reference to a person's religion should be eliminated from laws, on identity cards and in official papers. A ban on religious indoctrination and the religious interpretation of non-religious subjects in schools and colleges.

Exorcising Terror

From Bali to Karachi, and Riyadh to Casablanca, Islamic suicide bombers continue to carve an ever-widening swathe of death and devastation. Bombed, hounded, and evicted from former sanctuaries in Afghanistan, Al-Qaida nevertheless repeatedly demonstrates that it is well and alive. Like angry hornets that have survived the destruction of their nest, its members have spread far and wide. They are now drawing new recruits, and creating new havens. Vastly increased support in Muslim countries after the Iraq war for any organization fighting the United States makes their task easier.

Modern civilization will have to live with terrorism in the years to come, together with the reactions it provokes. This terrible fact cannot be changed. But key questions remain to be answered. What transformed former Islamic allies of the United States into unremittingly militant opposition? Is crushing Al-Qaida the answer? Is it at all possible?

The strong usually feel that a weaker enemy needs only force, not understanding. Indeed, the US establishment views terrorism as a form of incurable mental sickness whose origins and causes are beyond comprehension, and of little real interest. It has therefore chosen the path of exorcism - the violent expulsion of evil spirits from the possessed. This is a doubtful strategy. Medieval exorcists may have derived some satisfaction from their work, but little real success. On the contrary, they vastly increased the numbers of the mentally ill.

If terrorism is indeed a mental illness it must be treated the way scientific medicine begins treating any disease - ask the right questions, record the symptoms, examine the patient's history, and identify relevant environmental factors.

Is Islam the Problem?

Leaders of the Muslim community in the United States and Europe, imams (prayer leaders) in mosques throughout the world, and even President Bush, have routinely asserted that Islam is a religion of peace which has been hijacked by fanatics. This mantra is heard each time Islamic suicide bombers strike at civilian targets.

This assertion is simply untrue.

Islam - like Christianity, Judaism, Hinduism or any other religion - is not about peace. Nor is it about war. Every religion is about absolute belief in its own superiority and the divine right to impose its version of truth upon others. In medieval times, both the Crusades and the Jihads were soaked in blood. Today, there are Christian fundamentalists who attack abortion clinics in the United States and kill doctors; Muslim fundamentalists who wage their sectarian wars against each other; Jewish settlers who, holding the Old Testament in one hand and Uzis in the other, burn olive orchards and drive Palestinians off their ancestral land; and Hindus in India who demolish ancient mosques and burn down churches.

At first glance, the Quran - which Muslims accept as the literal and unchangeable word of God - makes it impossible for its followers to be the citizens of a modern, pluralistic state and peacefully coexist with peoples of different faiths. Take, for example, the verse:

O you who believe! Take not the Jews and Christians for friends. They are friends one to another. He among you who taketh them for friends is one of them.

The above became a subject of debate recently on a Pakistani television channel between Mufti Nizamuddeen Shamszai and me. Shamszai is a well-known and widely feared mullah who was Osama bin Laden's confidante, the tutor of Mullah Omar, and whose seminary in Karachi was a focal point of the Taliban movement. When Shamszai quoted the above verse, the anchorperson turned to me and asked whether I still thought it possible for Muslims and Jews to work together as colleagues? Most certainly, I replied, for although I am not well-versed in the nuances of Quranic exegesis yet there are certain irrefutable historical facts.

For example, between the 9th and 13th century, which was the Golden Age of Muslim civilization, Jewish and Christian scholars worked side-by-side with their Muslim counterparts and created new knowledge in the sciences and arts. They were actively encouraged to do by the great caliphs of that time - Harun-al-Rashid, Al-Mamun, and Abd-al-Rahman II. The caliphs were religious, as well as political, leaders and they had sanctioned collaborating with people of any religion.

The point of relating the above episode is that the practice of Islam has often, if not mostly, been at variance with the Quran. This, of course, is no surprise. Although all holy books were written millennia ago and are unchangeable, their followers have moved on. Today's Judaism is hardly the bloodthirsty Judaism of the Book of Joshua, in which God commands the Israelites to put all Canaanites, even children, to the sword. Nor is today's Christianity that of 13th century Europe - a time of bloody crusades and inquisitions, when Pope Innocent VIII issued the terrible papal bull that doomed countless women to unspeakable suffering and death - "Thou shalt not suffer a witch to live".

By the same token, I would argue that the accurate answer to the primary question - can Islam be made secular, democratic, and pluralistic - is also twofold. Islamic theology will not permit this either now or at any time in the future. But Islamic society may well accept it over a period of time - if the right conditions should somehow come about.

Therefore, we have no option but to delve into the historical experience of the Muslim peoples. We have to understand why today they stand in such sharp contrast with other peoples on this planet.

A Brilliant Past that Vanished

Martians visiting Earth between the 9th and 13th centuries - the Golden Age of Islam - would surely have reported back to headquarters that the only people doing decent work in science, philosophy or medicine were Muslims. Muslims not only preserved ancient learning, they also made substantial innovations.

Science flourished in the Golden Age of Islam because of a strong rationalist and liberal tradition, carried on by a group of Muslim thinkers known as the Mutazilites. To the extent that they were able to dominate over the traditionalists, science and culture flourished. But in the 12th century, Muslim orthodoxy reawakened, spearheaded by the Arab cleric Imam Al-Ghazali. Al-Ghazali championed revelation over reason, predestination over free will and he damned mathematics as being against Islam, an intoxicant of the mind that weakened faith.

Caught in the viselike grip of orthodoxy, Islam eventually

choked. The bin Ladens and Mullah Omar's of antiquity leveled the impressive edifice of Islamic cultural and scientific achievements. It was also the end of tolerance, intellect and science in the Muslim world. The last great Muslim thinker, Abd-al Rahman Ibn Khaldun, belonged to the 14th century.

Meanwhile, the rest of the world moved on. The Renaissance brought an explosion of scientific inquiry in the West. This owed much to translations of Greek works carried out by Arabs and other Muslim contributions. Mercantile capitalism and technological progress drove Western countries - in ways that were often brutal and at times genocidal - to rapidly colonize the Muslim world from Indonesia to Morocco.

The Rise and Fall of Muslim Modernisation

It soon became clear, at least to some of the Muslim elites in colonized countries, that they were paying a heavy price for not possessing the analytical tools of modern science and the social and political values of modern culture. Therefore, despite widespread resistance from the orthodox, the logic of modernity found 19th-century Muslim adherents. Modernizers such as Mohammed Abduh and Rashid Rida of Egypt, Sayyed Ahmad Khan of India, and Jamaluddeen Afghani (who belonged everywhere), wished to adapt Islam to the times, interpret the Qur'an in ways consistent with modern science, and discard the Hadith (ways of the Prophet) in favor of the Qur'an. Others seized on the modern idea of the nation-state.

When new nation states emerged in the 20th century, not even one of their leaders was a fundamentalist. Turkey's Kemal Ataturk, Algeria's Ahmed Ben Bella, Indonesia's Sukarno, Pakistan's Muhammad Ali Jinnah, Egypt's Gamal Abdel Nasser, and Iran's Mohammed Mosaddeq all sought to organize their societies on the basis of secular values. However, Muslim and Arab nationalism, part of a larger anti-colonial nationalist current across the Third World, included the desire to control and use national resources for domestic benefit.

The conflict with Western greed was inevitable. Indeed, America's foes during the 1950's and 1960's were secular nationalists, not fundamentalists. Mossadeq, who opposed Standard Oil's grab at Iran's oil resources, was removed by a CIA coup. Sukarno, accused of being a communist, was removed by US intervention and a resulting bloodbath that consumed about eight hundred thousand lives. Nasser, who had Islamic fundamentalists like Saiyyid Qutb publicly executed, fell foul of the US and Britain after the Suez Crisis. On the other hand, until very recently, America's friends were the sheikhs of Saudi Arabia and the Gulf states, all of whom practiced highly conservative forms of Islam but were the darlings of Western oil companies.

Pressed from outside, corrupt and incompetent from within, secular Muslim governments proved unable to defend national interests or deliver social justice. For example, Zulfiqar Ali Bhutto – Pakistan's popularly elected prime minister who soundly defeated the mullah's at the ballot box – coined "Islamic socialism" as the way of emancipating the masses. But obsessed with absolute power, Bhutto frustrated democracy. Such failures left a vacuum that Islamic religious movements grew to fill – in Iran, Pakistan and Sudan, to name a few. The expulsion of the PLO from Lebanon in 1982 paved the way for Hamas to dominate the Palestinian resistance. The times had begun to change, but what was only a trot changed into a gallop in 1979.

The Genesis of International Jihad

History may well have taken a different course if 1979, the year of the Soviet invasion, had not also been the year for presidential elections in the US. But with Ronald Reagan as the rival candidate, Jimmy Carter could not afford to appear soft on the Soviets. The Administration requested approval for a CIA. covert operation in Afghanistan, and offered Pakistan 400 million dollars in aid, which General Zia-ul-Haq, Pakistan's military ruler, dismissed as "peanuts" in an astute political move. Suddenly, Afghanistan had become the focal point of American global strategy. Officials like Richard Perle,

Assistant Secretary of Defense, saw Afghanistan not as the locale of a harsh and dangerous conflict to be ended but as a place to teach the Russians a lesson. Such "bleeders" became the most influential people in Washington.

Given the highly conservative nature of Afghan society and the spontaneous resistance to the Afghan communist resistance, it did not need a genius to suggest that Islamic international solidarity could be used as a powerful weapon. The task of creating such solidarity fell upon Saudi Arabia, together with other conservative Arab monarchies. The Jihad in Afghanistan provided an excellent outlet for the growing number of militant Sunni activists in Saudi Arabia, and a way to deal with the daily taunts of the Iranian clergy who were now ensconced in power.

Perhaps the most important contribution of the US was to create international linkages and bring in men and material from around the Arab world and beyond. The most hardened and ideologically dedicated men were sought on the logic that they would be the best fighters. Advertisements, paid for from CIA funds, were placed in newspapers and newsletters around the world offering inducements and motivations to join the Jihad.

Dr. Ayman al-Zawahiri and Ahmad Shawqi al-Islambuli were among the first Egyptians to arrive in Afghanistan. Zawahiri was an Egyptian pediatrician who was to become bin Laden's second-in-command. Islambuli too was a hard-core fundamentalist and brother of Khalid al-Islambuli, who later assassinated Sadat. Both men eventually became top-leaders of the Al-Qaida network.

In 1988 Soviet troops withdrew unconditionally and US-Pakistan-Saudi-Egypt alliance emerged victorious. Four years later the Soviet Union collapsed. Francis Fukuyama's thesis "The End of History" became wildly popular.

But appearances were illusory, and events over the next two decades were to reveal the true costs of the victory. Even in the mid 1990's it was clear that the victorious alliance had unwittingly created a dynamic now beyond its control. After the Soviet Union collapsed, the United States walked away from an Afghanistan in shambles. The Taliban emerged; Osama bin Laden and his al Qaeda made Afghanistan their base September 11 followed.

Learning The Wrong Lessons From 9/11

An impenetrable narcissism prevents most Americans from learning that the world does not share their self-image of a generous, libertarian, humane people whose innocence was injured by a savage attack on its cities. In spite of having fought 28 wars after 1945, maintaining 12 aircraft carrier groups that constantly prowl the oceans, stationing a million soldiers over five continents, and keeping thousands of nuclear weapons, a majority of Americans believes that the US seeks no more than self-defence. The peremptory dismissal of world opinion, contempt for international laws and treaties, and deliberate destruction of the United Nations, characterizes the American mood today.

Shortly after the collapse of the twin towers, George W. Bush rhetorically asked: "Why do they hate us?". After the Iraq war, that question is still more readily answerable. The daily televised bombardment of Baghdad with cruise missiles and bombs hailing down from the skies, smashed bodies and decapitated children, bombed out hospitals, women and children shot dead at checkpoints manned by the Marines, and the burning of Iraq's priceless architectural and literary heritage, have added to all older reasons. And each old reason gains new ferocity each time when, with American approval, Ariel Sharon's bulldozers plow into Palestinian homes and reduce towns like Jenin to rubble.

For its victims, America means invasion, occupation, and humiliation. Inevitably the US has become both a victim of terrorism and its godfather. But the slowest learners are undoubtedly the world's Islamists.

Each blow inflicted by America has led Islamists to predict that the pain and humiliation will make all Muslims to close ranks, forget old grudges, purge traitors and renegades from the ranks, and generate a collective rage great enough to take on the power of today's governing civilization. Each time they have been dead wrong.

The fact is that power does not lie in numbers. Nor do large armies and arsenals really matter. What Islamists fail to realize is that the awesome strength of Western civilization springs from accepting the paradigm of science and logic, respecting democratic institutions, allowing value systems to evolve, and boldly challenging dogma without being condemned as blasphemers. They cannot see why the West's success has anything to do with personal freedom and liberty, artistic and scientific creativity, the compulsive urge to innovate and experiment, or the nursery where such ideas are cultivated – the modern university.

This inability to learn can but lead to the one path – self-defeating and self-harming terrorism. Islamic militant organizations have done far greater harm to Muslims, whose causes they claim to promote, than to those who they battle against. Killing tourists and bombing churches is the work of moral cretins and is not just cowardly and inhumane, but also a strategic disaster. Indeed, fanatical acts can sting and provoke the American colossus but never seriously hurt it.

At the moment, if there is anything at all that can break the cycle of terror and counter-terror, and prevent the dreaded clash of civilizations; it is people of the western world.

Even as Bush's America wrapped itself in war frenzy, over ten million protested in the streets of London, Washington, Rome, and hundreds of other cities around the globe. They did not succeed in stopping the Iraq war, but they did broadcast an extremely important message. People in Pakistan – and I presume other Muslim countries too – were fascinated and touched by the demonstrations, especially since there was no way in which they could mobilize to do the same. They also saw Christian France bravely taking on the US in the Security Council, the Pope condemning the war as a sin, a beautiful white-American girl, Rachel Corrie, standing in the way of an Israeli bulldozer and being crushed to death, thousands courting arrest in the US, and more.

The overseas protests would have much impact on our mullahs. After all, Pakistanis are born into xenophobia, taught to believe that they are surrounded by enemies, and subjected to horrifically poisonous textbooks in schools. During the Iraq war there has been no repeat of extremist attacks on the Christian community in Pakistan. In previous months, anti-US feeling following the arrest of Al-Qaida members had sometimes translated into murders of Pakistan's terrified and helpless Christian minority.

Ultimately, the only way by which Muslim societies can become democratic, pluralistic, and free from violent extremism is by going through their own struggles. It cannot be done – as the failure of America's efforts in Afghanistan and Iraq demonstrates – by imposing colonial rule. But is there any reason to believe that indigenous reform is possible? Islam is immutable, but can Muslims change?

Astonishingly, the Muslim country which offers the most hope for reform is a declared member of Bush's axis-of-evil. Iran has the finest education system in the Muslim world, a population that is culturally more advanced and accepting of modernity than in Arab countries, and young people who abhor the Islamic theocracy that has ruled the country for over two decades. Even though America refused to take notice of the fact, but immediately after 9/11 nearly 40,000 Iranians came out to the streets in Tehran and lit candles in sympathy with the American people. Contrast that with celebrations held in countries like Pakistan that are declared US allies!

Religion in Education

It is an undeniable fact that education is one of the most important cornerstones of all human societies. The way a society regards raising the next generation is reflected first and foremost in its educational system. Here I will try to describe a complete religious education. My case is the Islamic educational system in Iran. I will discuss the effects of religious education on school curricula, on girl pupils and their rights, and on boys' and girls' relationships. I will examine the imposition of the veil on little girls and adolescents, the rule of sexual apartheid and the way sexual matters and sex education are treated in schools. At the end I stress and emphasize the necessity of a secular education that will enable the raising of healthy children and young people and the development of the whole community.

With the anti-secularist backlash and the rise of Political Islam, the last two decades have been some of the darkest Iran has seen, especially for women and children. Medieval beliefs and customs have found legal expression to oppress the people. Words can hardly do justice to the repression and backwardness of the Islamist movement and the Islamist government. For a long time Islam was kept at a relative arm's length from political power, but Political Islam is now the ideology in power in Iran, among other countries, and society has suffered serious setbacks in civil rights - especially women's and children's rights. One of these devastating setbacks has been in religious (radical Islamic) education. This system is reflected in school curricula, in the approach to science, in the school milieu, in the way girl pupils are treated, and in highly conservative teaching regarding the role of women.

School Curricula

In many societies children are taught to hold certain beliefs and religious values. Iran is an extreme case where education has given way to indoctrination. Political Islam rules every aspect of education and the school system. Belief in Islam is compulsory, and to live according to Islamic values, norms and thoughts is a pre-condition for survival. Learning the Qur'an is compulsory from the first year in primary schools. Teachers must pass a religious exam to be permitted to teach. This exam includes Islamic rules, prayers, the Qur'an and Hadith. Islamist propaganda is taught systematically. Free thoughts are forbidden and punishable. Superstition has influenced the school curricula. This has created a dark and stagnant milieu for children. Pupils are taught that if they do not obey the rules, they will be burned in hell (jahannam). This has deprived and continues to deprive children of learning about scientific advancements and the scientific approach. It kills their creativity and replaces their curiosity and desire for learning with the dark rules and values of 1400 years ago at the time of Mohammad.

Islamist teaching regarding women is one of the most devastating aspects of the educational system in Iran. Children are taught that women are inferior to and equal to only half of a man, that women belong to men, that men have the right to punish their wives if they do not obey them, that women are the potential source of corruption in society so the hijab must be imposed on them. They are taught that the veil is the legitimate physical border of a woman's existence in society to protect men and the community from any possible moral and social danger and the devastation they may cause. They learn that the main duty of women is to take care of the home and children. Teaching the oppression of women and male domination is an essential element of school education. Women are pictured only as mothers and housekeepers. In school, children are taught that the traditional male-female gender roles, women's segregation, and sexual apartheid are a desirable state for women in society.

Sexual Apartheid

Another important aspect of religious education in Iran is the rule of sexual apartheid. Sexual apartheid governs every area of people's lives including the workplace, libraries, transport, healthcare, education and schools. Girls and boys are separated from the very beginning in schools. According to the Islamist worldview, the basis of Iranian law, women are the source of corruption in the community and the agents of leading men astray. For this "crime" they are controlled and punished from early childhood to the moment of death.

Girl pupils are under enormous pressure in school as well as in society. The veil (hijab) is imposed on them by force. This deprives them of free movement, from playing freely, and from happily participating in social activities.

The schools authorities spy on girls to see if they wear make up, to hear if they talk about boys or if they carry pictures of stars and so on. Pupils are even intimidated into spying on their parents and to report to the school authorities about their parents' life style and whether their female relatives offend against Islamic rules at home. This has produced a system of inquisition in schools. The environment is full of repression and control, the control of children's minds and behaviour.

Friendship between girls and boys is forbidden, considered a sin and punishable. Girls are under strict scrutiny. Their talking, walking, laughing, and dress and movements are controlled and carefully monitored. Teachers and principals punish girls physically and psychologically if the veil is not worn properly even at play.

Takleaf Ritual

In Iran the legal age for girls to be married is nine. In law girls are considered to be mature women on reaching their ninth birthday. School authorities celebrate this day and hold a ceremony called the Takleaf celebration. In the Takleaf ceremony girls have to wear a complete white hijab which completely covers their bodies. A clergyman talks about girls' role in the society and warns them of evil, Fitna (which means chaos), and western culture. He reminds girls that their duty is to prevent corruption by wearing the proper hijab. From this day onward, girls are banned from playing with boys other than their brothers. It is forbidden for girls to laugh loudly. They have to pray to God five times a day. They are told that if they do not wear the proper veil or if their hair appears out of the veil, they will be punished in hell and snakes will grow on their heads.

Discussing sexual matters is treated as a serious crime and sex education is unacceptable. Any relationship among boys and girls is banned. In such a milieu it is a sin to talk about male and female organs. Everything related to male/female relationships is considered to be secretive, sinful and full of humiliation.

Children are normally keen to learn and experience, to know about the world, and learn about their bodies and their bodily functions. They want to know where babies come from and about the opposite sex. All these normal and necessary curiosities are answered by frightening tales about evil and hell. This system brings about nothing but backwardness and hypocrisy.

The Veil and the Rights of Girls Under 16

Veiling the heads and bodies of little girls and adolescents has a devastating impact on their minds and lives. Veiling children who have not come of age should be prohibited by law since it violates the rights of the child. Children are born without religion, tradition and prejudices. They have not joined any religious sect. They are new human beings who happen to have been born into a family with a specific religion, tradition, and prejudices. It should be the task of society to neutralize the negative effects of this blind lottery. Society is duty bound to provide fair and equal living conditions for children, for their growth and development, and for their active participation in social life. Anyone who tries to block the normal social life of a child is as guilty of abuse as those who would physically abuse a child because of their culture, religion or personal beliefs. No nine-year-old girl chooses to be married, sexually mutilated, serve as housemaid and cook for the male members of the family, or to be deprived of exercise, education, and play.

Children grow up in the family and society according to established customs, traditions and regulations, and automatically learn to accept these ideas and customs as the norms of life. It is not their choice to be veiled, and indeed to suggest that a girl child "chooses" to wear the veil of her own volition is a ridiculous joke.

Secular Education

Children have the right to be protected against the transgressions of religion and religious sects. It is an offence to prevent children from enjoying their social and civil rights such as a secular education, amusement and participation in social activities specific to children. The educational system in Iran and in other countries under the sway of Political Islam amounts to nothing less than systematic child abuse.

Society is duty-bound to defend the rights of children. We should demand that the standards that have become the norms in other countries as a result of the enlightenment and the just struggles of innumerable human beings in the secular democracies become the rules and norms in education in countries under Muslim rule. Society has the duty to protect children and persons under 16 from all forms of material and spiritual manipulation by religious institutions. Islamic society should guarantee freedom of religion, including atheism. Children must no longer be taught that Jews, Bahais and followers of other religions are somehow criminals and should not enjoy rights of Muslims. A complete separation of religion from the state guarantees this separation and protects children from manipulation by religion.

In my view, any struggle against Islamic child abuse in the educational system will have to confront state Islam and bring about the separation of religion from the state. This is a pre-requisite for a humane society that fulfils the needs and potential of children. Only a strong modern, secular and egalitarian social movement will enable us to sweep away the systematic child abuse that is the Iranian educational system.

We call for the complete separation of religion from education, for the prohibition of religious indoctrination and the religious reinterpretation of science and other subjects in schools and educational establishments, and for the abolition of any law, regulation or ritual that breaches the principles of secular education. These are the essential and necessary measures to ensure children rights, the health of the next generation and the development of society.

Bibliography

Abraham, A. J. *Islamic Fundamentalism and the Doctrine of Jihad*. Lima, OH: Wyndham Hall Press, 2002.

AbuKhalil, As'ad. *Bin Laden, Islam, and America's New 'War on Terrorism'*. Open Media Pamphlet Series. New York: Seven Stories Press, 2002.

. Ahmed, Nafeez Mosaddwq. *The War on Truth: 9/11, Disinformation and the Anatomy of Terrorism*. Northampton, MA: Olive Branch Press, 2005.

Aho, James. *Politics of Righteousness: Idaho Christian Patriotism*. Seattle, WA: University of Washington Press, 1995.

Alexander, Yonah. *European Terrorism Today & Tomorrow*. Brassey's Terrorism Library. Washington, DC: Brassey's, 1992.

Alexander, Yonah. *Middle East Terrorism: Current Threats and Future Prospects*. International Library of Terrorism; 5. New York: G.K. Hall & Co., 1994.

Alexander, Yonah. *Middle East Terrorism: Selected Group Profiles*. Washington, DC: Jewish Institute for National Security Affairs, 1994.

Alexander, Yonah. *Palestinian Religious Terrorism: Hamas and Islamic Jihad*. New York: Transnational, 2002.

Alexander, Yonah. *Terrorism in Europe*. New York: St. Martin's Press, 1982.

Alexander, Yonah. *Usama bin Laden's al-Qaida: Profile of a Terrorist Network*. Ardsley, NY: Transnational Publishers, 2001.

Alexander, Yonah; Latter, Richard, editors, *Terrorism and the Media: Dilemmas for Government, Journalists and the Public*. Washington, DC: Brassey's, 1990.

Bartholomeusz, Tessa J. *Buddhist Fundamentalism and Minority Identities in Sri Lanka*. New York: State University of New York Press, 1998.

Barton, Greg. *Indonesia's Struggle: Jemaah Islamiyah and the Soul of Islam*. Sydney, Australia: University of New South Wales Press, 2004.

Cateura, Linda Brandi. *Voices of American Muslims: 23 Profiles*. New York: Hippocrene Books, 2005.

Catholic Institute for International Relations, *Guatemala, Never Again*. Maryknoll, NY: Orbis Books, 1999.

Davies, Barry. *Terrorism: Inside a World Phenomenon*. London: Virgin Books, 2003.

Devji, Faisal. *Landscapes of the Jihad: Militancy, Morality, Modernity*. Ithaca, NY: Cornell University Press, 2005.

Devji, Mantoshe Singh. *The Mad Messiah: Osama bin Laden and the Seeds of Terror*. Scottsdale, AZ: Inkwell Productions, 2002. Emerson, Steven. *American Jihad: The Terrorists Living Among Us*. New York: Free Press, 2002.

Esposito, John L. *Islam: The Straight Path*. 3rd edition. New York: Oxford University Press, 1998.

Esposito, John L. *The Islamic Threat: Myth or Reality?*. New York: Oxford University Press, 1992.

Esposito, John L. *The Oxford Dictionary of Islam*. New York: Oxford University Press, 2003.

Esposito, John L. *Unholy War: Terror in the Name of Islam*. New York: Oxford University Press, 2002.

Etzioni, Amitai. *How Patriotic is the Patriot Act? Freedom Versus Security in the Age of Terrorism*. New York: Routledge, 2004.

Fandy, Mamoun. *Saudi Arabia and the Politics of Dissent*. New York: Palgrave, 2001.

Farah, Douglas. *Blood From Stones: The Secret Financial Network of Terror*. New York: Broadway Books, 2004.

Gardell, Mattias. *Gods of the Blood: The Pagan Revival and White Separatism*. Durham, NC: Duke University Press, 2003.

Gerges, Fawaz A. *The Far Enemy: Why Jihad Went Global*. New York: Cambridge University Press, 2005.

Habeck, Mary R. *Knowing the Enemy: Jihadist Ideology and the War on Terror*. New Haven, NY: Yale University Press, 2006.

Hoffman, Bruce. *Holy terror: The Implications of Terrorism Motivated by a Religious Imperative*. Santa Monica, CA: RAND, 1993.

Howard, Russell D. *Defeating Terrorism: Shaping the New Security Environment*. Guilford, CT: McGraw-Hill, 2004.

Jaimoukha, Amjad M. *The Chechens: A Handbook*. New York: Routledge Curzon, 2005.

Karawan, Ibrahim. *Islamic Impasse*. New York: Oxford University Press, 1997.

Miniter, Richard. *Losing Bin Laden: How Bill Clinton's Failures Unleashed Global Terror*. Washington, DC: Regnery, 2003.

Mishal, Shaul. *The Palestinian Hamas: Vision, Violence, and Coexistence*. New York: Columbia University Press, 2000.

Napoleoni, Loretta. *Modern Jihad: Tracing the Dollars Behind the Terror Networks*. Sterling, VA: Pluto Press, 2003.

Noorani, A. G. *Islam & Jihad: Prejudice versus Reality*. New York: Zed Books, 2002.

Nusse, Andrea. *Muslim Palestine: The Ideology of Hamas*. Amsterdam: Harwood Academic Publishers, 1998.

O'Ballance, Edgar. *Islamic Fundamentalist Terrorism: 1979-95*. Basingstoke: Macmillan, 1997.

Ojeda, Auriana. *Islamic Fundamentalism*. San Diego, CA: Greenhaven Press, 2003.

Randal, Jonathan C. *Osama: The Making of a Terrorist*. New York: Knopf, 2004.

Rapoport, David C. *The Rationalization of Terrorism*. Frederick, MD: University Publications of America, 1982.

Scheuer, Michael. *Through Our Enemies Eyes: Osama bin Laden, Radical Islam, and the Future of America*. Rev. ed., 2nd ed.. Washington, DC: Potomac Books, 2006.

Taheri, Amir. *Holy Terror: Inside the World of Islamic Terrorism*. Bethesda, MD: Adler & Adler, 1987.

Venske, Ben. *The al-Qaeda Threat: An Analytical Guide to al-Qaeda's Tactics & Targets*. Alexandria, VA: Tempest Publishing, 2003.

Venzke, Ben. *The al-Qaeda Threat: An Analytical Guide to al-Qaeda's Tactics & Targets*. Alexandria, VA: Tempest, 2003.

Waardenburg, Jacques. *Muslims and Others: Relations in Context*. New York: Walter de Gruyter, 2003.

Wiktorowicz, Quintan. *Global Jihad: Understanding September 11*. Falls Church, VA: 2002.

Zacharias, Ravi K. *Light in the Shadow of Jihad*. Sisters, OR: Multnomah Publishers, 2002.

Index